# Sleeping Giant: Awakening the Transatlantic Services Economy

*Edited by*

**Daniel S. Hamilton**

*and*

**Joseph P. Quinlan**

Hamilton, Daniel S. and Quinlan, Joseph P. (eds.), *Sleeping Giant: Awakening the Transatlantic Services Economy* (Washington, D.C.: Center for Transatlantic Relations, 2007)



**Center for Transatlantic Relations**
**American Consortium on EU Studies**
**EU Center of Excellence Washington D.C.**
**The Paul H. Nitze School of Advanced International Studies**
**The Johns Hopkins University**
1717 Massachusetts Ave., NW, Suite 525
Washington, D.C. 20036
Tel. (202) 663-5880
Fax (202) 663-5879
Email: transatlantic@jhu.edu
http://transatlantic.sais-jhu.edu

ISBN 10: 0-9788821-5-6
ISBN 13: 978-0-9788821-5-0

# Table of Contents

## Part III
## Opening the Transatlantic Services Economy: Global and Transatlantic Implications

# Introduction

*Daniel S. Hamilton and Joseph P. Quinlan*

Service activities are the sleeping giant of the transatlantic economy—an economic factor that, if awakened and unbound, would further deepen the commercial stakes between the United States and Europe and enhance the global competitiveness of both parties. At present, however, the full potential of the transatlantic service economy remains hampered by internal barriers, regulation, and obstacles in the U.S. and in Europe.

Removing barriers to trade and investment in services is a key challenge—but also a significant opportunity—for transatlantic policy makers. While services presently account for the largest share of gross domestic product in virtually all of the nations that comprise the transatlantic economy, the role of services could be even larger and growth-enhancing if the political will was present to push ahead with more service deregulation and reform.

The services economies of the United States and Europe have never been as intertwined as they are today, notably in such activities as financial services, telecommunications, utilities, insurance, advertising, computer services and other related functions. How important is this relationship to both sides of the Atlantic? What potential is there to open the transatlantic services economy even further? This volume addresses these questions. Part I sets the scene with chapters on the European and U.S. services economies. Part II offers a number of case studies for particularly important sectors—financial services, health services, and telecommunications. Part III examines the implications of greater liberalization of commerce in services across the Atlantic for both the transatlantic partners and the rest of the world.

This volume builds on the Center for Transatlantic Relations' work on U.S.-European economic relations, including its annual surveys of the transatlantic economy, and other previous volumes, including *Protecting Our Prosperity: Ensuring Both National Security and the Benefits of*

*Foreign Investment in the United States* (2006); *Deep Integration: How Transatlantic Markets are Leading Globalization* (2005); and *Partners in Prosperity: The Changing Geography of the Transatlantic Economy*, (2004) all by Daniel S. Hamilton and Joseph P. Quinlan.

Over past years we have worked together with a network of European and American scholars and experts to examine what accelerated integration of the U.S. and European economies means for key sectors of the economy, including services. This volume deepens our analysis. The Center for Transatlantic Relations asked a number of key experts to investigate specific aspects of this topic, and then sponsored a conference in February 2007 at which our authors presented their drafts for comment and critique by scholars and practitioners. We are grateful to those who participated, and in particular to Jacob Funk Kirkegaard of the Peter G. Peterson Institute of International Economics; Christine McDaniel of the Council of Economic Advisers in the White House; Christopher Boam of Verizon Communications; William Looney of Pfizer; Bruce Stokes of *The National Journal;* and Stephen Kobrin of the Wharton School of Business at the University of Pennsylvania, for their participation and considered critiques, which helped to improve our drafts enormously.

Particular thanks go to Katrien Maes and Gretchen Losee at the Center for Transatlantic Relations for their help throughout the project.

This project was made possible through the generous support of the German Marshall Fund of the United States, for which we are grateful. Each author writes in is or her own personal capacity; the views expressed are those of the authors and not their institutions.

# Part I

# The Setting: Understanding the European and U.S. Services Economies

# *Chapter 1*

# The European Market for Services: Patchwork

*Arjan M. Lejour*

*In Europe services markets are predominantly nationally oriented. In spite of the proclaimed free movement of services in the European treaty, foreign entry to national services markets is a cumbersome exercise or even an insurmountable hurdle. Cross-border trade in services remains low, albeit foreign direct investment is surging. The breakdown of capital controls, explicit ban on foreign discrimination and deregulation in national services markets, among others with respect to market entry, have contributed to the rise of FDI. However, current regulation procedures and country differences in regulation still hamper the full integration of services markets. Recent EU initiatives such as the Services Directive, action plan for financial services, and plans to integrate energy markets help to lower the market barriers. However, it will take many more initiatives before the free movement of services is realized and the economic benefits of a large market scale and a more competitive environment can be harvested.*

## Introduction[1]

Since January 2007, 27 countries form the European Union (EU), covering nearly the whole of Europe. This constitutes a market of about 500 million consumers, if national markets are integrated. One of the corner stones of the EU is the free movement of goods, services, capital, and labor. For goods the 500 million consumer market seems to be reality, but for services it is utopia. 27 Member States have implemented their own systems of regulating services; they regulate market entry, competition, quality and sometimes even prices. For some services, the degree of regulation isolates these markets from the rest of the world. In these services sectors cross-border trade and for-

[1] A substantial part of this chapter is based on joint work with my colleague Henk Kox. Comments by Jacob Funk Kirkegaard are highly appreciated. I want to thank Nico van Leeuwen for assistance with the data.

eign direct investment are hardly possible. These are extremes, most notably in the case of network services. For most sectors national regulatory systems do not isolate markets, but fragment them in 27 different markets per services sector.

If there is a European market for services it resembles patchwork, and Europeans need a lot of needles and thread to sew them together. The European treaty aims for the free movement of services, but this statement still expresses more ambition than reality. The basic idea of this chapter is to underpin the metaphor of the patchwork, and to discuss (recent) developments to integrate services markets. Although the European market for services is patchwork, the quilts are much more uniform than for the global market for services. In that respect Europe's efforts to integrate national services markets are an experiment to be applauded, and from which others could learn — such as the WTO with regard to the General Agreement on Trade in Services (GATS), and the EU and U.S. with respect to a transatlantic services market.

The fragmentation of European services industries does not represent a status quo situation. Cross-border trade and foreign direct investment in services are increasing. Section two presents recent trends. Some underlying causes for the increased interwovenness between services markets include deregulation of services industries and increased competition in many European countries. Section three presents recent patterns with regard to product market regulation in services using OECD indicators. These patterns clearly reflect deregulation policies.

Although less regulation promotes competition and even foreign competition, differences in country-specific regulation also hamper trade in services. Section four underscores the importance of reducing these differences in regulation. Section five describes some of the recent initiatives by the European Commission to integrate national services markets. The focus is on the Services Directive, but also some other initiatives for financial services, retail distribution and energy markets are discussed briefly. Section six discusses the prospects of further integrating national services markets in order to make the quilts more uniform.

**Figure 1.1 Shares of Types of International Transactions in World Services Trade**

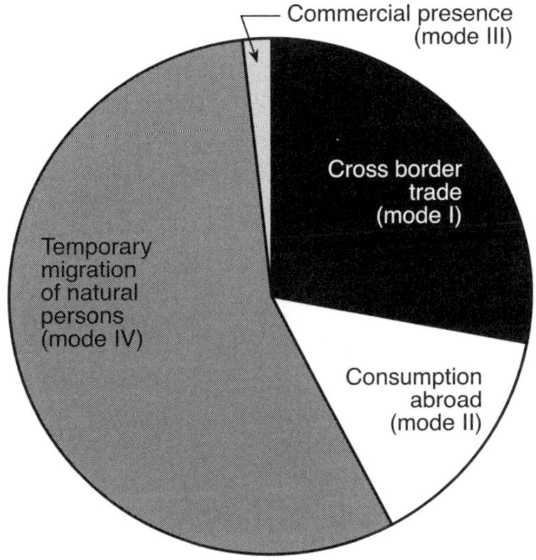


Source: Karsenty (2000).

## 1. Trends in Services Trade

Only a small fraction of services products, such as standard software packages, can be stored and shipped in boxes like traditional merchandise exports. In most other cases—think of vacations or hairdressers—it is difficult to separate production and consumption of the service in time and space. As a consequence, either the producer or the consumer must go abroad for an international transaction to take place. The producer can set up a production unit abroad or can have himself represented by an employee sent abroad on a temporary basis. While exporting and production abroad are optional supply forms for manufacturing firms, in some services industries the only feasible way to supply a foreign market is establishing a local subsidiary.[2] The GATS treaty therefore identifies four modes of international services supply, as shown in Figure 1.1.[3] The figure shows that international services deliveries through commercial presence abroad is the dominant sup-

---

[2] Sampson, G and R. Snape, "Identifying the issues in trade in services," *The World Economy*, vol. 8, 1985, pp. 171-181.

[3] White (2007) illustrates these four modes with some examples.

ply form (57 percent). This differs per services sector. Kirkegaard[4] argues that foreign commercial presence is eight to nine times as important as cross-border trade in computer and IT related services for the U.S. Also in financial services foreign commercial presence as much more important than cross-border trade.

## *Cross-Border Trade (and Consumption Abroad)*

In the period 1985 to 2001, EU cross-border trade in goods and services increased on average by about 8.4 percent per year. In 1985, the EU-15[5] countries exported about $173 billion in services—the equivalent of a quarter of EU goods exports. In 2001 the value of services trade increased to $633 billion, but still only 28 percent of EU goods exports.

Traditionally two services sectors, transport and travel, are responsible for the largest share in international services trade. In 2004, both sub-sectors accounted for half of total EU-25 exports in services. This held despite the fact that exports in transport grew less than total services exports in the EU,[6] as is shown in Table 2.1. External EU-25 services exports totalled about $450 billion in 2004, while the U.S. exported $381 billion in services in 2005.[7]

In recent decades, trade in business services has rocketed, recording annual growth of 15 percent since 1985.[8] Exports have also surged for computer and information services, royalties, other business services, financial services, insurance, and communication services.[9] The main subcategories with other business services are merchandising services, legal, accountancy and management services, architectural and engi-

---

[4] Kirkegaard, J.F., 2007, "Offshoring, Outsourcing and Production Relocations—Labor Market effects in The OECD and Developing Asia, *Singapore Economic Review*, forthcoming.

[5] The data only cover the 15 members of the EU before May 2004.

[6] This was in particular due to the modest growth in 'other transport' (mainly road transport).

[7] See White, L.J., "Reducing barriers to Services Trade: The U.S. Case," in this volume.

[8] Note that this growth rate is biased by a net increase in trade of about 80 percent in 1992 due to a change in the statistical classification system. Without this break in the data, the growth rates would be about five percentage points lower.

[9] OECD, *OECD Statistics on International Trade in Services; Partner Country Data and Summary Analysis* (Paris, 2003).

**Table 1.1 EU Exports in Services, 2004**

| | Value in billion U.S. dollars | Percent share in total exports | Percent of intra-EU exports to world exports | Percent value growth intra-EU exports 1985-2001 |
|---|---|---|---|---|
| Total services | 1064.0 | 100.0 | 57.7 | 10.5 |
| Transport | 230.1 | 21.6 | 50.2 | 8.2 |
| Sea transport | 101.6 | 9.6 | 39.6 | 10.3 |
| Air transport | 77.9 | 7.3 | 48.9 | 13.8 |
| Other transport | 50.6 | 4.8 | 73.5 | 3.5 |
| Travel | 276.2 | 26.0 | 69.8 | 11.1 |
| Communication services | 25.2 | 2.4 | 69.1 | 14.8 |
| Construction | 22.4 | 2.1 | 47.3 | 11.2 |
| Insurance | 35.7 | 3.4 | 56.0 | 15.3 |
| Financial intermediation | 71.3 | 6.7 | 55.7 | 16.9 |
| Computer and information | 56.4 | 5.3 | 61.2 | NA |
| Royalties and license fees | 41.9 | 4.0 | 42.5 | 14.6 |
| Other business services | 258.8 | 24.3 | 54.2 | 15.2 |
| Personal services | 13.5 | 1.3 | 54.1 | 10.8 |
| Government services | 21.7 | 2.0 | 48.4 | 6.4 |

Source: OECD (2006) and own calculations.

neering services, R&D and intra-firm services. Trade in government services and in personal services is relatively unimportant.

On average 58 percent of all EU-25 services exports is destined for other EU countries. The average is higher for travel, communication services, computer and information services and other transport. It is low for such sectors as construction, air transport, sea transport, government services, and royalties and license fees.[10] A large part of government services relates to defense material, which is often demanded by countries outside the EU.

[10] Royalties and license fees is not really a sub-sector; it consists of transactions related to patents, and copyrights.

**Table 1.2 Trade Orientation for Various EU countries, 2001**

| | France | Germany | Italy | NL | Spain | UK |
|---|---|---|---|---|---|---|
| Transport and communication | 20.4 | 17.7 | 9.2 | 70.8 | 13.1 | 20.2 |
| Financial intermediation and insurance | 3.2 | 7.8 | 2.2 | 4.0 | 6.4 | 52.6 |
| Other business services | 5.8 | 5.3 | 7.4 | 20.8 | 10.7 | 15.8 |
| Personal services | 3.1 | 0.4 | 1.3 | 4.1 | 2.4 | 3.4 |
| Government services | 0.5 | 3.7 | 0.9 | 3.2 | 1.0 | 5.2 |
| Total services | 5.3 | 6.1 | 5.2 | 13.1 | 7.5 | 7.7 |
| Total goods | 21.8 | 27.5 | 21.2 | 48.3 | 22.1 | 21.0 |

Source: OECD, fn 9; OECD, *Structural Analytical database* (Paris, 2003); own calculations. Trade orientation is defined as value of exports divided by value added times 100. Data in the last two rows are from Eurostat, *Structural Indicators; Economic Reform; Trade integration of Goods and Services* (2006), and reflect the average of exports and imports divided by GDP.

## *Trade Orientation*

To what extent are EU services sectors oriented towards foreign trade? In some services sectors cross-border trade is more important than in others. The differences in their openness to cross-border trade can be due to the nature of the service or to regulatory barriers.

For a trade-orientation indicator we use the value of exports by a services sector divided by value added in that sector.[11] This trade-orientation indicator shows the 'tradability' of services products in specific sectors. Table 1.2 presents the results. In business services, the picture is mixed. The Netherlands, the UK and to a smaller extent Spain have a strong trade orientation in this sector, whereas markets in France, Germany and Italy appear to be rather inward-oriented.

Table two also shows that exports in transport and communication are relatively high in all EU countries. Only in the UK is openness in finance higher than in transport and communication. That reflects the special position of the UK as a financial center. Its trade orientation is higher than that of the financial services sector in other EU countries.

[11] Note that this indicator only indicates the degree of internationalization with respect to exports. In principle the home market could be closed for imports, although in practice this situation does not occur very often. If home markets are closed to foreign competition, firms are often not very competitive, which restrains their export possibilities.

**Figure 1.2 Average Annual Growth FDI Stocks in EU15 between 1995-2003**

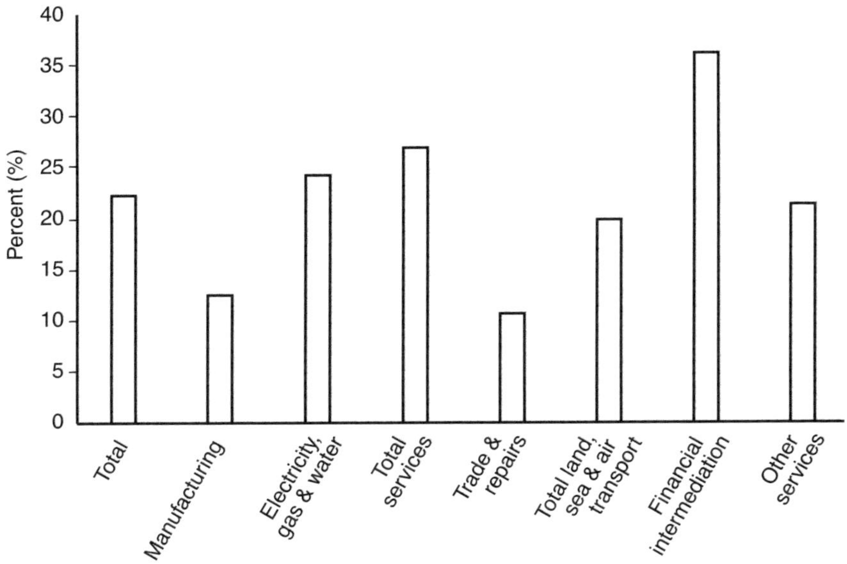


Source: Eurostat (2006).

Overall, however, the tradability of goods is much higher than that tradability of commercial services—except for transport services.

## *The Role of FDI in Services*

Services trade only reflects the internationalization of cross-border trade and consumers crossing the border (modes I and II), according to balance of payment data. It misses the degree of internationalization by foreign establishments in services markets (mode III). Data on sales of foreign establishments in services are rather scarce and incomplete. An indicator for foreign presence in a country is the foreign capital stock. Figure 1.2 presents the average annual growth of the FDI stocks in the EU15 between 1995 and 2003 for various economic sectors.[12] The figure shows that the FDI stock in services grew much faster than in manufacturing, in particular due to growth in financial intermediation. FDI also grew faster in such sectors as transport,

[12] For transport the data are between 1995 and 2002.

other services (mainly other business services) and network industries like electricity, gas and water than in manufacturing.

About two thirds of the FDI stocks in the EU are directed to services sectors.[13] Given the differences in FDI growth rates, the contribution of services will increase. UNCTAD[14] offers five underlying reasons for increased FDI in services sectors: the rising share of services in value added; the externalization of services of independent providers; the growing services intensity in the production of goods; the deregulation of services markets; and the liberalization of FDI policies. Moreover, greater competitive forces in services markets have led to market-seeking behavior abroad. Section 3 focuses on one of these arguments: the role of deregulation in services markets.

Activities of foreign services multinationals tend to be spread quite unevenly over domestic services industries in the EU. Kox *et al.*[15] illustrate this using the concept of "FDI inflow intensities," i.e. the share of a particular sector in total services FDI inflows to the sector's share of domestic services production. This indicator would total 1.0 if a services sector attracts a share of FDI inflows that corresponds with its share in domestic production. Table 1.3 indicates that services sectors such as retail and wholesale trade, tourism and transport account for far fewer FDI inflows than their corresponding share of domestic services production.

In the UK, the Netherlands and Spain other business services attracts a relatively low share of direct investment compared to the sector's size; the opposite holds for France and Germany. Communication gets relatively strong attention from foreign investors, which may well be due to deregulation that took place in the late 1990s, combined with the auctions for mobile phone licenses. Except in the Netherlands, financial intermediation attracts a relatively large amount of FDI.

[13] UNCTAD, *World Investment Report 2006* (Geneva, 2006). The relatively small difference in FDI stock growth rates between total services and total already reflects the importance of FDI in services in the total economy. The growth rate in manufacturing is much lower. It has a sizable but no large impact on the total growth rate, reflecting the shrinking importance of manufacturing.

[14] UNCTAD, *World Investment Report 2004* (Geneva, 2004).

[15] Kox, H.L.M., A.M. Lejour, R. Montizaan, *The Free Movement of Services within Europe*, CPB Document 69, 2004.

**Table 1.3 FDI inflow intensity: sectoral share of total service-FDI inflows divided by the sector's share of total domestic services production, selected countries, 1998-2000[a]**

| | Germany | France | UK | Spain[c] | NL | U.S.[b] |
|---|---|---|---|---|---|---|
| Retail and wholesale trade | 0.1 | -0.4[e] | 0.5 | 0.3 | 0.5 | 1.3 |
| Other business services | 1.9 | 1.5 | 0.4 | 1.9 | 0.2[d] | 0.4 |
| Travel | 0.0 | 0.1 | 0.2 | 0.1 | 0.2 | 1.0 |
| Communication | 1.2 | 0.8 | 6.4 | 4.3 | 3.0 | -1.3 |
| Transport services | 0.0 | 0.2 | 0.0 | 0.1 | 0.1 | 0.6 |
| Financial intermediation | 1.1 | 4.5 | 2.6 | 0.7 | 7.9 | 4.1 |
| Insurance (incl. auxiliary services) | -0.1 | 0.5 | 1.0 | 0.0 | 1.2 | 3.0 |
| Unweighted average | 0.6 | 1.0 | 1.6 | 1.1 | 1.9 | 1.3 |

**a.** services sector shares in total domestic services production are for the year 1999, except for Germany (1998). **b.** U.S. FDI inflow data refer to 1998. **c.** For Spain, production data for real estate and business services, and for tourism and other services refer to 1998, while data on communication, financial intermediation, and insurance refer to 1997. **d.** This does not count the FDI inflows in financial holding companies. **e.** The negative value reflects a net FDI outflow (disinvestment).

Source: Kox *et al.*, fn 15.

## 2. Regulation of Services Markets

Regulation is important in services markets. One reason is the need to provide universal services in energy and telecom sectors and to regulate the role of monopolies. A second reason is tied to asymmetries in information and the necessity to ensure quality for users. Quite often these regulations hamper competition because they deter market entry of domestic and foreign firms, restrict the behavior of firms and sometimes regulate prices.

Faini *et al.*[16] are quite pessimistic regarding market reforms in energy and telecom sectors and retail and professional services in Europe. They stress the need for more reform to increase competition and consequently productivity and innovation. However, most European countries have deregulated many services sectors since the 1980s, albeit at different speeds. This section presents recent trends in regulating services markets.

[16] Faini R., J. Haskel, G. Barba Navaretti, C. Scarpa, and C. Wey, "Contrasting Europe's Decline: Do Product Market Reforms Help?", paper presented at Breugel seminar, 2005.

**Figure 1.3 Regulatory Reform in Energy, Transport and Communications (1975-2003): Breakdown by Regulatory Area**

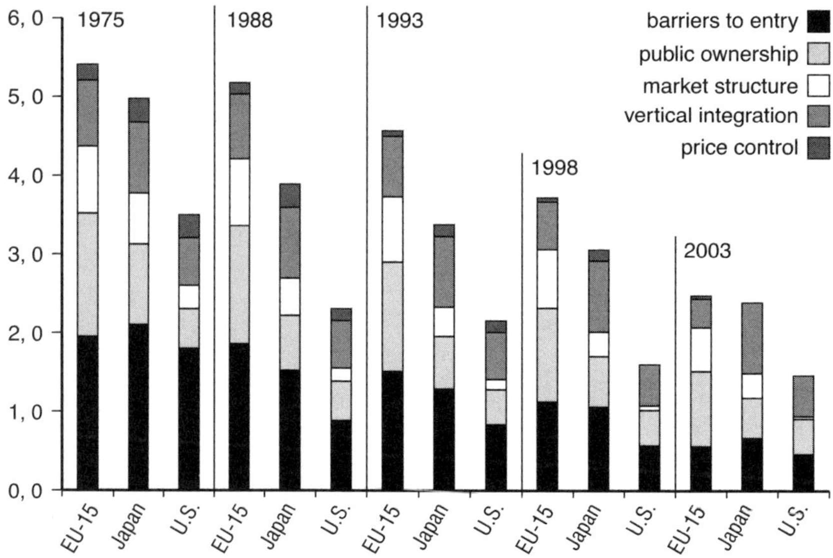


Source: Conway and Nicoletti, fn 17. Simple averages of the regulatory indicators for seven industries: electricity, gas, road freight, railways, air transport, post and telecommunications. Europe is defined as EU-15.

## *Regulatory Reform in Energy, Transport and Communication*

Conway and Nicoletti have recently updated regulatory indices for many services markets.[17] Telecoms and energy cover some of the industries in which anti-competitive regulation has traditionally been relatively strong in OECD countries, because these sectors were traditionally (and partly still are) characterized by natural monopoly segments and network externalities. Moreover, firms have typically been burdened with non-economic objectives (such as universal services obligations). Legal restrictions to entry, widespread public ownership,

---

[17] Conway, P. and G. Nicoletti, "Product Market Regulation in the Non-manufacturing Sectors of the OECD Countries: Measurement and highlights," *OECD Economics Department Working Papers No. 530,* (Paris, 2006). Although the quality of the OECD indicators is very high, these type of indicators are by definition imperfect, in particular if these are used to indicate their impact on the economy. Moreover, enforcement of regulation is important for the impact on competition. This is not measured by these indicators.

**Figure 1.4 The Timing of Reforms in Energy, Transport and Communication**

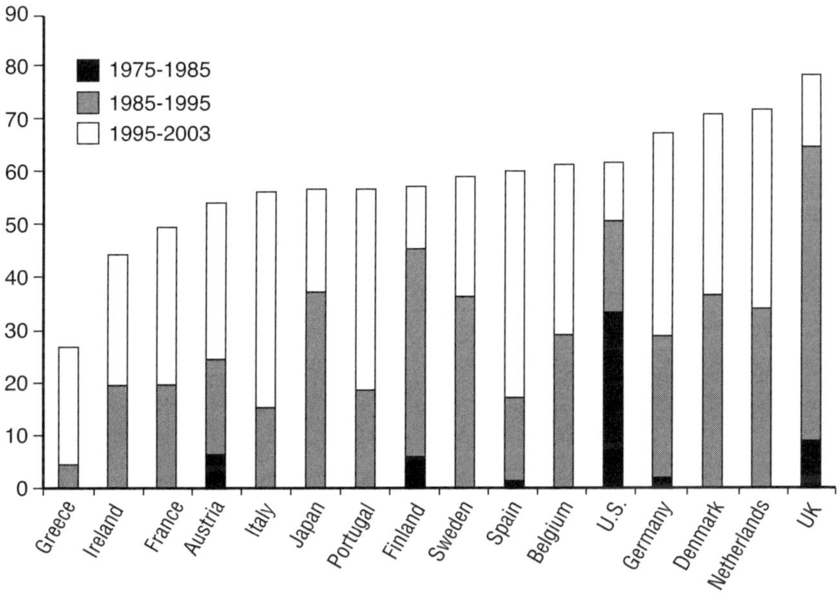


Source: Conway and Nicoletti, fn 17. Simple averages of the regulatory indicators for seven industries: electricity, gas, road freight, railways, air transport, post and telecommunications

and extensive cross-subsidies are common in these markets. Over time, technological advances, the evolution of governance and regulatory techniques, as well as increasing international exposure have made liberalization and privatization increasingly possible. According to these indicators, product market policies have become more market friendly recent decades as is shown by Figure 1.3.

The indicators suggest that regulation in these sectors was restrictive in all OECD countries in the 1970s, though more so in Europe and Japan. Since 1975, regulations have changed in most of the regulatory areas covered by the indicator, but were most pronounced in reducing entry barriers and, to a lesser extent, public ownership. Price controls are also almost completely eliminated. However, market and industry structures remain largely unchanged.

Eurostat data on gas and telecommunication price developments in EU member states show a substantial downward trend.[18] For some countries prices are even halved. This could be due to more competitive market forces, made possible by less restrictive regulation.

Figure 1.4 shows that the United States was the first country to begin reforming product market regulation in the early 1980s. Other countries, such as the United Kingdom, the Nordic European countries and Japan, started reforms a little later. In most other European countries product market reforms accelerated in the mid-1990s.

The cross-country dispersion product market regulation increased in relative terms until the late 1990s. In the EU countries this policy divergence appears to have been more pronounced, despite efforts to harmonize through the Single Market Program. From the beginning of this century, however, regulation in the EU has converged more rapidly than in the past.

As a result of these trends in product market reform, the aggregate product market indicator suggests that English-speaking countries, some small European countries and Germany have energy, transport and communication markets that are more open to competition than the rest of Europe. These services markets are less open to competition in France, Ireland and Greece in particular.

Conway and Nicoletti also conclude that there is considerable variation in the stringency of regulation across industries. In some industries, such as road freight, air transport, and telecommunications, regulation appears to have been completely overhauled. In other industries, such as gas, postal services, and rail transport, regulatory reforms appear to have been minor. The timing of reform has also varied widely across industries, with road freight and airlines being liberalized (and privatized) earlier than other industries and electricity and telecoms being reformed over the past decade.

## *Regulation in Retail Distribution and Professional Services*

In retail distribution and professional services markets are composed of many competing private firms. Hence, competition issues are

---

[18] Eurostat, "Economy and finance, Balance of payments - International transactions, EU direct investment positions, breakdown by country and economic activity," Luxembourg, 2006.

**Figure 1.5 Regulation in Retail Distribution in 2003**

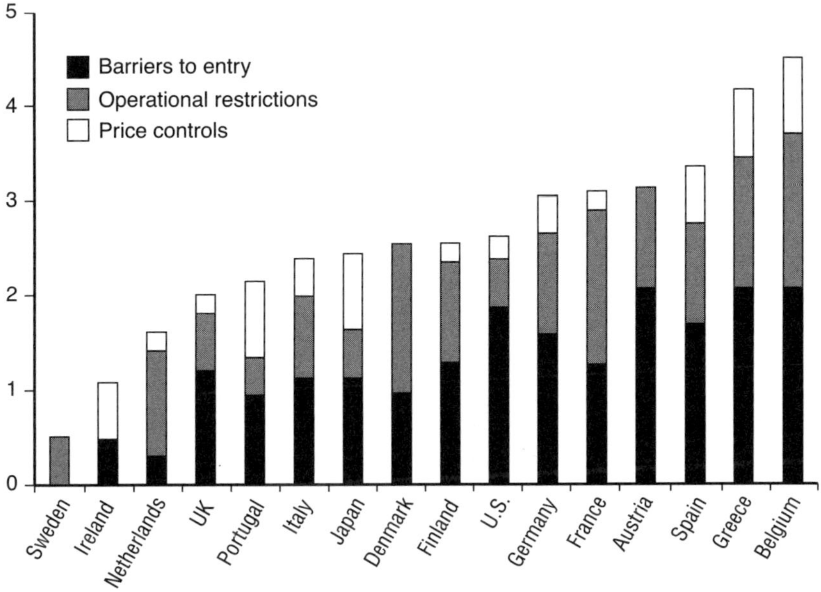


Source: Conway and Nicoletti, fn 17.

inherently different than in energy, transport and communications, where public legal monopolies have not been uncommon. Regulatory policies in retail distribution and professional services are based on either consumer protection or urban planning motivations or both. Being essentially country-specific, they have led to a wide dispersion of regulatory approaches, each being insulated by the low tradability of professional and retail trade services. Trade, technological developments and other global factors have less impact in these sectors. Reform trends have been less pronounced than in energy, transport and communication.

### *Retail Distribution*

Despite its generally fragmented market structure, the retail sector is often subject to numerous regulations that weaken competition. Conway and Nicoletti observe large differences in the indicator of retail regulation across OECD countries, suggesting very different policy approaches (Figure 1.5).[19] In addition, the large cross-country variation in retail regulation appears to have changed little between 1998 and 2003, implying little evidence of recent policy convergence in this sector. Operational restrictions and barriers to entry are the most common forms of regulation in retail distribution. Barriers to entry definitively hamper also market access of foreign providers, and operational restrictions are often also discriminatory, because the regulations often require companies to behave differently than in their home country.

***Professional Services***

Conway and Nicoletti[20] argue that regulation in the professional services often limits competition by restricting entry, allowing for price fixing, granting exclusive rights to perform particular services, and restricting advertising and business structures. These regulations are claimed to be in the interest of consumers because they improve quality of services and overcome information asymmetries. In practice, however, there is little empirical evidence that indicates a positive impact on consumer welfare, as Faini also concludes.[21]

The indicators of regulation in professional services (Figure 1.6) suggest that in Denmark, Sweden, Finland, UK, Ireland, and the Netherlands barriers to entry into professional services are less strict compared to other EU countries and Japan, while differences among restrictive countries mostly reflect differences in conduct regulation – that is restrictions on price setting, advertising, form of business, and inter-professional cooperation. On average entry regulation is more prominent than conduct regulation. In some countries conduct regulation is nearly absent. If the lack of conduct regulation does not affect the quality of the delivered services in these countries, it could also be eliminated in other countries.

For foreign competition in professional services it could be helpful that in 2005 the European Commission embarked upon a reform of

[19] Conway and Nicoletti, op. cit.

[20] Conway and Nicoletti, op. cit.

[21] Faini, *et. al.*, op. cit.

**Figure 1.6 Regulation of Professional Services in 2003**

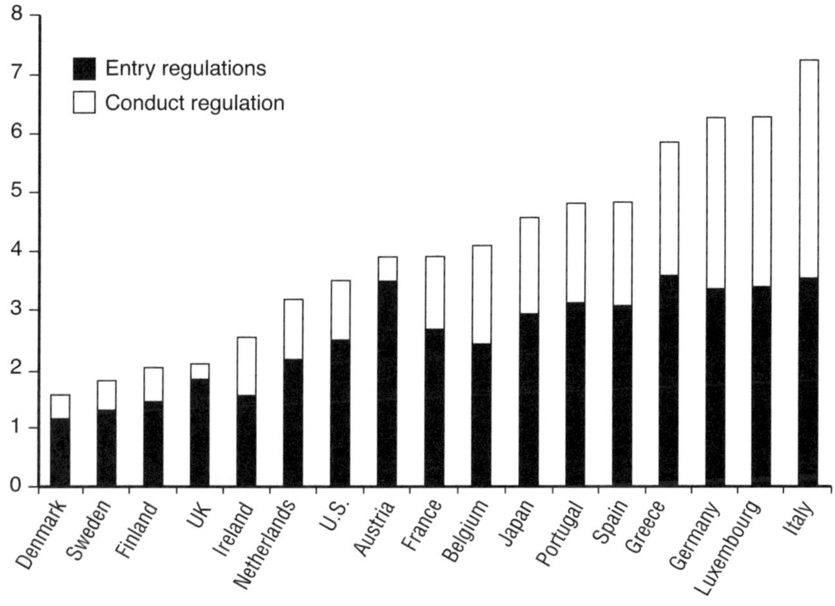


Source: Conway and Nicoletti, fn 17.

the system for the recognition of professional qualifications.[22] This will help to make labor markets more flexible, further liberalize the provision of services by encouraging more automatic recognition of qualifications, and simplify administrative procedures for those qualifications which are not automatically recognized.

Regulatory indicators for retail distribution and professional services are only available for the years 1998 and 2003. It is thus not possible to analyse regulatory reform over a longer period, as we did for telecoms and energy. The indicators suggest that entry barriers are relatively important. Conway *et al.* conclude that in recent years most European countries have not made much progress in lowering entry barriers according to the product market regulation indicators.[23]

[22] European Commission, *Directive 2005/36/EC of the European Parliament and of the Council of 7 September 2005 on the recognition of professional qualifications* (Brussels, 2005).

[23] Conway, P., V. Janod and G. Nicoletti, "Product Market Regulation in OECD Countries: 1998 to 2003," *OECD Economics Department Working Papers No. 419* (Paris, 2005).

These entry barriers not only hamper competition in national services markets, they hamper integrating these markets into European services markets.

The analysis of regulation in the sectors energy transport, communication, retail and professional services show that, by and large, regulation has decreased over the past few decades in most EU countries. This is helpful for integrating national services markets because regulatory systems are fragmenting the services markets. However, many barriers are still in place, in particular regarding market entry in retail distribution and professional services and public ownership in energy, telecommunication and transport markets. These barriers also hamper expansion of foreign services providers. Although the analysis above does not cover all services sectors and not all EU countries (such as many business services and the new EU countries), we have no indication that this analysis is not representative for Europe's other services markets.

## 4. National Regulatory Obstacles for the Internal Market

Section three concluded that market-reform policies reduced the degree of regulation in many services markets in Europe, but regulation did not disappear. We will not discuss the need for regulation, but focus here on the consequences of national regulation for integrating services markets. Many such (market-entry) regulations for services providers affect fixed costs of services firms (see the box below).

The fact that national services markets are regulated is not in itself an important barrier to international services trade. Kox and Lejour illustrate this with a thought experiment.[24] Suppose that all countries have the same type of regulation, for instance, a qualification requirement for providers producing a particular service product. Since qualification costs are mainly fixed costs, it would cost an exporting firm a one-off effort in its home country to comply with the qualification criteria. Once it incurred these fixed costs, it could allow the firm to reap economies of scale by expanding its market into additional EU member states.

[24] Kox, H.L.M. and A.M. Lejour, "Regulatory heterogeneity as obstacle for international services trade," CPB Discussion Paper 49, 2005.

**Examples of National Regulations for Services Providers that Affect Fixed Costs**

- Firm start-up licenses and associated authorization requirements
- Service-providing personnel must have locally recognized professional qualifications (may necessitate re-qualification)
- Obligatory membership of local professional association
- Owners or managers of service-providing firm must have local residence or nationality
- Firms must have a specific legal form
- Requirement that services providers have nationally recognized liability insurance or professional indemnity insurance
- All services activities in export destination country are fully subject to regular administrative and tax procedures
- Limitations on inter-professional co-operation or on the variety of services provided by one firm (may require unbundling)
- Temporary services personnel from origin country are subject to rules of the social security system of the destination country
- Impediments for material inputs, suppliers and personnel from origin country (necessitates search for new local suppliers)

Source: Kox, H.L.M. and A.M. Lejour, "Regulatory heterogeneity as obstacle for international services trade," CPB Discussion Paper 49, 2005, based on European Commission, *Report from the Commission to the Council and the European Parliament on the State of the Internal Market for Services* (Brussels, 2002).

However, such a uniform system of regulation does not exist in Europe. Countries developed their own systems of regulation rooted in their own culture and institutions. They have often have little confidence in the quality of each other's legal regimes and are reluctant to adapt their own regimes where necessary to facilitate cross-border activities. The result is that each national authority uses its own system of quality safeguards to protect services buyers. This is a great

**Figure 1.7 Cost Effect of Regulation Heterogeneity in EU Internal Market (perspective of exporting firm)**

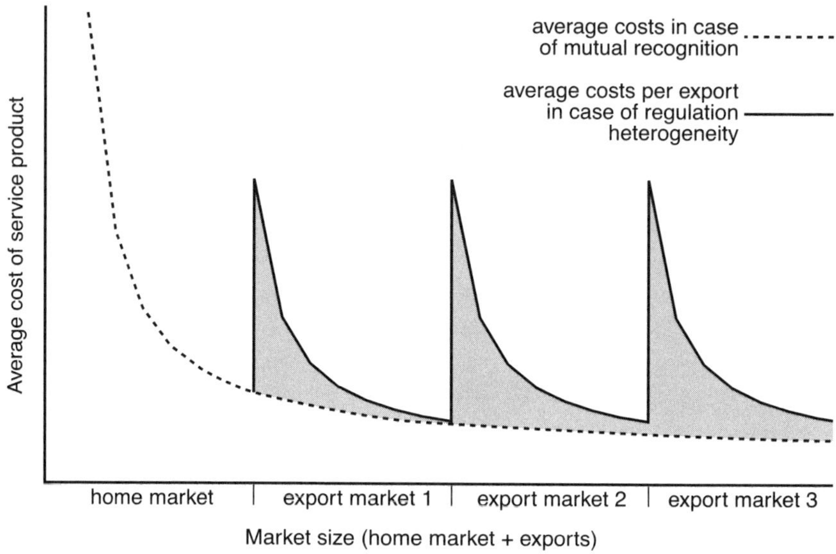


nuisance for international trade. Services exporters are confronted with different regulations and requirements, leading to additional costs when firms want to do business in other EU member states. These costs can be a prohibitive barrier for entering export markets.

Kox and Lejour argue further that the fact that these fixed qualification costs are specific for that national market implies that the costs cannot be spread out over production that is destined for other EU markets. The consequence is that the regulation heterogeneity limits intra-European economies of scale.

Figure 1.7 provides a picture of these effects for a services provider who subsequently enters a number of EU export markets. The presence of national qualification requirements gives rise to country-specific fixed transaction costs for the services exporter. Implicitly, the shaded area in Figure 1.7 shows the firm-level cost and efficiency gains that can be attained by a system that allows firms to achieve more economies of scale in dealing with regulation requirements.

Qualification requirements and associated costs for legal and other assistance are mostly independent of firm size. Hence, the market-entry deterring effect will be strongest for small and medium-sized firms. They form the large majority of services providers.

In a survey among a large number of business services firms in the EU, 44 percent of the firms mentioned costs as a "very important" barrier to setting up a local operation in other countries.[25] Those firms that were able to estimate the size of the start-up costs estimated them to be on the order of 6 months sales proceeds.[26] The European Commission has reached a similar conclusion:

> Evidence collected from SMEs and SME-supporting organisations suggests that many SMEs back off after initial inquiries about administrative requirements and procedures because they feel they do not have the necessary resources to deal with the current complexity. Such agencies report that micro enterprises in particular were easily dissuaded from engaging in cross-border activities.[27]

The heterogeneity in regulatory regimes doesn't only hamper services providers. Regulation heterogeneity suppresses foreign competition and the influx of new products and innovative working methods that foreign services providers can bring. It implicitly restricts the choice possibilities for domestic firms that want to purchase business services. The domestic price of business services will be higher than necessary (compared to the open-borders case). In the case of producer services, it leads to higher input prices for EU-based firms.

## 5. Current Initiatives to Integrate Services Markets

Section four argued that differences in national regulation negatively affect the internationalization of services providers and thereby contribute to fragmenting European services markets. However, recent developments indicate that the future could at least be a little

[25] *CSES, Barriers to international trade in business services—Final Report*, Study commissioned by the European Commission (Brussels: CSES / European Commission, 2001), p. 43.

[26] *Ibid*, p. 191.

[27] European Commission, *Report from the Commission to the Council and the European Parliament on the State of the Internal Market for Services* (Brussels, 2002).

bit different. Most European countries try to reform services markets by reducing entry barriers, barriers to competition and eliminating price controls (see section three). At the same time FDI is growing considerably. Moreover, the European Commission has taken initiatives to integrate services markets, and a common services market is also a key element of the EU's Lisbon reform program. These initiatives are of a much more recent date than the Single Market Program.

The Single Market Program focused mainly on the integration of goods markets. Services markets were not totally neglected, but for many commercial services single market policies lagged behind. Section two argued that cross-border trade in services has grown about the same speed as trade in goods, but given the rising share of services in GDP, the international market for services has opened more slowly than for goods. In identifying the role of the single market for various sectors, Nahuis demonstrated that for many services the internal market did not increase cross-border trade substantially, whereas the the internal market did stimulate trade for most goods sectors.[28] Lejour and de Paivra Verheijden (2007) show that services trade between the provinces of Canada is about twice as large as between the EU member states (measured as share of services value added).[29] An EC questionnaire of EC among services providers on the barriers to internationalization gives convincing anecdotic evidence to the statistical evidence mentioned above.[30]

This section discusses some of the recent Commission initiatives to integrate services markets. We concentrate on the highly-debated Services Directive, integration of financial markets, retail and wholesale markets and network industries.

## *The Services Directive*

In 2004 the European Commission proposed the Services Directive in order to slash regulatory barriers between national services markets.

---

[28] Nahuis, R., "One size fits all? Accession to the internal market, an industry-level assessment of EU enlargement," *Journal of Policy Modelling*, vol. 26, 2004, pp. 571-586.

[29] Lejour, A.M., and J-W. de Paiva Verheijden, "The Tradability of Services within Canada and the European Union,"Service Industries Journal, forthcoming, 2007.

[30] European Commission, *Report from the Commission to the Council and the European Parliament on the State of the Internal Market for Services* (Brussels, 2002).

Several studies indicate that bilateral trade and foreign direct investment in services could be boosted substantially. Kox and Lejour approach the issue by quantifying the market-entry costs of country-specific regulations, accounting for differences in product-market regulations between each EU country pair.[31] The degree of bilateral policy heterogeneity between countries is used as a proxy for sunken export costs; it may differ between each pair of countries. Applied in gravity equations for bilateral services trade in the EU, regulatory heterogeneity in policy areas like competition and trade regulation appears to have a robustly negative trade impact.

Kox and Lejour subsequently estimate in considerable detail the extent to which the Directive would affect bilateral policy heterogeneity. Intra-EU FDI in services could increase by 18 to 36 percent. In particular less heterogeneity in barriers to competition and a lower level of FDI restrictions would facilitate greater foreign direct investment. The Services Directive does not eliminate all heterogeneity in barriers to competition; some FDI restrictions in destination countries will remain in place. If all this heterogeneity in regulation would be eliminated, services FDI could increase by about 130 percent in Europe on average.

With respect to cross border trade, the heterogeneity in barriers to competition and explicit barriers to trade and investment hamper further market integration. The Services Directive would increase bilateral services trade within the EU by 30 to 62 percent, which is two to five percent of total EU trade. A complete elimination of heterogenous barriers would nearly triple intra-EU commercial services trade.

These numbers are stunning and we acknowledge that these are out-of-sample predictions. However, these numbers underpin the relevance of regulation and differences in regulation as barrier for international transactions in services.

In order to estimate the macro-economic importance of the Services Directive, De Bruijn *et al.* have fed the estimated trade impacts (not the FDI effects) into an applied general equilibrium model

---

[31] Using country-wise data on some 200 different items in product-market regulations from the OECD International Regulation database. The indicator is decomposed into five different areas of product-market regulation. See Kox, H.L.M. and A.M. Lejour, "The effect of the Services Directive on intra-EU trade and FDI," *Revue Economique*, vol. 57 (4), 2006, pp. 747-769.

WorldScan. They conclude that European consumption could increase on average by 0.5 to 1.2 percent.[32] If the effects of more FDI are added (derived from Lejour *et al.*)[33] consumption could increase by 0.5 to 1.5 percent. The limited openness of commercial services for trade and foreign investment explains why these macro-economic effects are relatively modest. However, expressed in terms of 2004 European GDP, the measures would total 35 to 95 billion euros. This still ignores the productivity and innovation impacts resulting from greater trade and FDI.

Copenhagen Economics also analyzed the EU proposals with an applied general-equilibrium model.[34] Their model also accounts for FDI effects. According to their simulation results, overall consumption in the European Union would increase by 0.6 per cent due to the Services Directive. This is somewhat smaller than the results reported by CPB.

### *Financial Services*

Financial integration in Europe has proceeded quickly. The introduction of the euro was an important landmark. It underpinned and stimulated integration of euro-derivative markets, equity and bond markets. In banking, however, integration proceeded less well. Some banks from different countries merged, but the efforts by ABN/AMRO to acquire a bank in Italy were seriously hampered in 2006. Moreover, the European Central Bank ECB has stressed that dispersion of national retail interest rates is also caused by differences in consumer protection rules, differing tax treatment, structural differences in the banking sector and the level of technology and competition in the national financial sectors.[35] The European Commission formulated proposals to address some of these issues. Ilzkovitz *et al.* point out that further efforts might be necessary in order to reduce the costs

---

[32] Bruijn, de R., H. Kox and A. Lejour, "The trade-induced effects of the Services Directive and the country-of-origin principle," *Working Paper 44*, ENEPRI (Brussels, 2006).

[33] Lejour, A.M., H. Rojas-Romagosa, and G. Verweij, "Opening up Services Markets within Europe: Modelling Foreign Establishments," *CPB Discussion Paper*, 2007.

[34] Copenhagen Economics, *Economic Assessment of the Barriers to the Internal Market in Services*, commissioned by the European Commission, 2005: www.copenhageneconomics.com.

[35] European Central Bank, "Differences in MFI interest rates across euro area countries," Statistics Publication, September 2006.

of cross-border clearing and settlement transaction, for which the costs are far higher than for domestic transactions.[36]

It is hard to assess the costs and benefits of financial integration. The London School of Economics estimated that GDP might increase by 1.1 percent in the long run caused by higher investment and private consumption and higher employment by integrating equity and bonds markets. The costs of capital are reduced by 0.5 percent points.[37] This study (as well as others) however, does not deal explicitly with the integration of the banking sector.

## *Retail and Wholesale Services*

Between 1994 and 2003 the average contribution of wholesale and retail trade to total productivity growth was 27 and 26 percent respectively in the U.S. and only 10 and seven percent respectively in Europe. Moreover, productivity growth in the U.S. was on average much higher than in the EU. McGuckin *et al.* explain the difference in performance by the early start of using ICT in the U.S. and the remaining regulatory obstacles within and between European countries.[38] The major obstacles to productivity growth are store opening hours, land usage restrictions (in particular on large stores) and labor laws. Land usage rules hamper entry and exit of firms and reduce the possibilities to economies of scale by larger firms. Dhyne *et al.* argue that the competitive pressure of larger retailers, like Wal-Mart, also stimulated other stores to improve technological and organisational structures.[39] These results suggest that regulatory reforms of land usage and opening hours could increase productivity growth in Europe. It has to be noted, however, that land usage laws are more rel-

[36] Ilzkovitz, F., A. Dierx, V. Kovacs and N. Sousa, "Steps towards a deeper economic integration: the Internal Market in the 21st century A contribution to the Single Market Review," *DG EcFin Economic Papers, 271* (Brussels, 2007).

[37] London School of Economics, 2002, "Quantification of the Macroeconomic Impact of Integration of EU Financial Markets, http://europa.eu.int/comm/internal_market/en/finances/mobil/ overview/summary-londonecon_en.pdf.

[38] McGuckin, R., H. Spiegelman, B. van Ark, "Can Europe match U.S. Productivity Performance? Perspectives on a Global Economy," *Conference Board Research report R-1358-05-RR*, 2005.

[39] Dhyne, E., L.J. Alvarez, H. Bihan, G. Veronese, D. Dias, J. Hoffmann, N. Jonker, P. Lünnemann, F. Rumler, J. Vilmunen, "Price Changes in the Euro-area and the US: Some Facts from Individual Consumer Price Data, *Journal of Economic Perspectives*, vol. 20, 2006, pp. 171-192.

evant in Europe. Land is scarcer because of the higher population density in Europe. Differences in taste could also hinder the development of standardized large retailers all over Europe.

### *Network Industries*

Section three showed that many countries have reformed their network industries, and tried to open up these industries to more competition. Initiatives of the European Commission have been helpful regarding reform efforts. However, the level of regulation within Europe is very uneven. The separation of vertically-integrated monopolies (often state-owned) sometimes meets fierce resistance because of vested interests and the fear that public interests are not taken sufficiently into account in liberalized network industries. It is necessary to introduce competition, however, which could finally lead to higher productivity and lower prices. The expansion of interconnections between national networks could at least reduce the physical barriers for foreign competition.

### *Dynamic Effects*

Most of the estimates on the effects of integration of European services markets only mention trade and investment effects or the static efficiency effects. Assessments of the dynamic effects are lacking because economists do not fully understand the mechanisms to measure them and data are nearly not available. However, Faini *et al.*, Ilzkovitz *et al.*, and Kox and Lejour[40] conclude that the prime economic gains come from more market entry. Improved market access will subsequently stimulate competitive selection and productivity growth. Competitive selection will lift average productivity, bolster the role of SME firms in exports, intensify knowledge spillovers, and strengthen innovation by incumbent firms. Moreover, increased FDI in liberalized services markets will also increase average productivity. This can be expected to be beneficial for the number of available services varieties, for services quality, and for the price of services.

[40] Op.cit; Kox, H.L.M. en A.M. Lejour, "Dynamic effects of European services liberalisation: more to be gained," in *Global Challenges for Europe*, Report by the Secretariat of the Economic council, PART 1, Prime Minister's Office Publications 18/2006, pp. 313-142, http://www.vnk.fi/hankkeet/talousneuvosto/tyo-kokoukset/globalisaatioselvitys-9-2006/en.jsp.

The literature on the relation between trade openness and income growth may offer some additional evidence regarding the size of the dynamic effects. The empirical relationship between openness and income is subject to debate. Some influential papers estimate that 1 percentage point more trade openness causes income to grow by 0.6 percent in the short term, and 1.1 percent when also long-term effects are counted.[41] Applying the latter estimate, the 2004 Services Directive could increase European GDP by two to five percent. These long-run effects incorporate the effects of extra competition, productivity spillovers, extra innovation and productivity growth. Nicoletti and Scarpetta estimate that entry liberalization in services towards the OECD average could boost productivity growth by 0.1 to 0.2 percent in some European countries.[42]

## 6. Prospects for Further Integration of Europe's Services Markets

In 2007, the European Union reviews its Single Market policies. Ilzkovitz *et al.*[43] state that the Single Market opened up perspectives to restore the confidence of European business and improve the performance of European companies through the formation of a better integrated and more competitive and innovative market place. The removal of barriers was intended to create an integrated market in which producers and consumers could reap the benefits of economies of scale. Moreover, fiercer competition was expected to result in efficiency gains and to stimulate innovation and the dynamic efficiency of the EU economy.

It is clear that the markets for goods are further integrated, but the EU has not yet taken the path towards a more dynamic and innovative economy. Comparisons with the United States show substantial gaps in growth rates in several services sectors. A higher level of regulation in Europe and the fragmented services markets explain a substantial part of these differences. The higher level of regulation in Europe and the differences in regulation which also hamper internationalization

---

[41] Frankel, J., and A. Rose, "An estimate of the effect of common currencies on trade and income," *Quarterly Journal of Economics* 117(2), 2002, pp. 437-466.

[42] Nicoletti, G. and S. Scarpetta, "Regulation, Productivity and growth: OECD evidence," *OECD Economic Department Working paper no. 347* (Paris, 2003).

[43] Op. cit.

require renewed single market policies for services markets if Europe wants to harvest the benefits of integrated services markets. After the laborious battle over the Services Directive this proposal will probably not meet much enthusiasm. Moreover, the horizontal approach of the Services Directive has to be abandoned, because more tailor-made proposals for market integration by services sector are needed. Such an initiative asks for a separate Directorate-General (DG) on the Internal Market for Services instead of the current DG on Internal Market and Services.

This analysis has demonstrated that many services markets have scope for further integration. Examples are retail and wholesale, network industries, financial services, and many business services. The Services Directive is a good start for business services, in particular the one shop idea to fulfill all administrative inquires for foreign firms. From the OECD indicators we know that many entry barriers remain. Eliminating these barriers would also stimulate foreign entry and introduce extra competition. The fierce debate over the Services Directive also showed that the acceptance of foreign regulation of imported services without domestic control is in many cases not acceptable at this moment. The alternative could be more detailed proposals on specific regulatory burdens to integrate national markets for each services market. This requires greater efforts. We have to accept that the low-hanging fruit is already harvested. Services markets by their nature are harder to regulate, but deregulation may be the only way to a more dynamic and innovative services economy. The large size of the U.S. market and fewer regulatory barriers are important causes for America's faster growing markets. It seems to be worthwhile to pursue further integration in order to try to grasp the large welfare effects possible by extra competition and effects on productivity and innovation. If not all EU member states are interested, enhanced cooperation between some member states could set the stage, although large scale markets are needed to generate larger economic effects.

## References

European Commission, 2004, Proposal for a Directive of the European Parliament and of the Council on Services in the Internal Market, SEC (2004) 21, Brussels.

Karsenty, G., 2000, Just how big are the stakes? An assessment of trade in services by mode ofsupply, in P. Sauvé, and R.M. Stern (eds.) *Services 2000: New Directions in Services Trade Liberalisation,* Washington D.C., Brookings Institution.

OECD, 2006, OECD Statistics on International Trade in Services; Detailed Tables by Service Category, Paris

# *Chapter 2*

# Reducing Barriers to Services Trade: The U.S. Case

*Lawrence J. White*[1]

*Though the U.S. economy is generally open with respect to international trade in services, there are some notable exceptions as well as some more subtle problems. This chapter provides a brief primer on trade in services, examines recent world and U.S. data, and highlights the major trade barriers, the opportunities, and the policy dangers that lurk in the current political climate.*

## 1. Introduction

Reducing the barriers to international trade in services provides all of the usual opportunities and challenges for the United States economy: the potential reductions in U.S. barriers provide the opportunities for improvements in the allocation of U.S. resources, with commensurate improvements in productivity and welfare. Further, because the U.S. has a comparative advantage in a number of major services areas—such as airline services, financial services, educational services, many professional services, entertainment services, etc.—the U.S. economy could also gain from reductions in services trade barriers abroad. But, because of the mercantilist orientation of most trade negotiations, the reductions in barriers abroad would likely require that the U.S reduce its barriers. But the losing parties from the reductions in the U.S. barriers have opposed and will surely continue to oppose such reductions.

All of this is standard stuff for trade barrier reductions. There are additional features, however, that make reductions in trade barriers for services—and the avoidance of the erection of new barriers—espe-

[1] This essay draws heavily in some places on White (2001, 2002b, 2005). I would like to thank Christine McDaniel for useful comments on an earlier draft.

cially interesting and worthwhile for the U.S.: international trade in services is an area that is growing faster than trade in goods—for the world generally and for the U.S. specifically. Also, unlike trade in goods, where for over a decade the U.S. has run ever-increasing annual net deficits, the U.S. continues to run surpluses in trade in services. Further, trade in services is a growth area in terms of the amount of attention—analytic as well as diplomatic—that is being paid to it.

This chapter will focus on trade in services and specifically on the recent U.S. experience and some U.S. issues.[2] Section two offers a brief primer on trade in services itself. Section three examines recent trade-in-services statistics for the world and for the U.S. Section four then turns to a description of the current orientation of the U.S. toward services trade, the major existing restrictions and the ripe opportunities for reductions in U.S. trade barriers, and the dangers of new restraints. Section five provides a brief conclusion.

## 2. Trade in Services—A Primer

Services are usually not the first thing that most people visualize when they think of international trade. Instead, it is trade in goods—represented by sacks of grain, rolls of steel, barrels of oil, boxes of toys and electronic goods, etc.—that is most readily visualized and that is often the subject of newspaper stories about trade and of policy debates about trade.

This is probably to be expected. Goods are concrete; their movement can be physically tracked as they cross borders from one country to another. Their concreteness helps in documentation and data gathering, as well as in understanding trade impediments such as tariffs and quotas.

By contrast, services are intangible; they can't be seen, touched, held, or felt. It is no accident that international flows of services used to be described as "invisibles". They flow internationally in different ways than do goods, so that the standard trade impediments (tariffs

[2] Since this essay focuses on the U.S., "foreign" corporations will mean those companies that are headquartered outside of the U.S., while "domestic" or "U.S." corporations will mean those companies that are headquartered in the U.S.

and quotas) usually don't apply. Also, services are more likely to be subject to direct domestic regulation of their delivery, which then opens opportunities for more subtle (or, perhaps, not so subtle) trade restrictive efforts through this regulation. In recognition of these differences, the inception of the World Trade Organization (WTO), as the successor to the General Agreement on Tariffs and Trade (GATT) in 1995, brought with it a separate document and negotiating forum (under the umbrella of the WTO): the General Agreement on Trade in Services (GATS).

These differences, and the likely lesser general familiarity with trade in services, make a brief discussion of the basics of trade in services worthwhile.

## *A. The Four Modes of Trade in Services*

As was noted above, services often don't flow across borders in the same way as goods flow. In recognition of this difference, a four-part classification system for services flows has developed and is generally accepted:[3]

1. cross-border;
2. consumption abroad;
3. commercial presence; and
4. temporary presence (presence of natural persons).

We expand on each category below.

1. **Cross-border.** Some services can and do actually originate in one country and "move" across a border to a user-recipient in another country. Examples include:

   - electricity;
   - telephone and similar telecommunications services;
   - the transportation and logistics services that attach to the physical movement of goods in international trade;

[3] These four modes are specified in article I of the GATS. Standard discussions of trade in services provide the examples listed below in the text, as well as other examples, and expand on them. See, for example, Bressand and Nicolaidis (1989), Hoekman and Braga (1997), Aharoni and Nachum (2000), Sauve and Stern (2000), Stephenson (2000), Findlay and Warren (2000), Hoekman (2000), Stern (2001), and Mattoo and Sauve (2003).

- the transportation of people across borders;
- the sales services that attach to a sale (of goods or services) across borders;
- the provision of a loan, deposit, insurance, or other financial services product across a border;
- distance learning, whereby a student in one country takes a course (e.g., via the Internet) offered by an educational institution in another country.

2. **Consumption abroad.** Some services are consumed through the travel of the customer from one country to the provider in another country. Examples include:

   - tourism;
   - education abroad;
   - repair services abroad;
   - medical treatment abroad.

3. **Commercial presence.** For many services, the service is most effectively provided/sold to the customer through a local physical establishment in the country of the consumer. For example, though a loan could (in principle) be made by a bank that was located solely in country X to a borrower who was located solely in country Y (and thus be a "cross-border" transaction along the lines of number one above), the bank's ability to assure itself that the borrower was a good risk who would be likely to repay the loan would usually be enhanced by the bank's having a local branch ("commercial presence") in country Y for interviewing and monitoring the borrower. As another example, a restaurant chain or a hotel chain in country X may believe that its services would be attractive also to customers in country Y, but few of the latter would be willing to travel to country X just for those services. In this case, the establishment of local outlets in country Y may be the only way for those services to be delivered.

   More generally, examples of services providers through "commercial presence" would include:

   - banks and other financial services providers;

- restaurant chains;
- hotel chains;
- retail merchandise chains;
- accountancy branches;
- legal services branches.

Since "commercial presence" does require a physical presence, the provision of services through this channel will usually require investment in the host country from the services firm in its home country (i.e., foreign direct investment, or FDI). Also, home country personnel may need to travel to the location abroad (i.e., the host country) so as to initiate the operations, train local personnel, periodically monitor the operations, etc. Thus, this mode brings other international transactions—FDI and labor movement—with it. In turn, these additional international flows mean that there are more (and more subtle) opportunities for host countries to impede the flow of services from abroad through restrictions on FDI and restrictions on immigration, as well as through more direct limitations on commercial location and establishment itself.

4. **Temporary presence (presence of natural persons).** Some services may be best delivered through the temporary presence of an individual or a group of individuals who deliver the service while abroad. Examples include:

- visiting entertainers (e.g., visiting orchestras, theater companies, rock stars);
- temporary consultancies;
- short-term construction projects.

Again, because individuals from a home country must travel to a host country in order to deliver the service, immigration policy can become an indirect means of impeding the flow of the service.

## B. *Domestic Regulation*

Services are often subject to extensive regulation by governments. As one illustration, consider the set of industries that were considered to be extensively regulated in the U.S. in the 1960s and 1970s and that were the targets of major efforts at deregulation or regulatory reform during the last quarter of the twentieth century:[4]

- air transport;
- rail transport;
- truck transport;
- water transport;
- natural gas pipeline transport;
- petroleum pipeline transport;
- telephone;
- broadcasting;
- electricity;
- banking;
- securities;
- insurance.

All of these industries are services providers. Further, though this list is drawn from the U.S. experience, in other countries these same industries were either also heavily regulated or were under government ownership.

Though these industries are considerably less regulated today in the U.S. than they were three decades ago, a remnant of regulation—modest in some industries, still substantial in others—persists today. Similarly, in many other countries, the partial deregulation or privatization over the past few decades has meant that greater or lesser remnants of regulation persist.

For another broad category of services—e.g., professional services, such as medical services, legal services, accountancy services, architectural services, etc.—government regulation occurs through licensing boards (or through delegation to professional associations, with government oversight) that are intended to maintain quality standards, prevent fraud, and protect the public.

Government regulation of the various kinds of services industries adds a layer of complexity to efforts to reduce impediments to interna-

[4] See, for example, Joskow and Rose (1989), Noll (1989), Winston (1993), and Joskow and Noll (1994).

tional trade in services, since the regulatory regimes themselves can become separate centers of resistance to the removal of barriers.

## C. *A Paucity of Data*

Another special feature of services is the relative paucity of detailed data with respect to services, as compared with manufacturing in the U.S. and elsewhere. Despite the fact that services in the U.S. now account for over 75 percent of private-sector GDP and 75 percent of private-sector employment, while manufacturing accounts for only 15 percent and 12 percent, respectively, the quantity of data and the levels of detail that are available for the manufacturing sector—say, from the semi-decennial economic censuses or from international trade data—far exceed those that are available for the services sector. This disparity is a legacy from the 1930s, when the basic statistical-gathering functions of the federal government were established and manufacturing was substantially more important in the U.S. economy. Though efforts are being made to rectify this disparity,[5] it still hobbles efforts to understand services—and trade in services—at a deeper level.

## D. *The GATS*

Through the mid 1970s there was little perception that trade in services was an important enough phenomenon to warrant substantial attention.[6] Instead, virtually all of the post-World War II multilateral effort at trade liberalization was focused on trade in goods through the General Agreement on Tariffs and Trade (GATT).

In the late 1970s, however, as the U.S. began the deregulation of its domestic airline industry, the same commitment to greater competition (and the dawning realization that the U.S. had a comparative advantage) began manifesting itself internationally through U.S. efforts to negotiate bilateral "open skies" arrangements to reduce the impediments that U.S. airlines faced abroad. Further, the U.S. was also increasingly concerned about how other countries were treating the overseas branches of U.S. banks and how U.S. entertainment services,

5 See, for example, Lazear (2007).

6 A more extensive treatment of the diplomatic history that eventually led to the GATS can be found in Nicolaidis (1989).

such as movies and syndicated television programs, were being treated. In addition, the European Common Market (ECM) was recognizing that the flows of various kinds of services, among its member countries and between the ECM and the rest of the world, was a major task that warranted substantial attention. In the early 1980s the U.S. began a concerted effort to bring trade in services into the realm of multinational negotiation and bargaining.

During the Uruguay Round of GATT negotiations in the late 1980s and the early 1990s there was a more general international realization that trade in services needed to be brought into a more formal multilateral negotiating arena. As a consequence, along with the formation of the World Trade Organization (WTO) itself as the successor to the organization that had administered the GATT, a general agreement on trade in services—the GATS—was negotiated, and the GATT and the GATS became parallel pillars of the newly formed WTO.[7] The GATS (with a Council on Trade in Services to administer it) came into effect on January 1, 1995.

The GATS is a broad set of principles that has the goal of encouraging freer trade in services among the WTO member countries. It applies to virtually all services, with the exception of government services that are non-commercial in nature (e.g., social insurance, public safety, national defense) and air traffic rights. It establishes general commitments toward most-favored nation (MFN) treatment, transparency in the domestic regulation of services, market access, and national treatment of services suppliers. It formally recognizes that services can be delivered through any of the four modes discussed above.

Unfortunately, the GATS is also riddled with loopholes and exceptions, which are the formal recognition in the GATS of the sensitivities and difficulties that come with many services sectors, especially those that are regulated along the lines discussed above. The most important loophole is that each country can choose which of its services sectors, through which mode, will be subject to the specific provisions of the GATS (and, implicitly, which will be exempt). Further, the leadership of the GATS and of the WTO, in deference to national sensitivities

---

[7] An "Agreement on Trade-Related Aspects of Intellectual Property Rights" (TRIPS) was also negotiated during the Uruguay Round and also placed within the WTO.

about domestic regulatory issues, have stressed the ability of governments to limit their commitments to removing barriers.[8]

Actual progress in effecting reductions in services trade barriers—because of all of the sensitivities to regulatory issues—has been slow.[9] The GATS has been in existence for about twelve years. After an initial set of statements and commitments at its inception, the "serious" negotiations were supposed to occur after 2000 in what has come to be called the Doha Round, with the negotiated reductions to be put in place at the end of the Round. Unfortunately, the Doha Round fell apart in July 2006 over a range of issues, and it is unclear what will happen next and also unclear whether any negotiated reductions will actually occur.

Further, the structure of the GATS and its substantial deference to domestic regulation has created a seemingly inherent bias toward inaction.[10] The efforts aimed at reducing barriers to trade in accountancy services are a good example.[11] Early in its existence the Council on Trade in Services chose accountancy as a lead sector (among the heavily regulated professional services sectors) for more detailed and extensive negotiations aimed at reducing trade barriers, because accountancy already had substantial international presences through the international expansions of a (literal) handful of large accountancy firms. In 1998 the Council adopted "disciplines" (rules) on the domestic regulation of accountancy that were intended to provide greater detail on issues of transparency, licensing requirements and procedures, qualification requirements and procedures, and technical standards. The disciplines were not to come into force, however, until the conclusion of the Doha Round (which has fallen apart). When the GATS announced a "Workshop on Domestic Regulation" that was to be held on March 29-30, 2004, and highlighted accountancy, the most recent progress that it could cite in that area was the 1998 disciplines.

---

[8] See, for example, WTO (2001).

[9] This is the clear tenor of the essays in Mattoo and Sauve (2003), with the possible exception of the essay (Roseman, 2003) on telecommunications.

[10] The arcane and opaque terminology of the GATS—"schedules", "bindings", "disciplines", "negative lists", etc.—surely does not enhance outsiders' understanding and monitoring of the process.

[11] More details can be found in White (2001, 2005) and Trolliet and Hegerty (2003).

Excerpts from the "Abstract" and "Introduction" sections of two recent GATS Working Papers[12] provide excellent expressions of the exceedingly modest progress that has been achieved under the GATS:

> "… Members have more scope than under the GATT to depart from common horizontal obligations, in particular the MFN principle; they are able to adjust the breadth and depth of their trade commitments (market access and national treatment) to particular sector conditions; and they face less constraints, if any, in the use of trade-related policies such as subsidies, export restrictions, or domestic regulatory interventions… [T]he basic (built-in) flexibility elements of the Agreement… will, of course, persist.… However, flexibility may come at a cost: lack of meaningful obligations across a reasonably broad range of service sectors. Vested interests may find it far easier than under the GATT to defend their privileges and defy more rational and harmonized trading conditions..." (Adlung, 2004, p. 1)

> "The… absence of major problems [within the GATS] to date may be attributed to at least three factors:... Second, the lack of stringent, non-modifiable trade obligations. There are virtually no requirements that individual Members might find difficult to meet or, otherwise, elude under relevant exemptions. The GATS offers more scope for departures from most-favored-nations (MFN) treatment—one of the few horizontal obligations that apply across virtually all services—than is the case under relevant GATT Articles. Moreover, traditional building blocks of the GATT, including the prohibition of quantitative restrictions and the automatic guarantee of national treatment with regard to domestic rules and regulations, are negotiable under the GATS…" (Adlung, 2004, p. 2)

> "Over the past months, it has become increasingly clear that the services negotiations under the Doha Develop-

[12] See Adlung (2004) and Adlung and Roy (2005).

ment Agenda will not produce significant improvements on current commitments unless major new impetus is provided.... [T]his paper discusses various impediments, from the perspective of the participating governments, that may explain the lack of negotiating momentum to date..." (Adlung and Roy, 2005, p. 2)

"The services commitments that resulted from the Uruguay Round (1986-1993/94), the first such round to cover trade in services as well, apparently have not had significant liberalization effects. Barring a few exceptions in basic telecommunications and financial services, where negotiations continued until February and December 1997, respectively, the commitments inscribed in Members' schedules remained essentially confined to binding existing regimes in a limited number of sectors. Further, many commitments may have been overtaken by autonomous liberalization moves in individual countries.... This paper seeks to explore why commitments under the GATS have generally remained modest..." (Adlung and Roy, 2005, p. 3)

## III. Some Data

A priori, one would expect to see rising levels of international trade in services, for at least five reasons. First, services generally appear to have an income elasticity of demand that is substantially greater than 1.0, especially in developed economies. As developed countries grow, they tend to produce and consume more-than-proportionately greater levels of services. To the extent that any services can cross borders, we would expect the growing demand for services to affect these cross-border services as well, which would be captured in economic statistics as growth in international trade in services.[13]

Second, the technologies—telecommunications, data processing and digitization, transportation, biological sciences—that underlie many important categories of services have experienced rapid

[13] For recent estimates of the income and price elasticities of demand that pertain to major categories of U.S. exports and imports of services, see Marquez (2005).

**Table 2.1 World Trade and GDP Data, 2005**

| | Levels — 2005 trillions of dollars ($) | Average annual percent (%) change, 1980-2005 |
|---|---|---|
| World trade: services | 2.415 | 7.85 |
| World trade: goods | 10.539 | 6.74 |
| World GDP | 44.455 | 5.47 |

Note: All values in nominal dollars ($); average annual percent change is calculated as simple annual compounding of last year/first year.

Sources: WTO; IMF

improvements in the past few decades.[14] As a consequence, better quality services, with greater variations and variety, can be offered by more firms at lower costs over longer distances; more effective competition among providers follows. The real prices (quality-adjusted and inflation-adjusted) of many services has surely decreased, which reinforces the income-elasticity effects to encourage greater consumption of services. And, again, some of this greater consumption should spill over to international trade in services.

Third, the improvements in telecommunications, data processing, and transportation technologies have also allowed firms to operate effectively over longer geographic distances and thus to allow services providers (such as hotel and restaurant chains) that require a commercial presence to be able to expand their reach and offerings.

Fourth, digitization of various kinds of information—e.g., credit scores of potential borrowers, the X-rays of medical patients, etc.—and reduced telecommunications costs have permitted some services (credit assessment, X-ray reading) that were previously vertically integrated with the final service (making a loan, health care) to be "outsourced". With low-cost telecommunications extending internationally, the outsourced services can become "offshored" internationally traded services.[15]

Finally, to the extent that countries have reduced their barriers to trade in services, those reductions too should encourage greater growth.

[14] See Bosworth and Triplett (2004) for a general discussion.

[15] For further discussions along these lines, see Mann (2005), Jensen and Kletzer (2006), Van Welsum and Reif (2006), and (more generally) Collins and Brainard (2006).

**Table 2.2 Leading World Exporters and Importers, 2005**

| Goods Exports | Services Exports | Goods Imports | Services Imports |
|---|---|---|---|
| Germany | U.S. | U.S. | U.S. |
| U.S. | U.K. | Germany | Germany |
| China | Germany | China | U.K. |
| Japan | France | France | Japan |
| France | Japan | U.K. | France |

Source: WTO

As we will see, the data strongly support these predictions. We will first present briefly some world trade data and then some more extensive U.S. data.

## *A. World Data*

Table 2.1 shows the experience of the world trading system for the past quarter century for goods and services. Consistent with the brief discussion above, trade in services has grown substantially: faster than trade in goods, and faster than the growth in world GDP. It is worth noting that these data exclude the "commercial presence" mode (mode number three above) of services exports, which has probably grown even faster (at least as is indicated by the U.S. data that are discussed below).

Table 2.2 shows the identity of the leading exporters and importers of goods and services, as of 2005. As would be expected, the world's largest economies are the world's leading traders as well, with the U.S. holding first place in three of the four categories and second in the fourth.

## *B. U.S. data*

Table 2.3 shows the experience specifically of the U.S. over this same quarter century. Again, consistent with the discussion above, trade in services has grown substantially: faster than trade in goods and faster than U.S. GDP, as well as faster than world trade in services.

Table 2.4 provides the year-by-year annual trade data for goods and services for 1992-2005. As can be readily seen, trade in services has

**Table 2.3 U.S. Trade and GDP Data, 2005**

| | Levels — 2005 billions of dollars ($) | Average annual percent (%) change, 1980-2005 |
|---|---|---|
| Services exports | 381 | 8.67 |
| Services imports | 315 | 8.44 |
| Goods exports | 895 | 5.69 |
| Goods imports | 1,677 | 7.92 |
| GDP | 12,479 | 6.18 |

Note: All values are in nominal dollars ($); average annual percent change is calculated as simple annual compounding of last year/first year.

Sources: BEA; CEA

**Table 2.4 U.S. Trade Data, 1992-2005 in billions of dollars ($)**

| | Services | | | Goods | | |
|---|---|---|---|---|---|---|
| Year | Exports | Imports | Balance | Exports | Imports | Balance |
| 1992 | 177 | 120 | 58 | 440 | 537 | -97 |
| 1993 | 186 | 124 | 62 | 457 | 589 | -132 |
| 1994 | 200 | 133 | 67 | 503 | 669 | -166 |
| 1995 | 219 | 141 | 78 | 575 | 749 | -174 |
| 1996 | 239 | 153 | 87 | 612 | 803 | -191 |
| 1997 | 256 | 166 | 90 | 678 | 876 | -198 |
| 1998 | 263 | 181 | 82 | 670 | 917 | -247 |
| 1999 | 282 | 199 | 83 | 684 | 1030 | -346 |
| 2000 | 299 | 224 | 75 | 772 | 1224 | -452 |
| 2001 | 286 | 222 | 64 | 719 | 1146 | -427 |
| 2002 | 292 | 231 | 61 | 682 | 1165 | -482 |
| 2003 | 303 | 250 | 52 | 713 | 1261 | -547 |
| 2004 | 344 | 290 | 54 | 808 | 1473 | -665 |
| 2005 | 381 | 315 | 66 | 895 | 1677 | -783 |
| **Average annual percent (%) change, 1992-2005** | | | | | | |
| | 6.05 | 7.73 | | 5.62 | 9.16 | |

Note: All values are in nominal dollars ($); average annual percent change is calculated as simple annual compounding of last year/first year; average annual percent change in nominal U.S. GDP, 1992-2005 is 5.35 percent.

Source: BEA

**Table 2.5 U.S. Services Trade Data, 1992-2005 in billions of dollars ($)**

| | Travel | | | Passenger Fares | | | Other Transportation | | | Royalties & License Fees | | | Other Private Services | | | U.S. Military | | | U.S. Gov. Misc. | | | Total Services | | |
|---|---|---|---|---|---|---|---|---|---|---|---|---|---|---|---|---|---|---|---|---|---|---|---|---|
| Year | Ex | Im | Bal | Ex | Im | Bal | Ex | Im | Bal | Ex | Im | Bal | Ex | Im | Bal | Ex | Im | Bal | Ex | Im | Bal | Ex | Im | Bal |
| 1992 | 55 | 39 | 16 | 17 | 11 | 6 | 22 | 24 | -2 | 21 | 5 | 16 | 50 | 25 | 25 | 12 | 14 | -1 | 1 | 2 | -1 | 177 | 120 | 58 |
| 1993 | 58 | 41 | 17 | 17 | 11 | 5 | 22 | 25 | -3 | 22 | 5 | 17 | 54 | 28 | 26 | 13 | 12 | 1 | 1 | 2 | -1 | 186 | 124 | 62 |
| 1994 | 58 | 44 | 15 | 17 | 13 | 4 | 24 | 26 | -2 | 27 | 6 | 21 | 61 | 32 | 29 | 13 | 10 | 3 | 1 | 3 | -2 | 200 | 133 | 67 |
| 1995 | 63 | 45 | 18 | 19 | 15 | 4 | 26 | 27 | -1 | 30 | 7 | 23 | 65 | 35 | 30 | 15 | 10 | 5 | 1 | 3 | -2 | 219 | 141 | 78 |
| 1996 | 70 | 48 | 22 | 20 | 16 | 5 | 26 | 27 | -1 | 32 | 8 | 25 | 73 | 40 | 34 | 16 | 11 | 5 | 1 | 3 | -2 | 239 | 153 | 87 |
| 1997 | 73 | 52 | 21 | 21 | 18 | 3 | 27 | 29 | -2 | 33 | 9 | 24 | 84 | 43 | 41 | 17 | 12 | 5 | 1 | 3 | -2 | 256 | 166 | 90 |
| 1998 | 71 | 56 | 15 | 20 | 20 | 0 | 26 | 30 | -5 | 36 | 11 | 24 | 92 | 48 | 44 | 17 | 12 | 5 | 1 | 3 | -2 | 263 | 181 | 82 |
| 1999 | 75 | 59 | 16 | 20 | 21 | -2 | 27 | 34 | -7 | 40 | 13 | 27 | 104 | 56 | 48 | 16 | 13 | 3 | 1 | 3 | -2 | 282 | 199 | 83 |
| 2000 | 82 | 65 | 18 | 21 | 24 | -4 | 30 | 41 | -12 | 43 | 16 | 27 | 108 | 61 | 47 | 14 | 13 | 0 | 1 | 3 | -2 | 299 | 224 | 75 |
| 2001 | 72 | 60 | 12 | 18 | 23 | -5 | 28 | 39 | -10 | 41 | 17 | 24 | 114 | 66 | 48 | 13 | 15 | -2 | 1 | 3 | -2 | 286 | 222 | 64 |
| 2002 | 67 | 59 | 8 | 17 | 20 | -3 | 29 | 38 | -9 | 45 | 19 | 25 | 122 | 73 | 50 | 12 | 19 | -7 | 1 | 3 | -2 | 292 | 231 | 61 |
| 2003 | 64 | 57 | 7 | 16 | 21 | -5 | 32 | 45 | -13 | 47 | 19 | 28 | 131 | 80 | 51 | 13 | 25 | -13 | 1 | 3 | -2 | 303 | 250 | 52 |
| 2004 | 75 | 66 | 9 | 19 | 24 | -5 | 37 | 54 | -17 | 53 | 23 | 29 | 145 | 90 | 54 | 15 | 29 | -14 | 1 | 4 | -3 | 344 | 290 | 54 |
| 2005 | 82 | 69 | 13 | 21 | 26 | -5 | 42 | 62 | -20 | 57 | 25 | 33 | 158 | 99 | 60 | 19 | 30 | -11 | 1 | 4 | -3 | 381 | 315 | 66 |
| Average annual percent (%) change, 1992-2005 | | | | | | | | | | | | | | | | | | | | | | | | |
| | 3.13 | 4.60 | | 1.79 | 7.16 | | 5.32 | 7.67 | | 8.11 | 12.73 | | 9.22 | 11.01 | | 3.36 | 6.15 | | 1.99 | 4.44 | | 6.05 | 7.73 | |

Note: All values are in nominal dollars ($); average annual percent change is calculated as simple annual compounding of last year/first year; average annual percent change in nominal U.S. GDP, 1992-2005 is 5.35 percent. Source: BEA

**Table 2.6 Sales of Services through Affiliates in billions of dollars ($)**

| Year | Sales to foreign persons by foreign non-bank affiliates of U.S. Companies | Sales to U.S. persons by U.S. non-bank affiliates of foreign companies | Difference |
|---|---|---|---|
| 1992 | 141 | 128 | 13 |
| 1993 | 143 | 135 | 8 |
| 1994 | 159 | 145 | 14 |
| 1995 | 190 | 150 | 40 |
| 1996 | 223 | 168 | 55 |
| 1997 | 255 | 223 | 32 |
| 1998 | 286 | 246 | 40 |
| 1999 | 353 | 294 | 59 |
| 2000 | 414 | 344 | 70 |
| 2001 | 422 | 368 | 54 |
| 2002 | 424 | 368 | 56 |
| 2003 | 452 | 374 | 78 |
| 2004 | 490 | 383 | 107 |
| | **Average annual percent (%) change 1992-2004** | | |
| | 10.94 | 9.56 | |

Source: Koncz *et al.* (2006).

maintained a consistent annual surplus, while the annual deficit in trade in goods has grown progressively larger.

Table 2.5 provides annual data for 1992-2005 for finer categories of services trade.[16] Travel (i.e., tourism) has shown modest growth rates on both the export and import sides. Passenger fares (largely airline fares plus cruise lines) showed slow growth in exports but much larger growth in imports. Other transportation (i.e., ocean shipping, air freight, ocean port services, and airport services) showed faster growth of imports than of exports. Royalties and license fees (mostly fees paid to affiliates for intellectual property, plus fees paid for broadcasting international sports events) grew substantially, especially on the import side. Other private services (including education; financial services; insurance; telecommunications; film and television tape rentals; and business, professional, and technical services) grew rap-

[16] Greater detail and discussion can be found in Koncz *et al.* (2006) and USITC (2006).

idly;[17] finally, U.S. military and other government services grew at slow to medium rates.

Finally, Table 2.6 shows the annual data for 1992-2005 for sales of services through nonbank affiliates—in essence, sales of services through a commercial presence (mode number three discussed above). As can be seen, the flows in both directions grew faster than did the services flows shown in Table 2.4. Further, sales by foreign affiliates of U.S. companies to non-U.S. persons grew faster than did the sales by the U.S. affiliates of foreign companies to U.S. persons, and the net balance was a growing and sizable surplus. It is also worth noting that for recent years the absolute sizes of the services sales in each direction have been larger than the counterpart services exports and imports listed in Table 2.4, and the annual surpluses for 2003 and 2004 in Table 2.6 are also larger than the services surpluses in Table 2.4 for the same years.

## 4. Opportunities for Reductions in Trade Barriers

### *A. The general landscape*

The U.S. economy—with some notable exceptions—is generally open to non-U.S. providers of services through any of the four modes.[18] Even in relatively open areas, however, there are some subtle problems.

Financial services provide a good example. As a general matter, with respect to financial services the U.S. generally does not discriminate against non-U.S. banks or securities firms or insurance companies, and non-U.S. firms have developed sizable shares of the U.S. market (as measured by assets or other standard metrics).[19] As a first subtle problem, however, since financial services are frequently regulated by the 50 states as well as by the U.S. Government,[20] anomalous state regula-

[17] The persistent annual surpluses in this category are prominently noted in USCEA (2005, pp. 178-179).

[18] See the discussions in Brewer and Young (2001), Mann (2005), WTO (2006b), and USITC (2006).

[19] See, for example, the data and discussion in White (2002a).

[20] Insurance is an exception, in that it is regulated solely by the states.

tions sometimes make entry and establishment by foreign firms somewhat harder than is true for U.S. firms.[21]

Second, in the area of housing finance, the U.S. has chartered three large "government-sponsored enterprises" (GSEs)—Fannie Mae, Freddie Mac, and the Federal Home Loan Bank System—that are private companies with special privileges and advantages.[22] The most important advantage is the reduced borrowing costs that these GSEs enjoy as a consequence of their GSE status and the financial markets' perception that the U.S. Government would likely "bail them out" and thus make their creditors whole in the event of financial difficulties at any of the GSEs. Only these three GSEs have these special charters, and the Congress is unlikely to create more such charters. Consequently, this special area of housing finance[23] is effectively barred to new entry and competition from new firms with such charters—whether the firms are foreign or domestic.

Third, the major bond rating companies (e.g., Moody's, Standard & Poor's, and Fitch) have been protected since 1975 by a little-known set of Securities and Exchange Commission (SEC) regulations.[24] These regulations created a category "Nationally Recognized Statistical Rating Organization" (NRSRO) and "grandfathered" the three major firms into the category. Though the SEC subsequently designated four more firms as NRSROs, by 2000 mergers among the four and with Fitch had reduced the number of NRSROs back to the original three.

The importance of the NRSRO designation lies in the following: Many categories of regulated financial services firm are restricted as to the quality of bonds that they can hold in their portfolios (i.e., in which they can invest). For example, commercial banks and other depository institutions are permitted to hold only "investment grade" bonds. Crucially, only the NRSROs' designations of quality (e.g., their designations of "investment grade") matter for the financial institu-

[21] Further discussion on this point can be found in USITC (2002, ch. 5) and WTO (2006b).

[22] Further discussion of these GSEs can be found, for example, in Frame and Wall (2002), Frame (2003), White (2003, 2004), Frame and White (2004, 2005), and Frame and Flannery (2006).

[23] It is important to note, however, that entry into housing finance more generally is open to foreign firms as well as to domestic firms.

[24] For expansion on this topic, see White (2002b, 2006, 2007).

tions' choices—and thus the absence of the NRSRO designation causes a would-be bond rating firm to be at a substantial disadvantage.

Moody's and S&P are U.S. companies; Fitch is the subsidiary of a French conglomerate. There is no evidence that the SEC has any "home company" bias. Indeed, when (under Congressional pressure) in early 2003 the SEC designated a fourth NRSRO, it chose a Canadian bond rating company, Dominion Bond Rating Services (DBRS).[25] Nevertheless, it is clear that the SEC's NRSRO designation is a barrier to entry into the bond rating business in the U.S. and thus a restriction on trade in services if a foreign firm would otherwise want to enter and provide bond rating services in the U.S. (as DBRS had desired prior to 2003, and as other foreign firms have indicated to the SEC).[26]

There are likely other such subtle restrictions on trade in services that are strewn across the regulatory landscape in the U.S.

## *B. The Major Restrictions*

There are four major areas for which there are notable restrictions on trade in services in the U.S.: air transport; water transport; truck transport; and satellite broadcasting spectrum licenses. We will discuss each in turn.[27]

**1. Air transport.** Under the Civil Aeronautics Act of 1938 and the Federal Aviation Act of 1958, any company that provides point-to-point passenger or freight air service within the U.S. ("cabotage") must be a U.S. carrier. This means that the company must be under the actual control of U.S. citizens, and foreign ownership is limited to a maximum of 25 percent of voting shares. Also, the president and at least two-thirds of the board of directors and other managing officers must be U.S. citizens. The crews of a U.S. carrier must be U.S. citizens or resident aliens.

---

[25] When the SEC designated a fifth NRSRO in early 2005, it chose A.M Best, an insurance company specialist. In May 2007 the SEC designated two Japanese rating companies as the sixth and seventh NRSROs.

[26] In the late summer of 2006 new legislation was passed that was intended to loosen the SEC's restrictions on entry into the bond rating business. Whether that intent will be converted into actuality will be determined by how the SEC drafts and implements the new regulations that are required by the legislation. For further discussion, see White (2007).

[27] Extensive discussions of these restrictions and their consequences can be found in USITC (1999, ch. 5; 2002, ch. 5; 2004, ch. 5)

All of these requirements effectively prevented foreign carriers from offering domestic service in the U.S. until Virgin America, a subsidiary of the Virgin Group, succeeded in satisfying the requirements and began offering service in August 2007.

In addition, the Fly America Act of 1974 requires that U.S. government-financed international transportation of passengers and cargo be on a U.S.-flag carrier (although exceptions are possible).

**2. Water transport.** The Jones Act of 1920 restricts the domestic point-to-point transport of cargo to ships that are registered and built in the U.S., on which at least 75 percent of the employees are U.S. citizens, and that are owned by a U.S. corporation. Domestic passenger service (essentially, cruise lines) must meet similar requirements under the Passenger Vessel Services Act of 1886. Though foreign companies could, in principle, establish a shipping company in the U.S. through a holding company arrangement, the other requirements have effectively discouraged such actions, and U.S. water-borne cabotage is a U.S. preserve.

In addition, various pieces of legislation require that 50 to 100 percent (depending on the category) of "government-impelled" international cargoes—such as military cargo, oil for the Strategic Petroleum Reserve, and foreign aid cargo—be carried in U.S.-flag ships (that are built in the U.S., on which at least 75 percent of the employees are U.S. citizens, and that are owned by a U.S. corporation). Despite these restrictions, 98 percent of U.S. international water-borne cargo travels in non-U.S. flag ships. Nevertheless, the restrictions on the remaining two percent are effectively a restraint on trade.

**3. Truck transport.** Realistically, the import of trucking services is likely to occur largely from Canada and Mexico. Neither country's trucks are permitted to provide domestic point-to-point freight service within the U.S.;[28] thus, yet another category of cabotage is reserved for U.S. firms.

The use of foreign-owned trucks for the delivery of international cargo to points within the U.S. is a separate, and important, category

[28] A modest exception is available to Canadian trucks that are delivering or picking up international cargoes in the U.S.; they can transport goods between points within the U.S., so long as the local shipment is incidental to an immediately prior or subsequent international trip.

of concern. About 70 percent of goods imports from Canada enter the U.S. by truck; the comparable figure for goods imports by truck from Mexico is over 80 percent.

Efforts began in the 1980s to harmonize regulations between the U.S. and Canada. These efforts continued under the U.S.-Canada Free Trade Agreement of 1988 and the North American Free Trade Agreement (NAFTA) of 1992, so that delivery of international cargoes by Canadian trucks is currently not considered to be a major problem.

With respect to the use of Mexican-owned trucks for the delivery of international cargoes, however, the picture has been quite different. Despite specific provisions in NAFTA for the progressive expansion of the reach of Mexican trucks to all points in the U.S., until 2007 Mexican trucks were restricted to deliveries within a few miles of the border, necessitating costly and inefficient cargo transfers for most cargoes from Mexico. Only in September 2007 were the first few Mexican trucking companies allowed to operate thoughout the U.S. under a one-year pilot program.

**4. Satellite broadcasting spectrum.** The Communications Act of 1934 restricts the granting of electromagnetic spectrum licenses to U.S. citizens or corporations; but it is possible for a foreign company to establish a holding company that owns a U.S. corporation that has such licenses.

However, the Communications Act also restricts foreign ownership of one-way satellite transmissions of direct-to-home (DTH), direct broadcasting systems (DBS), and digital audio services, and the holding company work-around does not appear to be available to undo this restriction.

## *C. Opportunities and Challenges*

As is true in other areas of international trade, the U.S. Government's position with respect to trade in services is a mixture of export boosterism and import protectionism. On the one hand, in areas in which the U.S. has a comparative advantage—such as international airline services, financial services, and entertainment services—the U.S. has been actively promoting "open skies" and its financial and entertainment equivalents. On the other hand, in areas where the U.S.

has a comparative disadvantage, such as ocean shipping, or where important national interests are seen to be at stake, such as domestic airline service or satellite services, the U.S. remains protectionist.

This bifurcation in perspective is largely typical of the mercantilist perspective that continues to dominate national policy-making: Exports are good; imports are bad; "jobs" saved and created are all-important; we will (maybe) lower our trade barriers only if you promise to lower yours; etc. It pervades the U.S. policy perspective with respect to trade in goods. There's no reason to expect that it wouldn't pervade trade in services as well.

It is clear that there would be net gains in U.S. social welfare if the major restrictions identified above were relaxed, even unilaterally.[29] Further, because the U.S. has a comparative advantage in many important services—e.g., airline services, educational services, financial services, entertainment services, etc.—the U.S. economy could also gain from reductions in services trade barriers abroad. These latter reductions could well require, as a quid pro quo, the reductions in the major U.S. barriers. However, the reduction or removal of these major restrictions—which would require contentious legislation[30]—do not seem to be "on the table" for discussion and negotiation.[31]

There are two other trade-in-services issues that are of concern. First, as a consequence of the events of September 11, 2001, the U.S. clearly tightened its immigration procedures, which must make it harder for foreign services providers to maintain their efforts in the U.S. Substantial levels of illegal immigration into the U.S. have generated calls for a general reform of immigration policy. There are always dan-

---

[29] The "national defense" argument for retaining these restrictions on domestic air service and waterborne trade are weak, at best, and the goals could be achieved at lesser social costs through various contingent contracting arrangements by the U.S. Department of Defense. The "highway safety" arguments that are used to justify the restrictions on Mexican trucking in the U.S. are similarly weak.

[30] Beginning in late 2005 the U.S. Department of Transportation (DOT) explored the possibility that it could (through a liberal interpretation of the relevant legislation) find a way around the foreign ownership restrictions on domestic airline service (so as to accommodate the possibility of the Virgin Group's establishing domestic service) but ultimately abandoned the effort in December 2006. However, as was noted above in the summer of 2007 the Virgin Group succeeded in satisfying the DOT's requirements and Virgin America began service in August 2007.

[31] In its initial policy statement that was preliminary to the WTO's 2006 "Trade Policy Review", the U.S. did not mention any of its major services trade restrictions. See WTO (2006a).

gers that changes in immigration policy could further restrict the inflow of foreign workers, with unfortunate consequences for trade in services.

Second, there has been a rising level of political attention to the offshore outsourcing of some services, such as telephone call centers, backoffice data processing, software development, and other information technology functions. This outsourcing has grown as a consequence of decreasing telecommunications and data processing costs and the generally increasing scope, breadth, and quality of digitization technologies.[32] Fortunately, this greater political attention has not (yet) been translated into any restrictive actions or policies. But the possibility of restrictions surely continues as a worrisome threat to freer trade in these services.

## 5. Conclusion

Trade in services is a growing and worthwhile area for the U.S. and the world. Though the U.S. is a comparatively open economy with respect to trade in services (as well as trade in goods), there are some major restrictions that are worthy of relaxation, as well as some more subtle problems. Further, since the U.S. has a comparative advantage in a number of major services areas, the U.S. economy would benefit from the relaxation of restrictions abroad. Finally, policy concerns about immigration (which is essential for many forms of trade in services) and about the offshore outsourcing of some services could lead to new restrictions, with unfortunate consequences for trade in services.

Though the long-run trends of reduced restrictions on and expanded flows of trade in services have been favorable and probably will continue to be so, the attractiveness of protectionism and mercantilism should never be underestimated. Wary optimism and watchful readiness may well be the best attitudes for those who care about maintaining an open environment for trade in services.

---

[32] See Mann (2005) and Van Welsum and Reif (2006).

## References


Adlung, Rudolf, "The GATS Turns Ten: A Preliminary Stocktaking," Staff Working Paper ERSD-2004-05, WTO, August 2004.

Adlung, Rudolf and Martin Roy, "Turning Hills into Mountains? Current Commitments under the GATS and Prospects for Change," Staff Working Paper ERSD-2005-01, WTO, March 2005.

Aharoni, Yair and Lilach Nachum, *Globalization of Services: Some Implications for Theory and Practice.* London: Routledge, 2000.

Bressand, Albert and Kalypso Nicolaidis, eds., *Strategic Trends in Services: An Inquiry into the Global Service Economy.* New York: Ballinger, 1989.

Brewer, Thomas L. and Stephen Young, "The USA in the WTO," in Alan M. Rugman and Gavin Boyd, eds., *The World Trade Organization in the New Global Economy: Trade and Investment Issues in the Millennium Round.* Northampton, Mass.: Edward Elgar, 2001.

Collins, Susan M. and Lael Brainard, eds., *Brookings Trade Forum 2005: Offshoring White-Collar Work—the Issues and the Implications.* Washington, D.C.: Brookings, 2006.

Findlay, Christopher and Tony Warren, eds., *Impediments to Trade in Services: Measurement and Policy Implications.* London: Routledge, 2000.

Frame, W. Scott, "Federal Home Loan Bank Purchases: Implications for Mortgage Markets," *Economic Review*, Federal Reserve Bank of Atlanta, 88 (Third Quarter 2003), pp. 17-31.

Frame, W. Scott and Mark J. Flannery, "The Federal Home Loan Bank System: The 'Other' Housing GSE," *Economic Review*, Federal Reserve Bank of Atlanta, 91 (Third Quarter 2006), pp. 33-54

Frame, W. Scott and Larry Wall, "Financing Housing through Government-Sponsored Enterprises," *Economic Review*, Federal Reserve Bank of Atlanta, 87 (First Quarter 2002), pp. 29-43.

Frame, W. Scott and Lawrence J. White, "Regulating Housing GSEs: Thoughts on Institutional Structure and Design," *Economic Review*, Federal Reserve Bank of Atlanta, 89 (Second Quarter 2004), pp. 87-102.

Frame, W. Scott and Lawrence J. White, "Fussing and Fuming over Fannie and Freddie: How Much Smoke, How Much Fire?" *Journal of Economic Perspectives*, 19 (Spring 2005), pp. 159-184.

Hoekman, Bernard M., "Towards a More Balanced and Comprehensive Services Agreement," in Jeffrey J. Schott, ed., *The WTO after Seattle.* Washington, D.C.: Institute for International Economics, July 2000, pp. 119-135.

Hoekman, Bernard M. and Carlos A. Primo Braga, "Protection and Trade in Services: A Survey," in *Open Economies Review*, 8 (July 1997), pp. 285-308.

Jensen, J. Bradford and Lori G. Kletzer, "Tradable Services: Understanding the Scope and Impact of Services Offshoring," in Susan M. Collins and Lael Brainard, eds., *Brookings Trade Forum 2005: Offshoring White-Collar Work—the Issues and the Implications.* Washington, D.C.: Brookings, 2006, pp. 75-117.

Joskow, Paul L. and Roger G. Noll, "Economic Regulation: Deregulation and Regulatory Reform during the 1980s," in Martin Feldstein, ed., *American Economic Policy in the 1980s.* Chicago: University of Chicago Press, 1994, pp. 367-440.

Joskow, Paul L. and Nancy L. Rose, "The Effects of Economic Regulation," in Richard Schmalensee and Robert D. Willig, eds., *Handbook of Industrial Organization*, vol. 2. Amsterdam: North Holland, 1989, pp. 1449-1506.

Koncz, Jennifer, Michael Mann, and Erin Nephew, "U.S. International Services: Cross-Border Trade in 2005 and Sales through Affiliates in 2004," *Survey of Current Business*, 86 (October 2006), pp. 18-74.

Lazear, Edward P., "Remarks," Chicago Council on Global Affairs: Chicago, IL, February 1, 2007; available at: http://www.whitehouse.gov/cea/lazear_cga020107.pdf

Mann, Catherine L., "Offshore Outsourcing and the Globalization of U.S. Services: Why Now, How Important, and What Policy Implications," in C. Fred Bergsten, ed., *The United States and the World Economy.* Washington, D.C.: Institute for International Economics, 2005, pp. 281-311.

Marquez, Jaime, "Estimating Elasticities for U.S. Trade in Services," International Finance Discussion Paper No. 836, Board of Governors of the Federal Reserve System, August 2005.

Mattoo, Aaditya and Pierre Sauve, eds., *Domestic Regulation and Service Trade Liberalization.* Washington, DC: World Bank, and Oxford University Press, 2003.

Nicolaidis, Kalypso, "Learning while Doing: How Services Got on the Uruguay Round Agenda," in Albert Bressand and Kalypso Nicolaidis, eds., *Strategic Trends in Services: An Inquiry into the Global Service Economy.* New York: Ballinger, 1989, pp. 161-179.

Noll, Roger G., "Economic Perspectives on the Politics of Regulation," in Richard Schmalensee and Robert D. Willig, eds., *Handbook of Industrial Organization*, vol. 2. Amsterdam: North Holland, 1989, pp. 1253-1287.

Roseman, Daniel, "Domestic Regulation and Trade in Telecommunications Services: Experience and Prospects under the GATS," in Aaditya Mattoo and Pierre Sauve, eds., *Domestic Regulation and Service Trade Liberalization*. Washington, D.C,: World Bank, and Oxford University Press, 2003, pp. 83-107.

Sauve, Pierre and Robert M. Stern, eds., *GATS 2000: New Directions in Services Trade Liberalization*. Washington, D.C.: Brookings Institution, 2000.

Stephenson, Sherry M., ed., *Services in the Western Hemisphere: Liberalization, Integration, and Reform*. Washington, D.C.: Brookings Institution, 2000.

Stern, Robert M., ed., *Services in the International Economy*. Ann Arbor: University of Michigan Press, 2001.

Triplett, Jack E. and Barry Bosworth, *Productivity in the U.S. Services Sector*. Washington, D.C.: Brookings, 2004.

Trolliet, Claude and John Hegerty, "Regulatory Reform and Trade Liberalization in Accountancy Services," in Aaditya Mattoo and Pierre Sauve, eds., *Domestic Regulation and Service Trade Liberalization*. Washington, D.C.: World Bank and Oxford University Press, 2003, pp. 147-166.

U.S. Council of Economic Advisers, *Economic Report of the President*. Washington, D.C.: USCEA, February 2005.

U.S. International Trade Commission, *The Economic Effects of Significant U.S. Import Restraints*, Second Update, Publication 3201. Washington, D.C.: USITC, May 1999.

U.S. International Trade Commission, *The Economic Effects of Significant U.S. Import Restraints*, Third Update, Publication 3519. Washington, D.C.: USITC, June 2002.

U.S. International Trade Commission, *The Economic Effects of Significant U.S. Import Restraints*, Fourth Update, Publication 3701. Washington, D.C.: USITC, June 2004.

U.S. International Trade Commission, *Recent Trends in U.S. Services Trade: 2006 Annual Report*. Washington, D.C.: USITC, June 2006.

Van Welsum, Desiree and Xavier Reif, "Potential Offshoring: Evidence from Selected OECD Countries," in Susan M. Collins and Lael Brainard, eds., *Brookings Trade Forum 2005: Offshoring White-Collar Work—the Issues and the Implications*. Washington, D.C.: Brookings, 2006, pp. 165-194.

White, Lawrence J., *Reducing the Barriers to International Trade in Accounting Services.* Washington, D.C.: AEI Press, 2001.

White, Lawrence J., "The Credit Rating Industry: An Industrial Organization Analysis," in Richard M. Levich, Giovanni Majnoni, and Carmen M. Reinhardt, eds., *Ratings, Rating Agencies, and the Global Financial System.* Boston: Kluwer, 2002a, pp. 41-64.

White, Lawrence J., "Unilateral Trade Openness: The Experience of the U.S. Financial Services Sector," in Jagdish Bhagwati, ed., *Going Alone: The Case for Relaxed Reciprocity in Freeing Trade.* Cambridge, Mass.: MIT Press, 2002b, pp. 445-481.

White, Lawrence J., "Focusing on Fannie and Freddie: The Dilemmas of Reforming Housing Finance. *Journal of Financial Services Research*, 23 (February 2003), pp. 43-58.

White, Lawrence J., "Fannie Mae, Freddie Mac, and Housing Finance: Why True Privatization is Good Public Policy," *Policy Analysis*, No. 528, Cato Institute, October 7, 2004.

White, Lawrence J., "International Trade in Services: More than Meets the Eye," in E. Kwan Choi and James C. Hartigan, eds., *Handbook of International Trade: Economic and Legal Analyses of Trade Policy and Institutions*, Vol. II. Malden, Mass.: Blackwell Publishing, 2005, pp. 472-498.

White, Lawrence J., "Good Intentions Gone Awry: A Policy Analysis of the SEC's Regulation of the Bond Rating Industry," *Policy Brief* #2006-PB-05, Networks Financial Institute, Indiana State University, 2006.

White, Lawrence J., "A New Law for the Bond Rating Industry" *Regulation*, 30 (Spring 2007), pp. 45-52.

Winston, Clifford, "Economic Deregulation: Days of Reckoning for Microeconomists," *Journal of Economic Literature*, 31 (September 1993), pp. 1263-1289.

World Trade Organization, Council for Trade in Services, "Accountancy Services," December 4, 1998.

World Trade Organization, "GATS—Fact and Fiction," 2001.

World Trade Organization, "Trade Policy Review: Report by the United States," March 3, 2006a.

World Trade Organization, "Trade Policy Review: Report by the Secretariat —United States," June 20, 2006b.

# Part II

# Opening the Transatlantic Services Economy: Sectoral Case Studies

# *Chapter 3*
# A Single Market in Financial Services

*Randal K. Quarles*

In this volume dedicated to examining overall market integration between the United States and the European Union, I was asked to address the question "A Single Market in Financial Services?" In preparing this chapter, it quickly became clear that there were three ways of understanding this question, each of which was an appropriate topic for discussion. The first was a simple question of fact: "***Is*** there an integrated market in financial services between the U.S. and the EU—or is such a market inevitably and speedily evolving?" The second is a question of norms: "Whether or not there is such a market, ***ought*** there to be a single market in financial services between the U.S. and the EU?" And the third and final question is one of means: "***How*** might such a single market be brought about?" Looked at in this way, of course, the third question does not arise until the first and second have been answered—we needn't consider how to create a single market in financial services unless we conclude that this integration is desirable, but will not evolve in a timely fashion without help.

## Progress toward a Single Market in Financial Services

Let me begin, then, with the first question: "Is there already effectively a single market in financial services, or is the rapid development of such a market inevitable?" At first, it might seem that the simple answer to this question of fact is, "Yes." Gross transactions in U.S. equities by investors from the European Union were over $3 trillion last year, up from $144 billion in 1990. Similarly, transactions in EU equities by investors based in the United States were well over $2 trillion, up from $141 billion in 1990. Well over half of all foreign portfolio equity investment both in the U.S. and in the European Union is held in the stocks of companies headquartered in the other's jurisdiction, and the percentages are nearly as high for bond assets. Nearly 30 U.S. banks operate in the European Union with aggregate assets in the EU of over $650 billion; 66 EU-based banks with U.S. assets of over $1.7 trillion conduct commercial banking operations in the United States. The increasingly ambitious efforts to combine financial exchanges across borders between the U.S. and the EU in the last few years are a demonstration both of the degree of integration that participants in these markets find them to have and of the further integration that these participants proximately expect.[1]

Yet, notwithstanding these facts, there are still significant obstacles to cross-border financial transactions between the United States and the European Union, and those obstacles impose substantial costs—or in some cases create impenetrable barriers—that prevent a truly single market in financial services from evolving between these two jurisdictions. There are different and sometimes conflicting frameworks for licensing financial firms and financial instruments, not only between the United States and the EU, but also (particularly in the United States) between different local jurisdictions on the same side of the Atlantic. There are differing rules governing access to market infrastructure and the conduct of trading activities. There are different practices of prudential regulation and supervision. Last, but certainly not least, there are different tax regimes, which can create substantially different incentives for traders in one jurisdiction versus another, even when their economic position is virtually identical. While the degree of integration that has managed to develop despite these obstacles is significant, it does not amount to a single market, and cannot grow into one without positive and difficult action taken to address these obstacles.

## Benefits of a Single Market in Financial Services

Which brings us, then, to the second preliminary question: *should* we make the effort to create a single transatlantic market in financial services? Or is the existing degree of integration sufficient? While it is difficult to quantify the economic benefits that would result from further market integration between the U.S. and the EU, credible estimates by various observers suggest that the gains to be realized are substantial. Creation of a single market between the U.S. and the EU could reduce

[1] Securities Industry and Financial Markets Association; Treasury International Capital Data; *Transatlantic Financial Market Integration: Ambition Needed*, Deutsche Bank Research, November 2005; "A Look Into the Future," *The Economist*, March 22, 2007; "Looking for Options," *The Economist*, April 15, 2007

transaction costs by 60 percent, increase trading volume (and thus the efficiency of asset re-allocation) by 50 percent, and reduce the cost of equity capital by roughly nine percent.[2] This certainly suggests that the existing market linkages still preserve substantial inefficiencies and are by no means "close enough for government work."

Whatever the precise validity of these efforts to quantify the economic benefits, it is conceptually clear that there would be structural advantages to further integration. Increased competition would reduce cost and improve the quality of financial services, just as it does for any other product or service. In addition, facilitating the trading of assets across a broader jurisdiction would assist diversification and thus risk reduction, increasing the stability of the financial markets generally. Finally, a single market would promote more efficient asset allocation in the real economy, with attendant benefits for economic growth.

## Concerns about a Single Market in Financial Services

If the benefits of a single transatlantic market in financial services are both clear and material, however, why has it not yet come about? The chief obstacles appear to be regulatory, but this is not just a question of bureaucratic inertia or shortsightedness, although those certainly play a role. Rather, there are legitimate regulatory concerns arising from transatlantic market linkages that merit careful consideration. These fall into three principal categories:

1. investor protection,
2. systemic risk, and
3. regulatory choice.

Let us look at each of these in turn.

To sum up one of the major investor protection concerns in one phrase, it would be that "The bigger the stream, the harder it is to find

[2] "The US-EU Economic Relationship: What Comes Next?", Testimony of Marc E. Lackritz, President, Securities Industry Association Before the Subcommittee on Domestic and International Monetary Policy, Trade and Technology, June 16, 2005; "The EU-US Financial Markets Dialogue: From Damage Control to Pro-active Integration", European Parliamentary Financial Services Forum, October 2005; Ben Steil, "Building a Transatlantic Securities Market," Council on Foreign Relations, New York 2002.

the fish." Certainly the most blatant types of fraud and deception could be made both easier and more profitable by the larger field of activity that would be covered by a truly single financial services market in the United States and European Union (the same technology that facilitates cross-market integration can facilitate cross-market fraud), and effective enforcement could be made correspondingly harder by the simple geographic scope of the jurisdiction. On top of that, there are fair grounds for concern about differing levels of enforcement standards and resources, particularly with the enlargement of the EU to include not just the markets of London and Frankfurt, but newly acceded countries where capital markets and their regulation are—if not in their absolute infancy—still in early adolescence. There is also the mundane but important problem of information overload: the sheer volume of activity that would affect—and therefore require assessment by—each participant in an integrated market would inevitably require market participants to rely even more heavily on information aggregators and processors, with attendant potential conflicts of interest. This would place an even greater emphasis on reliably effective supervision and regulation of those entities.

With regard to systemic risk, I have noted above that financial stability is enhanced by the improved scope for diversification of an integrated market, but this is not a one-way street. Ours is not a world where all good things are compatible, and while integration can facilitate diversification, it will almost certainly also facilitate further consolidation among financial services firms themselves. While this brings theoretical benefits of efficiency and cost reduction of its own, it is also true that the increased prevalence of extremely large, systemically important financial institutions is one of the characteristics of the system that gives pause to those responsible for promoting financial stability.[3]

Finally, some differences in regulatory approach will inevitably result from differing views on the most effective way to achieve regulatory goals, even where those goals are shared. In the same way that the federal governance structure of the United States as a whole is

---

[3] "Remarks to the Global Association of Risk Professionals," Randal Quarles, March 1, 2006; "Changes in the Structure of the U.S. Financial System and Implications for Systemic Risk," Remarks before the Conference on Systemic Financial Crises at the Federal Reserve Bank of Chicago by Timothy Geithner, President of the Federal Reserve Bank of New York, October 1, 2004.

often described as creating a beneficial "laboratory of the states" to test differing pragmatic approaches to the attainment of objectives that might be broadly shared among the nation's citizens, differing regulatory approaches of various financial market jurisdictions can result in valuable lessons about which measures are most effective and least burdensome in attaining shared regulatory goals. While there are certainly short-term efficiency costs to regulatory variation, it is at least conceivable that the long-term benefit could offset those costs.

Is the tension between the pros and cons of transatlantic market integration reconcilable? Given that there seems to be substantial and increasing integration already, given the clear benefits of further integration, and given that the principal obstacles to a truly single market are regulatory (and thus addressable by government action), can a cross-border regulatory framework to facilitate this result be formed that still addresses the genuine concerns outlined above?

## Regulatory Framework for Further Market Integration: Harmonization vs. Mutual Recognition

Conceptually, there are two basic approaches to creating a regulatory approach that addresses this tension: 1) harmonization, and 2) mutual recognition. Each of these is pretty much what it sounds like. Harmonization aims, through cooperation of governments and regulatory bodies between the U.S. and the EU, to create a set of rules in the two jurisdictions that are in important ways largely identical—similar not merely in objective but in detail. The substance of those harmonized rules would be negotiated to address each side's concerns in the regulatory areas of investor protection, enforcement, and financial stability described above, and also negotiated to leave some scope for each jurisdiction to have a modest choice of means in certain areas deemed compatible with a single market.

Mutual recognition, on the other hand, presupposes that each jurisdiction will maintain separate regulatory regimes that may in some cases materially differ from each other, but that are designed and administered in a way that gives each jurisdiction comfort that the other's rules are adequate to address the investor protection and financial stability objectives that both jurisdictions share. In a mutual recognition regime, the choice of regulatory means—and thus the benefit of the "laboratory"—is more clearly maintained than in a harmonized regime, but at the cost of a higher degree of discomfort in each jurisdiction about the adequacy of the other's regulation of activities that have substantial cross-jurisdictional effects.

In the modern history of cross-border financial regulation, we have examples of each of these two types of regulatory approach. Traditionally, banking regulators were more open to a "mutual recognition" approach: banks in developed countries have generally been able to open branches in other developed jurisdictions rather than separately incorporated subsidiaries, and while a branch is generally subject to some host country regulation it is not a separate legal entity from the parent bank, and supervision of the branch's safety and soundness is therefore fundamentally dependent on the home country regulatory regime. Securities regulators, on the other hand, have historically been more insistent on harmonization as a condition of cross-border market access—particularly in the United States, where the standard to which harmonization was required to converge was always that of the U.S. itself.

Recently, however, these traditional positions seem to have been reversed. Banking regulators in the developed world have been spending nearly a decade seeking to harmonize an extremely complex and sophisticated system of capital regulation across the bulk of the systemically important financial jurisdictions in the so-called "Basel II" process. Securities regulators, on the other hand, now seem open, at least rhetorically, to a form of mutual recognition (or "substituted compliance", as the preferred phrase now seems to be) in the licensing and supervision of exchanges and broker dealers. This approach has been laid out in detail in an article by Ehtiopis Tafara, who heads the International Office of the SEC's staff, together with his Senior Counsel Robert J. Peterson, in a recent issue of the *Harvard International Law Journal*.[4] The securities regulators are also now open to what amounts to mutual recognition of differing accounting regimes in the U.S. and the EU once a certain point of incomplete convergence has been reached.[5] If we want to consider the relative effectiveness of har-

---

[4] Ethiopis Tafara and Robert J. Peterson, "A Blueprint for Cross-Border Access to U.S. Investors: A New International Framework." *Harvard International Law Journal*, Vol. 48, No. 1, Winter 2007.

[5] "Chairman Donaldson Meets with EU Internal Market Commissioner McCreevy," SEC press release announcing "roadmap" to elimination of U.S. GAAP reconciliation requirement, April 21, 2005; "U.S. and EU Edge Closer on Accounting Rules", *International Herald Tribune*, April 23, 2005.

monization as against mutual recognition in fostering financial market integration, then, we have at hand recent examples of both approaches to compare against each other. With Basel II representing harmonization on the one hand, and "substituted compliance" representing a form of mutual recognition on the other, these two examples may provide lessons about how the approach each exemplifies might help or hinder increased market integration between the U.S. and the EU.

## Basel II: Harmonization without Harmony

The genesis and content of the draft Basel II Accord have been described in great detail by others, and are too well known to require much review here.[6] In brief summary, the principal bank regulatory authorities of the world's major financial jurisdictions—meeting in a regular forum called the Committee on Banking Supervision, known popularly as the Basel Committee because it meets at the headquarters (though not actually under the auspices) of the Bank for International Settlements in Basel, Switzerland—have developed a harmonized framework for the measurement and maintenance of bank capital, generally referred to as "Basel II." This framework is designed to replace the earlier capital accord agreed by the Basel Committee in 1988 ("Basel I"), which required banks to assign specified assets to one of a handful of categories and then weighted the capital to be held against those assets by a fixed percentage that had been agreed to account roughly for that category's perceived risk. While Basel I was straightforward in both concept and application, it did not account for various important risks facing banks (such as market and operational risk), did not cover all off-balance sheet assets, and was subject to gaming because of the relative crudeness of the available categories.[7] Basel II is designed to address these deficiencies by requiring banks to

---

6 The most comprehensive discussion of the development of the Basel II Accord will be found in a forthcoming book by Daniel Tarullo tentatively titled *Banking on Basel*, manuscript on file. See also Hal S. Scott, ed., *Capital Adequacy Beyond Basel: Banking, Securities and Insurance*, Oxford University Press, 2005.

7 To take only the most well known example of gaming, Basel I required substantially more capital to be held against loan commitments of more than one year than for short-term commitments. Within only a few months after adoption of the accord, it had become virtually universal market practice for all loan commitments to have an initial term of one year less one day, which the bank would then routinely extend for an unlimited number of identical periods. Although the economic and practical effect was essentially the same as a longer-term commitment that could be cancelled if certain financial covenants were not met, the regulatory capital held against these exposures in the aggregate was now actually less than had been usual before the Basel I accord.

hold capital against a broader range of risks, and by providing for the measurement of an asset's risk (and thus the appropriate capital charge) through materially more sophisticated methods than the handful of "capital buckets" of Basel I.

Basel II achieved these aims, however, at the cost of a substantially more complicated mechanism than the original Basel I accord. The Basel I capital rules spanned about five pages in the Federal Reserve Regulatory Service. The Basel II framework is several hundred pages long, and has taken roughly a decade to develop and negotiate. In addition to the sheer complexity of the framework, Basel II appears to illustrate a variety of other lessons about regulatory harmonization efforts, particularly those involving increasingly sophisticated financial measures.

First, and perhaps most obviously, much time can be spent on harmonizing rules, but if the implementation of the rules is not uniform, the effect of this effort can be significantly undermined. As an example, there has been much controversy over the decision by the U.S. and EU regulatory authorities to apply the Basel II framework to different groups of banks. The EU authorities decided they would apply Basel II to all banks in their jurisdiction, while the U.S. authorities decided to limit application to the 20 largest U.S. banks. This has caused much angst—particularly in the EU—about competitive inequity between the two jurisdictions because of differences in implementation of elaborately harmonized rules. While I think the angst over this particular difference is overdone on the part of the Europeans (Basel II is intended to apply to "internationally active" banks, which is a very small number of banks in the U.S.—far fewer than the 20 largest to which the U.S. authorities will apply Basel II), it is an example of how the harmonization of standards among many banks actually exacerbates the effect of inconsistent application between jurisdictions, and thus magnifies any competitive inequity that inconsistent application may cause. In that way, a harmonization effort can end up increasing rather than reducing concerns about a level playing field. Moreover, the more complicated the regulatory standard in question, the greater will be the likelihood of inconsistent implementation or application across jurisdictions. There will just be too many interpretive questions that arise in a complicated regulatory scheme for cross-jurisdictional interpretation to be uniform.

Second, the Basel II process shows that political obstacles to harmonization can be substantial. Many members of the U.S. Congress—both Democrat and Republican—have been suspicious of the Basel II process almost from the outset. Some of this concern has been directed at the potential creation of a competitive disadvantage for small banks in the U.S., who will not generally have their capital measured under Basel II. Ironically, while the Europeans have been concerned that the small banks in the U.S. might have some competitive advantage because they were not required to measure capital under Basel II, those small banks themselves fear that they will be at a disadvantage versus banks that can use the more sophisticated capital measures. These banks have used their considerable political clout to generate concern on Capitol Hill over the details of the Basel II accord, raising the threat of direct political intervention in this complex regulatory process. On top of these competitive equity issues are additional concerns about the overall safety and soundness of the banking system, measured by the rough standard of aggregate systemic capital. Some of the preliminary quantitative impact studies of the prospective effect of Basel II suggest that aggregate capital in the system could decline quite substantially once risks in the system are evaluated by Basel II measures, and this has raised concern among some—particularly at the FDIC—that the system as whole could be less resilient to unexpected stress if Basel II were implemented as designed. While some of these concerns would exist even absent a harmonization effort (the competitive equity issue is raised even more starkly in a mutual recognition regime), the necessary degree of technical complexity involved in harmonizing a sophisticated regulatory regime inevitably produced an almost gnostic level of arcane detail that was fully understood by only a small number of apolitical technicians, which magnified the distaste and suspicion of the politicians who dealt with it.[8]

The political issues surrounding harmonization are not merely on the U.S. side, however. The Europeans believed that they could not begin implementing the Basel II Accord without approval from the European Parliament, and once that approval was granted they have consistently maintained that obtaining it was so politically difficult

[8] On more than one occasion, members and senior staffers of the relevant Congressional committees have spoken with disdain of the Basel II framework as appearing to be what happened when "the Math Club went to Switzerland."

that they could not and would not bring the issue back to Parliament again. This stance has made the necessary flexibility in the final stages of preparing a complex harmonized regulatory framework extremely difficult.

In addition to these risks of politicization, the fragmented structure of the regulatory institutions on each side of the U.S.-EU divide makes reaching a harmonized stance almost impossible—and certainly very time consuming. These institutional complexities are a large part of the reason that the Basel II effort has so far taken roughly a decade. To take only the most recent example, the tension between the FDIC and the Federal Reserve on certain implementation safeguards—most specifically the so-called 10 percent threshold[9]—has resulted in such divergence between the United States and the rest of the world that some large banks have suggested they want the ability to opt out of the relevant provisions of Basel II.[10] But while the differing views of the U.S. regulators have been more public and consequential, the EU institutional framework is similarly fragmented, with the European Commission, various member state regulatory authorities, and certain of the principal finance ministries and central banks all having views, and similar tensions over interpretation and implementation are operating there as well.

Finally, on top of these practical obstacles to harmonization, it is not clear that harmonization is a theoretically desirable goal, even were it obtainable as a practical matter. Regulatory competition—like competition in any area—is a good thing. If there were one single regulator—or one outcome of a single regulatory process involving multiple regulators—it could end up imposing needlessly onerous (but bureaucratically convenient) regulations without practical recourse. If the regulatory framework of a single market allows at least some regulatory choice, however, overreach by any one regulator could be met with migration of regulated entities to another supervisory entity. This is something with which U.S. financial institutions are quite familiar having operated for over a hundred years in a regu-

9 The FDIC, as a result of concerns that the Basel II framework might allow aggregate capital in the system to decline substantially, has insisted that the U.S. should place a limit on the amount to which bank capital can decline, requiring at the very least a thorough review of the framework if capital would otherwise fall by more than 10 percent.

10 "Settled Issue on Basel Now a Roadblock," *American Banker*, July 31, 2006.

latory system with a quite complex institutional structure. The issue in the transatlantic context is similar to the one that arises when considering harmonization or consolidation of this domestic structure—the goal must be to limit as much as possible the costs of regulatory fragmentation, while preserving the benefits of regulatory competition.

## Substituted Compliance: Mutual Recognition with a Twist

This review of the Basel II harmonization process provides a good context in which to examine the Tafara/Peterson proposal for cross-border access to U.S. investors for non-U.S. exchanges and broker-dealers. As I noted at the outset, this proposal is a departure from the long tradition at the SEC of allowing only very limited flexibility for foreign financial firms in their compliance with U.S. rules as a condition for entering our markets. Under this proposal, non-U.S. exchanges and broker-dealers could obtain exemptions from registration with the SEC if they complied with "substantively comparable" non-U.S. securities regulations and were supervised by a "substantively comparable" non-U.S. securities regulator.[11] The SEC would determine whether the regulations and the supervisor were "substantively comparable" by a review of several factors, including:

1. exchange oversight,
2. broker-dealer oversight,
3. issuer requirements,
4. general legal and enforcement comparability,
5. reciprocity, and
6. the negotiation of a supervisory and enforcement memorandum of understanding with the SEC.

Since regimes and enforcement practices that are comparable at one time might not be in the future, the exemptions thus obtained would be subject to a five-year "comparability review."[12] While only an unof-

[11] Tafara and Peterson, "A Blueprint for Cross-border Access to U.S. Investors," op. cit.

[12] *Ibid.*

ficial proposal at this stage, this approach is similar in concept to mutual recognition regimes that have been instituted by other U.S. financial regulatory agencies.[13]

This approach would have a number of advantages over a harmonization effort, as illustrated by our review of the Basel II process above. Most obviously, it requires substantially less effort from all the regulatory entities involved. It is an enormous amount of work to harmonize differing regulatory regimes, and returns on this investment of resources diminish rapidly—much of the time in any harmonization project tends to get spent in areas with only a modest benefit when looked at from the standpoint of the regulatory regime as a whole. Merely ensuring comparability of principles while allowing for differing practical mechanisms, however, requires far fewer resources and is therefore more likely to get done.

As important as that it get done, however, is the speed with which it is done, and a mutual recognition regime is faster to implement than harmonization. Speed of implementation is particularly important in the area of financial regulation, in order to allow regulators to keep up with the continual rapid innovation in the financial sector without imposing rules that stifle innovation because they are obsolete by the time they can be formulated.

One of the principal benefits of a well-designed mutual recognition approach is that it maintains useful aspects of regulatory competition. By allowing firms supervised by different regulatory institutions to be active across the entire geographic market, it imposes discipline on the ability of those regulatory institutions to impose rules with costs that greatly exceed benefits. Firms might either reorganize so as to be subject to a different regulator or, more likely, market activity will migrate to firms that are regulated more responsibly. At the same time, the requirement of "substantive comparability" and "comparability

---

[13] Before embarking on the Basel II process, for example, the Federal Reserve implemented a requirement that foreign bank branches seeking access to the U.S. market be subject to "comprehensive consolidated supervision" by their home regulator, allowing access after a determination by the Fed that the home country regulatory regime and the foreign regulator provided this level of supervision, even though the means each regulator chose to achieve this goal might be quite different. The Tafara/Peterson proposal is conceptually very similar to this precedent. In addition, the Commodities Futures Trading Corporation's "Part 30 Rules" may grant an exemption from various U.S. registration requirements when a comparable regulatory system exists in a subject firm's home country.

review" in the Tafara/Peterson proposal seems a satisfactory way of limiting the potential for a race to the bottom and other costs of regulatory fragmentation.

Mutual recognition does, however, have its own set of drawbacks. For example, precisely because it maintains the possibility of regulatory competition, it could be even more vulnerable to politicization. Firms subject to regulation they believe burdensome compared to that applicable to other market participants, but unwilling or unable to take the necessary steps to change regulators, can be expected to seek political intervention. While it is logically conceivable that this intervention could be entirely beneficial, experience tells us that getting legislators involved in the details of complicated financial regulation runs a high risk of shipwreck. A healthy system of mutual recognition (even when limited by "substantive comparability") would require strong commitment from the U.S. financial services industry to prevent these political reactions.

Another potential drawback of the Tafara/Peterson proposal is that —like the Federal Reserve "comprehensive consolidated supervision" regime on which it appears to draw—the SEC would be required to act only as requests for exemption were received. When the Federal Reserve was implementing the CCS regime in the early 1990s, for example, it became a huge bottleneck for several years as it dealt with the initial wave of CCS determination requests, and it was over a decade before firms based in some jurisdictions were able to obtain the necessary imprimatur.

## Next Steps?

What can we conclude from these comparisons? I believe that recent experience has shown us that cross-border regulatory frameworks based on mutual recognition are more likely than those based on harmonization to be fruitful in furthering transatlantic financial integration—both for reasons of practicality and for reasons of policy design. They require fewer resources to implement, are more nimble in a fast-changing financial services sector, and preserve the important benefit of regulatory competition. With the publication of the Tafara/Peterson proposal, there are indications that the SEC is willing to go further along the road of a type of mutual recognition that it has ever been willing to before. This should be encouraged.

In addition, the Basel II experience in particular makes clear that regulatory cooperation of the sort necessary for either harmonization or mutual recognition is hindered by the overly fragmented regulatory structure on both sides of the Atlantic. While regulatory competition is a benefit, excessive regulatory fragmentation imposes costs that can exceed that benefit, and policymakers must continually be looking to ensure that the balance between the two is being struck appropriately in light of changing circumstances. Both the U.S. and the EU made progress in the 1990s in regulatory reform that permitted needed industry consolidation. But the U.S. has lagged the EU in reforms that further reduce fragmentation costs, and the consequences have been thrown into relief in the negotiations between the U.S. and the EU on an entire range of cross-border financial regulatory issues, of which the convolution in implementing Basel II arising from infighting between the various U.S. regulators is merely one example.

An important element in creating a regulatory framework that will promote further transatlantic integration, then, is for the United States to make a serious effort at further domestic regulatory consolidation. An obvious first step would be to rationalize our kaleidoscopic insurance regulatory regime with the creation of an optional federal insurance charter. Europeans have increasingly complained that our state-centered insurance regulatory regime is not just a burden on the industry as a whole, but a particular barrier to foreign firms. An optional federal charter would streamline this system and reduce the regulatory burden, while maintaining the benefit of regulatory competition from the continuing ability of any particular firm to choose a state charter rather than a national one. A second step would be some rationalization of the four federal banking regulators—at least a merger of the bank and thrift charters, and ideally a merger of all bank supervisory functions in one federal regulator. Finally, the jurisdictional lines between the SEC and the CFTC are increasingly arbitrary and counterproductive. Until now, merger of any functions between the two agencies has been impossible because of turf battles between the relevant committees of jurisdiction in the Congress (the SEC answers to the Financial Services and Banking Committees; the CFTC to the Agriculture Committees), but if this becomes one element of a comprehensive effort at regulatory consolidation with the vision of a single transatlantic financial services market, there may be more scope for creativity.

## Conclusion

A truly integrated transatlantic financial services market is a worthy and achievable goal. Much remains to be done, however—particularly making some fundamental choices about basic approaches to regulatory interaction. In the contest between harmonization and mutual recognition, mutual recognition (along the lines of the Tafara/Peterson "substituted compliance" proposal) seems the better approach, avoiding harmonization's resource drain and mire of detail, and maintaining a healthy scope for regulatory competition and innovation.

There is, however, important groundwork to be laid for either harmonization or mutual recognition, particularly in attitude and structural changes in our own regulators. The proffer of the Tafara/Peterson proposal suggests that the attitude change at least is underway. Structural change in our regulatory institutions will be more difficult and would almost certainly be the work of many years. This change would, however, be among the most concrete and consequential steps we could take to further transatlantic regulatory cooperation in the financial services area—which would in turn inevitably further market integration. In light of the benefits we would expect from that integration, we should begin those changes now.

# *Chapter 4*

# Health Services in an Open Transatlantic Market: A European Perspective

*Fabio Pammolli, Massimo Riccaboni, Chiara Bonassi*

## Introduction

Markets for health care services are much more complex than markets in other highly regulated industries, such as public utilities, due to asymmetric information. Unlike most publicly regulated goods and services, consumers often do not know, and can not ascertain themselves, the quality of health care service, and may not even be able to observe whether a suggested treatment quality was actually provided or not. "Credence goods" are goods and services whose quality is better understood by an expert than the consumer himself (Darby and Karni, 1973; Dulleck and Kerschbamer, 2006). Depending on market and institutional settings, information problems in the provision of health care services could lead either to undertreatment or to overtreatment and overcharging.

Traditionally, the provision of services has been mainly a domestic activity, while the pharmaceutical industry has been highly internationalized. However, technological change, trade liberalization and patient mobility are progressively opening up service markets to foreign competition. Thus, offshoring and trade of professional health services has been recognized to be a prominent example of a new type of trade (Bhagwati *et al.*, 2004; Mankiw *et al.* 2004; Markusen, 2005; Amiti and Wei, 2005). Medical services such as teleradiology (Levy and Yu, 2006) and arthroscopy (Baldwin 2006) are often cited as paradigm examples of how globalization might threaten highly educated workers both in Europe and the U.S.

Meanwhile, increasing consolidation of insurers, providers, and the health industry, including pharmaceutical companies, device manufacturers, and other suppliers of health services, is transforming national health care markets. The reduction of information asymmetries and patients' switching costs is affecting productivity and is modifying the sources of market power in health care.

Above all, health care is an innovation based, R&D intensive sector. Technical change is embedded in both goods, such as drugs and medical devices, and health care services, with important consequences in terms of static and dynamic efficiency conditions (see Ahn, 2002). Thus, markets for health care services have to provide incentives for both cost-reducing and quality-enhancing technological change. In other terms, the allocation of resources devoted to R&D and the direction of technical change are influenced by the way in which health care is financed.

The demand for health care is a function of the state of technology, and hence of previous R&D undertakings (Weisbrod, 1991). Historically, public coverage and insurance have sustained the development of quality-improving technologies. In his work in 1992, Newhouse states that almost three-fourths of the increase of health care spending in the last century is attributable to technological change. Jones (2002) finds that technological progress may have accounted for as much as half of total spending growth over recent decades throughout the OECD.

Finally, the health care sector is heavily regulated. In the past, regulation was designed to guarantee safety, efficacy, and quality and, moreover, to deal with potential market failures and need for complex chains of principal agent relations — patient-physician, physician-payer, payer-society — to deal with market and administrative inefficiencies associated with credence goods.

Regulation is not only meant to guarantee and improve access to better health services, but also to control health care expenditure, both on the supply side (tariffs, price controls), and on the demand side (co-payment schemes, formularies, contract design).

Historically, health policy has been under the responsibility of national state authorities. In almost all EU Member States health care is tax funded: healthy young workers pay for the care of sick, usually older citizens. Moreover, European countries have opted for different financial frameworks and regulation schemes to control health care costs, for both pharmaceutical products and hospitals.

Such a fragmentation of the European institutional and regulatory framework is preventing both the European Union and Member States from taking an active and positive role in balancing and aligning different interests through managed competition (see Abbott, 1995).

The current equilibrium is neither efficient nor sustainable. The total level of health spending and its allocation among different services and products tend to perpetuate national historic patterns of care and consumption, instead of responding to the interest of European patients in opening up health care markets to trade and dynamic competition. At the same time, universal tax funded systems and strict public regulation of health care markets in many Member States prevent the rise of a pluralistic system in which public coverage coexists with a complementary private insurance sector. In the past, young generations relied on future generations to pay for their care. At present, demographic changes—a falling birth rate and growing life expectancy—are likely to cause severe funding problems within the existing framework, which will worsen over the years.

Both in Europe and in the U.S. the key challenge for governments is how to design pluralistic systems of health care delivery and financing, in which multiple plans and market forces can act to promote competition.

Public and private programs can converge to make patterns of care responsive to individual preferences balancing different incentives, without imposing excessive financial burdens on individuals or denying necessary care because of inability to pay (see Feldstein, 1995).

In this context, public authorities should design fine-tuned regulatory policies in health care markets, stimulating innovation and dynamic competition and, at the same time, dealing with market imperfections and asymmetric information.

Against this background, this chapter focuses on some of the existing barriers to market integration and trade liberalization in health care. Institutional fragmentation in the regulation of health care markets tends to be remarkably high, since both health provision and financing are considered as key components of fiscal and redistributive policies by individual States.

There is growing demand for reducing administrative barriers to market integration in Europe. In 2005 the European Parliament, in its

"Report on Patient Mobility and Healthcare Developments in the EU," called for the Commission to act on a wide range of issues related to patient mobility and cooperation among national health systems, starting for harmonization of health payment schemes across member states. Coordination among European countries to deal with patient mobility starts to be perceived as a priority by an increasing number of European Countries and citizens, since intra-EU mobility has been increasing dramatically as a consequence of progresses in the EU labor market enlargement and integration. Such harmonization can be achieved only by reducing transaction costs and regulatory barriers and promoting a pluralistic system in health financing, with international private actors complementing the role of the public and contributing to both cross border mobility of patients and to a better integration of health services markets across the Atlantic.

## The Institutional Context of Health Care Services in Europe

The regulatory framework governing cross border provision of health services within the European Union has become more and more complex over the last decade. Cross-border provision of services (such as remote diagnosis and prescription and laboratory services), and the use of services abroad are covered by Article 22 of Regulation 1408/71, now replaced by Articles 19-20 of Regulation 883/2004, under the primary purpose of granting social security coordination across member states. Permanent as well as temporary presence of providers in host countries is admitted under Directive 36/05, which regulates the recognition of professional qualifications. Thanks to better transportation and communications and lower cross-border restrictions, patient mobility is becoming the easiest way to benefit from cross-border provision of health care. At the same time, it calls for coordination among Member States' health care and funding systems.

In hospital markets, different schemes have been introduced both in the U.S. and in European countries to pursue allocative efficiency among providers. Diagnosis-related groups (DRGs) and prospective payment schemes have replaced cost-plus reimbursement schemes, stimulating efficiency in the use of inputs and competition among providers. Price regulation via "prospective-payment" insurance schemes can induce competition and mobility, provided that hospitals compete for contracts with multiple institutional health purchasers. Providers are forced to compete reducing inefficiencies and "differentiating" their own services through specialization, instead of performing cost-shifting among patients (Anderson *et al.* 1993; Wallack *et al.* 1996).

Discussions on how to promote access to health care and hospital services in the Single European Market started in 1998, following a series of case law judgments by the European Court of Justice. Until then, the Community mechanism enabling patients to receive treatment abroad was designed by Regulation 1408/71. Urgent medical treatments were provided to EU citizens temporarily visiting a Member State according to the recipient statutory scheme, applying the reimbursement conditions and tariffs of the hosting country. Financial compensations between Member States were cleared either by computing current costs or on a flat rate basis.

According to the Community legislation, patients needed prior authorization from their competent institution in order to be reimbursed by their home country. In some cases national discretion has been limited as authorization has to be released whenever health treatments can be covered at home but with undue time delay.

This legal framework still remains in place, but in 1998, through the *Koll and Decker* rulings, the European Court of Justice established new principles on the reimbursement of health services provided to patients abroad. When health services are provided for remuneration, the fundamental principle of free movement of goods and services, set out in Articles 30 and 49-50 of the EC Treaty, must apply.

An important element of modernization has been introduced by Regulation 883/2004, with the European Health Insurance Card (EHIC), designed to assure direct provision of occasional and "necessary" health treatment in any EU country.

Moreover, the Court ruled that for non-hospital services patients may move in any other Member State without requiring prior authorization, and be reimbursed according to the rules of their home health system. However, in case of hospital services, state authorization is still required, subject to the condition that the home health care system cannot provide medical care within a reasonable limit of time.

In general, legal uncertainty still affects cross border health care provision in Europe. Available case studies[1] highlight that procedures under the EHIC scheme do not work efficiently; sometimes patients do not receive direct health care treatments and are forced to out of pocket payments. Furthermore, stringent national authorization policies for planned care have been undue obstacles of cross border provisions, limiting the choices of patients and the opportunities offered by the Single Market.

Information asymmetries can harm the negotiating process between health care purchasers and providers. In particular, when the quality of a service cannot be clearly identified ex-ante (i.e. before service delivery), a problem of incomplete markets arises. Incomplete contracts, in turn, increase the likelihood that further reductions in costs are made at the expense of quality (*quality-shading hypothesis*, Domberger and Jensen 1997).

As stated by the European Commission (2006) "a key concern about the application of internal market rules is clarity over which Member States' authority is responsible for supervising health services for each of the different kinds of health service.... For example, which authority is responsible for ensuring the quality and safety of health services provided to people from other Member States, whose complaints and how patients will be compensated when they suffer harm, and if there are errors, whose liability rules apply and how those errors will be followed up?"

Another important issue related to contracting in an international context is continuity of care. As a result, contracting with foreign providers should include arrangements for follow-up assessment and exchange of medical records and practices.

To deal with these issues, the European Parliament and the Council invited the Commission to develop specific proposals by the end of 2007.

---

[1] See M. Rosenmoller, M. McKee and R. Baeten (2006), *Patient mobility in the European Union—Learning from Experience.*

## Fragmentation and Convergence in Pharmaceuticals

Control on public expenditure in pharmaceuticals has been pursued in most European countries mainly through price regulation schemes (price cap regulation, reference pricing, price volume agreements, price negotiations, cost effectiveness criteria, ex post price cuts). Traditional approaches to price regulation combined with the fragmentation of the regulatory framework have induced a bias toward static versus dynamic efficiency, thus reducing the price premium and market incentives for new innovative drugs *vis-à-vis* the U.S. market.

Since R&D activities in pharmaceuticals are more and more concentrated in the U.S. (see Pammolli and Riccaboni, 2007; European Commission, 2006), the current international division of labor does not appear to be sustainable, and a coordination effort between Europe and the U.S. has to be undertaken.

The pharmaceutical industry accounts for a large fraction of both private and public health expenditure. Kyle (2006) reports that the share of pharmaceuticals in total health care ranges from four percent in the U.S. to around 18 percent in France and Italy, while, according to OECD (2006), total health care expenditure as percentage of GDP is above 15 percent in the U.S., while for France and Germany it is higher than 10 percent.[2]

European markets are highly regulated, heterogeneous and fragmented. In France, Belgium and Spain cost-sharing is a proportion of the price of drugs. In the United Kingdom, Germany and Italy, co-payment is determined on a flat rate basis. Similarly, exemption schemes are highly differentiated: some countries such as Germany provide a maximum co-payment level; others, such as the UK, exempt the poor and elderly; and still other Member States specify particular categories of "essential drugs" for which there is no charge (Italy and France).

Other measures tend to influence physicians' prescription behavior through positive lists of reimbursable drugs or negative lists of non-reimbursable pharmaceuticals, clinical guidelines and financial incentives. Moreover, pharmacists sometimes have generic substitution rights if doctors have not formally opposed substitution of the branded products.

---

[2] For the U.S. and France the reference year is 2004, while for Germany it is 2003.

**Figure 4.1 Price convergence in EU25, median prices, 1994-2004 (EU-15 average price = 1).**

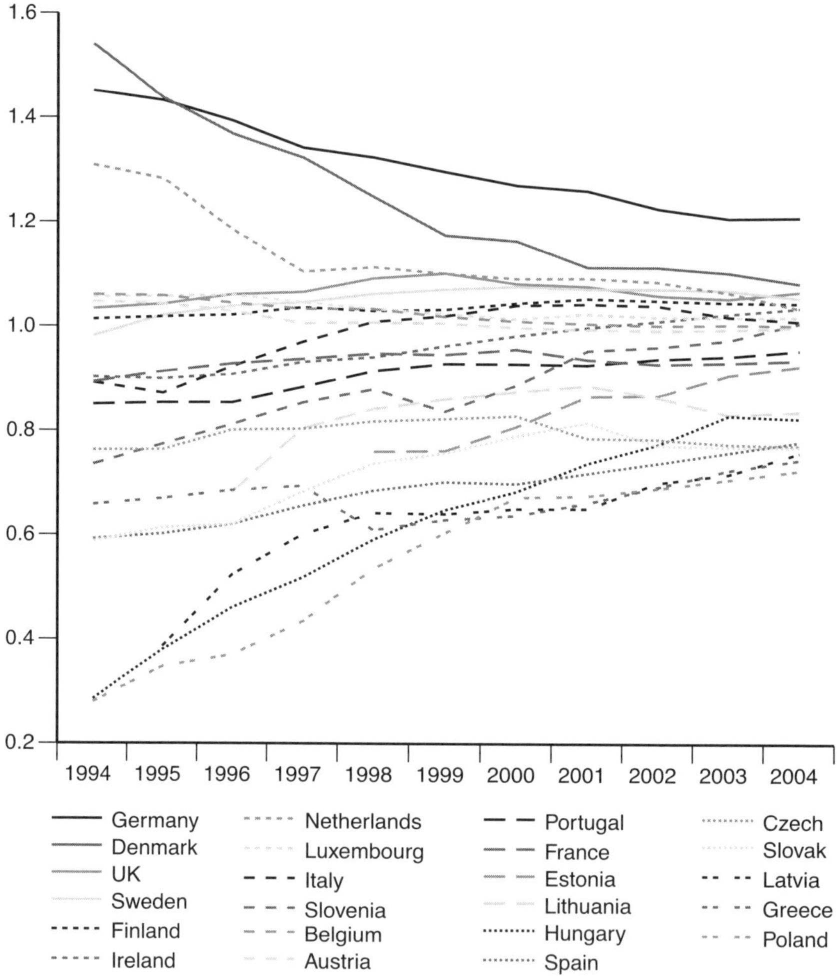


Source: our computations on IMS Health.

In this context, price convergence across national pharmaceutical markets has been driven by cross country reference pricing schemes and parallel trade rather than by regulatory integration and free market competition (Figure 4.1).

So far, efforts aimed at developing a Single Market for pharmaceuticals have failed. Excess fragmentation of pricing and reimbursement schemes, as well as cost containment policies in Europe, had a negative effect on both incentives to innovate and the introduction of new drugs.

Although there has been a gradual move towards harmonization of regulatory standards on market authorization (Mutual Recognition and Centralized Procedures), pharmaceutical companies still must negotiate with individual countries on price and reimbursement. Cross-country differences in price regulation schemes imply an excessive market fragmentation and, moreover, tend to delay the launch of innovative products.

Table 4.1 shows market concentration and relative prices of the first three products in each anatomic therapeutic class of pharmaceuticals (ATC4). Concentration is measured by the concentration ratio of the first n firms/products $C_n$ (n=1,...,10) in the market. The one-firm/product concentration ratio $C_1$ corresponds to the market share of the largest firm/product, while the $C_n$ index equal the sum of the market shares of the top n firms/products in terms of sales. Market concentration of the first product in nominal values can be broken down into two components: the concentration in real values—i.e. the number of standard units sold—multiplied by its relative price (the price of the first product divided by the mean price in the market).

Table 4.1 shows that the U.S. market is less fragmented than the EU market as a whole and all the most important national markets in Europe (Germany, France, Italy and Spain), with the exception of the UK. On average, the three leading products in each of the top one hundred therapeutic categories account for 85.6 percent of total market share in the U.S., as compared with a total market share of 77.3 percent in the EU-25.

The gap between the U.S. and the EU is wide in terms of sales, while the U.S. market is as concentrated as the European one in terms of volume. Thus the higher concentration of the U.S. market is due to the "premium price" that leading products can command. Indeed, the relative price of the market leader in the U.S. is 44 percent higher than the market average price (see Pammolli and Riccaboni, 2006).

The analysis of market shares of the leading companies confirms this view (Table 4.2).

**Table 4.1 Average market concentration (sales and volumes) and relative prices of the first three products on the market, top 100 ATC4 classes, 1994-2004**

| | $C_1(S)$ | $C_1(Q)$ | $P_1$ | $C_2(S)$ | $C_2(Q)$ | $P_2$ | $C_3(S)$ | $C_3(Q)$ | $P_3$ |
|---|---|---|---|---|---|---|---|---|---|
| **EU-25** | 41.72 | 34.70 | 1.20 | 64.61 | 56.95 | 1.13 | 77.31 | 71.47 | 1.08 |
| **EU-15** | 41.18 | 34.17 | 1.21 | 63.83 | 56.05 | 1.14 | 76.53 | 70.49 | 1.09 |
| **U.S.** | 49.72 | 34.63 | 1.44 | 74.96 | 59.48 | 1.26 | 85.56 | 70.74 | 1.21 |
| **Germany** | 29.97 | 22.94 | 1.31 | 47.42 | 38.49 | 1.23 | 58.87 | 50.95 | 1.16 |
| **Italy** | 36.68 | 33.49 | 1.10 | 57.57 | 54.07 | 1.06 | 71.49 | 67.14 | 1.06 |
| **France** | 39.01 | 31.21 | 1.25 | 64.88 | 54.45 | 1.19 | 78.18 | 71.16 | 1.10 |
| **Spain** | 40.36 | 32.62 | 1.24 | 62.37 | 52.72 | 1.18 | 75.94 | 67.92 | 1.12 |
| **Czech Rep.** | 46.26 | 40.80 | 1.13 | 72.70 | 66.68 | 1.09 | 86.77 | 83.83 | 1.04 |
| **Portugal** | 46.73 | 39.65 | 1.18 | 70.41 | 61.34 | 1.15 | 84.32 | 79.63 | 1.06 |
| **Belgium** | 48.33 | 42.24 | 1.14 | 76.64 | 70.27 | 1.09 | 92.24 | 86.65 | 1.06 |
| **Austria** | 48.43 | 41.12 | 1.18 | 74.19 | 66.51 | 1.12 | 87.70 | 82.03 | 1.07 |
| **Netherlands** | 48.56 | 37.60 | 1.29 | 72.35 | 58.42 | 1.24 | 86.24 | 76.38 | 1.13 |
| **Luxembourg** | 49.54 | 39.93 | 1.24 | 76.49 | 68.20 | 1.12 | 89.91 | 83.20 | 1.08 |
| **Slovak Rep.** | 50.02 | 42.52 | 1.18 | 76.77 | 72.70 | 1.06 | 90.69 | 90.27 | 1.00 |
| **Poland** | 50.16 | 39.71 | 1.26 | 76.55 | 68.63 | 1.12 | 89.29 | 85.30 | 1.05 |
| **Ireland** | 51.19 | 43.77 | 1.17 | 77.50 | 72.42 | 1.07 | 91.76 | 87.10 | 1.05 |
| **Latvia** | 45.07 | 35.23 | 1.28 | 68.63 | 63.24 | 1.09 | 82.96 | 79.67 | 1.04 |
| **Lithuania** | 51.53 | 44.06 | 1.17 | 77.37 | 72.95 | 1.06 | 90.67 | 88.95 | 1.02 |
| **Finland** | 52.30 | 45.58 | 1.15 | 78.95 | 73.26 | 1.08 | 92.65 | 89.54 | 1.03 |
| **Greece** | 52.73 | 43.08 | 1.22 | 78.00 | 69.76 | 1.12 | 88.90 | 83.08 | 1.07 |
| **Denmark** | 53.50 | 45.22 | 1.18 | 80.34 | 75.33 | 1.07 | 93.07 | 91.05 | 1.02 |
| **Sweden** | 53.68 | 44.70 | 1.20 | 79.70 | 75.51 | 1.06 | 91.60 | 89.95 | 1.02 |
| **Estonia** | 54.71 | 45.13 | 1.21 | 80.74 | 75.51 | 1.07 | 93.32 | 91.67 | 1.02 |
| **Hungary** | 54.85 | 52.29 | 1.05 | 84.04 | 82.19 | 1.02 | 96.11 | 95.72 | 1.00 |
| **UK** | 55.69 | 48.34 | 1.15 | 79.61 | 75.16 | 1.06 | 90.20 | 87.75 | 1.03 |
| **Slovenia** | 61.25 | 54.13 | 1.13 | 88.25 | 84.98 | 1.04 | 97.89 | 97.47 | 1.00 |

Source: our computations on IMS Health.

**Table 4.2 Market shares of the leading company ($C_1$) and top three companies ($C_3$) and firm turnover, sales and volumes, 2004**

| | $C_1$ | | $C_3$ | | Turnover* | |
|---|---|---|---|---|---|---|
| Country | Sales | Quantity | Sales | Quantity | Sales | Quantity |
| EU-15 | 9.59 | 8.43 | 25.00 | 21.11 | 5.77 | 5.23 |
| EU-25 | 9.40 | 8.29 | 24.78 | 21.24 | 5.76 | 5.04 |
| U.S. | 15.14 | 9.33 | 31.06 | 20.12 | 9.48 | 10.55 |
| Italy | 10.20 | 7.33 | 23.85 | 19.22 | 5.46 | 4.91 |
| Belgium | 12.31 | 8.02 | 29.14 | 21.16 | 5.71 | 5.42 |
| Spain | 9.84 | 6.34 | 21.96 | 16.70 | 6.17 | 5.24 |
| France | 16.95 | 14.77 | 30.92 | 29.94 | 6.22 | 5.69 |
| Portugal | 8.43 | 7.80 | 23.93 | 19.10 | 6.83 | 5.32 |
| Germany | 7.60 | 12.20 | 19.88 | 26.77 | 7.23 | 6.92 |
| Finland | 11.79 | 23.94 | 31.14 | 38.60 | 7.25 | 4.91 |
| Ireland | 14.88 | 15.61 | 33.45 | 30.95 | 7.41 | 6.45 |
| Luxembourg | 12.35 | 7.17 | 32.03 | 21.16 | 7.56 | 6.07 |
| Austria | 7.95 | 10.18 | 23.03 | 23.74 | 7.80 | 5.74 |
| Greece | 10.63 | 13.49 | 28.00 | 29.06 | 8.34 | 8.31 |
| Sweden | 14.52 | 21.87 | 32.96 | 43.88 | 8.84 | 7.16 |
| UK | 15.72 | 19.56 | 35.73 | 35.83 | 9.16 | 5.22 |
| Hungary | 9.86 | 19.34 | 28.96 | 38.38 | 9.84 | 7.68 |
| Netherlands | 10.72 | 15.55 | 27.37 | 33.42 | 10.05 | 8.70 |
| Denmark | 9.96 | 34.72 | 26.48 | 55.36 | 10.23 | 17.86 |
| Slovenia | 17.93 | 21.10 | 40.54 | 47.41 | 10.96 | 9.53 |
| Poland | 7.62 | 12.33 | 21.72 | 29.59 | 11.42 | 8.97 |
| Czech Rep. | 14.30 | 26.03 | 27.64 | 36.79 | 12.26 | 9.56 |
| Estonia | 9.33 | 7.04 | 24.36 | 19.36 | 13.94 | 16.72 |
| Slovak Rep. | 10.97 | 22.44 | 25.83 | 38.70 | 14.78 | 11.68 |
| Lithuania | 7.73 | 7.00 | 21.60 | 18.35 | 21.23 | 19.05 |
| Latvia | 7.58 | 6.20 | 19.39 | 16.83 | 21.98 | 22.89 |

*computed as in Hymer, Pashigian, 1962.

Source: our computations on IMS Health, Copyright 2005.

**Figure 4.2 Product mobility statistics over all ATC4 therapeutic markets***

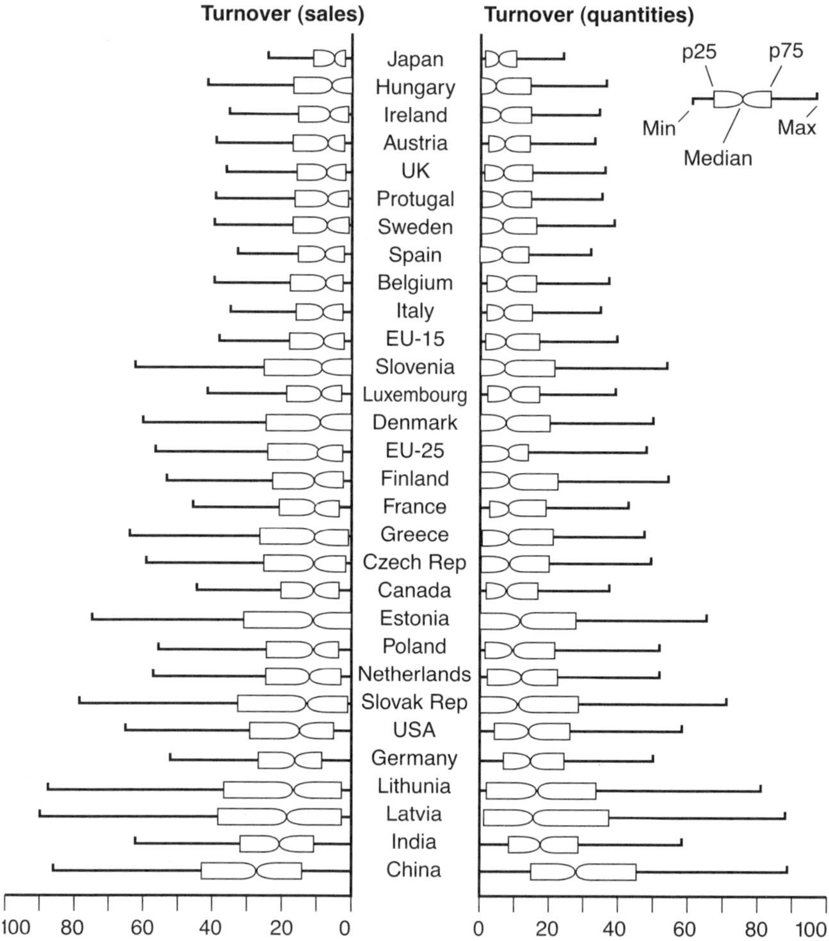


*The product mobility index is computed as in Hymer, Pashigian (1962).

Source: our computations on IMS Health.

Interestingly enough, higher concentration levels in the U.S. market do not imply less competition. Figure 4.2 shows the product mobility index for each therapeutic market (ATC4 class), defined as the sum of the annual change in the product market share (Hymer, Pashigian, 1962). Boxplots highlight the median value of the index and the 75th and 25th percentiles of the distribution. The most striking

**Table 4.3 The persistence of the leading product in top 100 ATC4 markets**

| | Leadership change (%) | | | | | | | | | | |
|---|---|---|---|---|---|---|---|---|---|---|---|
| **Country** | **1995** | **1996** | **1997** | **1998** | **1999** | **2000** | **2001** | **2002** | **2003** | **2004** | **AP** |
| **Portugal** | 6.42 | 6.36 | 7.62 | 9.26 | 7.74 | 4.95 | 5.86 | 9.88 | 8.72 | 9.06 | 13.18 |
| **Spain** | 6.50 | 9.97 | 7.20 | 10.37 | 7.33 | 9.74 | 7.95 | 6.98 | 8.55 | 8.53 | 12.03 |
| **Italy** | 7.40 | 9.72 | 8.14 | 9.14 | 7.79 | 7.01 | 9.84 | 7.51 | 9.66 | 7.41 | 11.96 |
| **Sweden** | 4.99 | 10.69 | 9.62 | 7.93 | 10.56 | 8.62 | 7.43 | 10.70 | 9.30 | 8.66 | 11.30 |
| **UK** | 10.46 | 8.92 | 8.00 | 8.71 | 10.16 | 8.38 | 9.11 | 9.50 | 8.16 | 7.24 | 11.28 |
| **Ireland** | 11.39 | 10.00 | 11.39 | 9.17 | 9.01 | 6.61 | 8.16 | 10.91 | 11.82 | 7.42 | 10.43 |
| **Belgium** | 8.36 | 7.24 | 7.56 | 9.58 | 9.78 | 11.36 | 9.86 | 10.31 | 11.52 | 11.08 | 10.35 |
| **Finland** | 7.76 | 9.67 | 9.85 | 9.79 | 10.88 | 9.50 | 7.19 | 11.24 | 11.31 | 12.06 | 10.08 |
| **Austria** | 7.32 | 9.38 | 10.09 | 11.31 | 8.92 | 10.54 | 13.84 | 9.53 | 11.78 | 9.82 | 9.75 |
| **EU-15** | 10.70 | 10.94 | 9.84 | 10.71 | 10.15 | 9.34 | 10.23 | 10.25 | 10.81 | 10.16 | 9.70 |
| **EU-25** | 10.95 | 11.14 | 10.05 | 10.97 | 10.43 | 9.52 | 10.30 | 10.36 | 10.89 | 10.40 | 9.52 |
| **France** | 9.30 | 10.57 | 9.82 | 12.01 | 10.42 | 10.28 | 10.00 | 11.00 | 12.76 | 11.28 | 9.31 |
| **Luxembourg** | 12.30 | 10.71 | 13.44 | 11.08 | 11.05 | 9.89 | 8.11 | 10.33 | 10.11 | 10.63 | 9.29 |
| **Hungary** | 14.46 | 14.98 | 13.67 | 12.67 | 10.67 | 9.86 | 5.26 | 9.73 | 7.07 | 10.93 | 9.15 |
| **Netherlands** | 9.61 | 10.59 | 11.54 | 10.18 | 14.24 | 10.85 | 11.08 | 10.39 | 9.04 | 12.28 | 9.11 |
| **Denmark** | 12.33 | 13.38 | 11.18 | 12.54 | 13.61 | 9.81 | 8.97 | 10.03 | 13.03 | 9.90 | 8.71 |
| **Greece** | 7.63 | 10.38 | 11.72 | 14.97 | 9.54 | 12.53 | 11.66 | 11.65 | 14.83 | 12.63 | 8.51 |
| **Germany** | 16.49 | 14.16 | 12.66 | 11.94 | 12.14 | 10.02 | 12.96 | 13.12 | 12.12 | 12.94 | 7.78 |
| **Slovenia** | 16.17 | 14.99 | 13.91 | 14.08 | 15.67 | 11.94 | 12.81 | 8.72 | 9.89 | 14.67 | 7.53 |
| **Poland** | 17.47 | 12.66 | 15.22 | 14.95 | 17.45 | 12.76 | 11.26 | 13.54 | 13.25 | 16.02 | 6.92 |
| **Estonia** | 0.00 | 0.00 | 0.00 | 66.67 | 11.59 | 11.55 | 16.52 | 19.46 | 16.77 | 13.69 | 6.40 |
| **Czech Rep.** | 18.37 | 18.55 | 15.27 | 15.74 | 18.58 | 15.82 | 13.56 | 11.65 | 16.58 | 13.42 | 6.35 |
| **U.S.** | 17.20 | 17.12 | 17.35 | 19.67 | 18.59 | 15.65 | 15.85 | 17.48 | 16.40 | 14.87 | 5.88 |
| **Slovak Rep.** | 22.22 | 21.35 | 18.86 | 26.32 | 21.28 | 14.74 | 13.76 | 13.31 | 14.66 | 18.70 | 5.40 |
| **Lithuania** | 0.00 | 73.10 | 28.03 | 25.23 | 22.09 | 19.51 | 28.19 | 16.57 | 17.83 | 19.29 | 4.00 |
| **Latvia** | 83.16 | 25.08 | 23.49 | 24.14 | 18.36 | 24.65 | 20.17 | 24.23 | 15.45 | 18.85 | 3.60 |

AP = Average Persistency.

Source: our computations on IMS Health.

**Table 4.4 Product turnover as a share of existing products (top 100 ATC4 classes, 1995-2004)**

| | 1995 | 1996 | 1997 | 1998 | 1999 | 2000 | 2001 | 2002 | 2003 | 2004 | Avg. |
|---|---|---|---|---|---|---|---|---|---|---|---|
| | | | | | | **Product entry rate (%)** | | | | | |
| **U.S.** | 12.15 | 16.64 | 18.81 | 15.30 | 15.45 | 9.05 | 14.13 | n.a. | 11.00 | 12.29 | *13.87* |
| **EU-15** | 9.12 | 9.53 | 9.15 | 11.78 | 11.07 | 10.62 | 9.41 | 9.98 | 10.28 | 10.71 | *10.17* |
| **EU-25** | 9.30 | 9.54 | 9.33 | 11.91 | 11.11 | 10.67 | 9.46 | 10.00 | 10.31 | 10.65 | *10.23* |
| | | | | | | **Product exit rate (%)** | | | | | |
| **U.S.** | 13.39 | 7.51 | 7.44 | 6.25 | 8.38 | 13.43 | 6.87 | 7.61 | 6.09 | 6.37 | *8.33* |
| **EU-15** | n.a. | 4.92 | 4.51 | 4.29 | 4.60 | 4.03 | 3.87 | 4.04 | 4.66 | 5.39 | *4.48* |
| **EU-25** | n.a. | 4.92 | 4.57 | 4.38 | 4.64 | 4.15 | 4.11 | 4.17 | 4.68 | n.a. | *4.45* |
| | | | | | | **Product turnover (%)** | | | | | |
| **U.S.** | 25.54 | 24.14 | 26.25 | 21.55 | 23.84 | 22.47 | 21.00 | n.a. | 17.10 | 18.66 | *22.28* |
| **EU-15** | n.a. | 14.44 | 13.66 | 16.07 | 15.67 | 14.65 | 13.28 | 14.02 | 14.94 | 16.10 | *14.76* |
| **EU-25** | n.a. | 14.46 | 13.91 | 16.29 | 15.76 | 14.82 | 13.57 | 14.17 | 15.00 | n.a. | *14.75* |
| | | | | | | **Product net entry (%)** | | | | | |
| **U.S.** | -1.24 | 9.13 | 11.37 | 9.05 | 7.07 | -4.38 | 7.26 | n.a. | 4.91 | 5.92 | *5.45* |
| **EU-15** | n.a. | 4.61 | 4.64 | 7.49 | 6.47 | 6.59 | 5.54 | 5.94 | 5.62 | 5.32 | *5.80* |
| **EU-25** | n.a. | 4.62 | 4.76 | 7.53 | 6.47 | 6.52 | 5.35 | 5.83 | 5.63 | n.a. | *5.84* |

Reported n.a. correspond to computed entry and exit rates outside the range of average turnover +/– two times the standard deviation interval, computed on the basis of observed product entry and exit rates.

Source: our computations on IMS Health.

result is that firm turnover in the U.S. is almost double that of the EU-15 and EU-25.

The lower turnover of EU markets means higher persistency and lower market contestability. As an average, the persistency of the leading product in the U.S. is slightly less than six years, while in the EU it is almost 10 years (Table 4.3).

U.S. product turnover is more intense than in Europe (Table 4.4). Product exit rate and turnover are almost double in the U.S. than in the EU-15 (8.3 and 4.5 percent, 22.3 and 14.8 percent respectively). Product entry rates are more than 3 percentage points higher in the U.S. than in the EU-15. All in all, the process of creative destruction seems to be much less intense in the European markets than in the U.S., where new and improved products displace old ones in any given

**Figure 4.3 Introduction lag (in months) from launch on the U.S. market of all molecules launched since 1975**

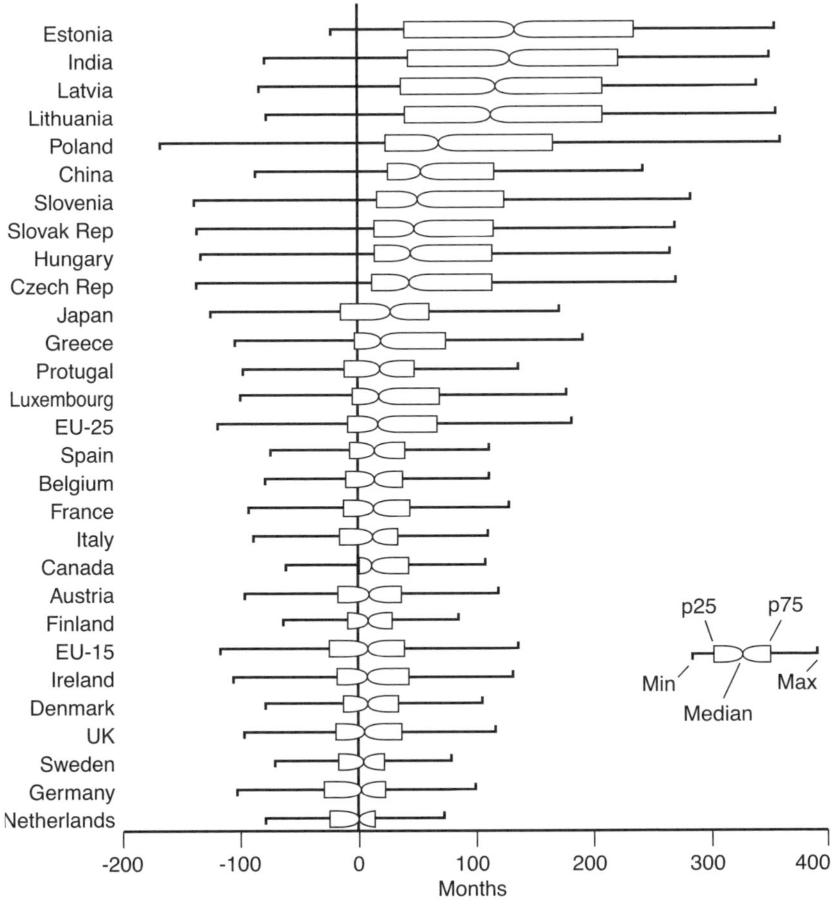


Source: our computations on IMS Health.

therapeutic market. Low market contestability in Europe is one of the most striking consequences of market fragmentation and price regulation that undermines the productivity of European companies, since national barriers still limit, to a certain extent, the breadth of the market segment within which they can draw customers away from rivals.

Moreover, differences in price levels, as well as in reimbursement and co-payment schemes across countries, account for the delay in the launch of new molecules in EU countries with respect to the U.S. (Danzon *et al.*, 2003; Gabrowski and Wang, 2006; Kyle, 2006).

Figure 4.3 shows that, with the exception of the Netherlands, European countries experience a time lag in the launch of new molecules. The median delay from the U.S. launch is eight months for EU-15,[3] which increases to 17 months for the EU-25.

In conclusion, EU health care markets are more fragmented and less dynamic *vis-à-vis* the U.S. due to regulatory barriers, which prevent market integration, competitive turnover, contestability, and dynamic competition. As a result, since patient, product and firm mobility are limited, price differences among countries persist to favor parallel trade and hinder product innovation.

## Conclusions

Heterogeneous national regulatory frameworks, price regulation mechanisms and cost containment policies in Europe have a negative impact on market integration as well as on productivity and innovation in health care markets for goods and services.

The key challenge for EU governments is to design and coordinate pluralistic systems of health care delivery and financing, in which market forces and mechanisms of managed competition can act to generate an environment favorable to investment and innovation, while public and private programs can perform complementary functions to make patterns of care responsive to individual preferences without imposing excessive financial burdens on individuals or denying necessary care because of inability to pay.

The uneven geographical distribution of research efforts in pharmaceuticals, together with the differences in price levels for innovative drugs between Europe and the U.S., calls for revival of a transatlantic dialogue on the political economy of pharmaceuticals and medical technologies, through the lens of trade policy and protection of intellectual property rights.

---

3 When considering the European aggregate, the comparison is made between the median launch across the European countries and the launch in the U.S.

Moreover, for Europe and the U.S. both productivity and the rate and direction of medical innovation will be affected by the interplay between technological advances and patterns of demand, especially in relation to the effective management of health and pharmaceutical expenditures to encourage innovation while preserving access and fiscal sustainability.

In the health care sector, Europe is suffering at the supranational level from the sort of institutional fragmentation that hindered transactions and stifled economic growth for centuries within European states themselves. In each country, the power of the state to set health and pharmaceutical policy is intertwined with political autonomy. Fearful of yielding power to the EU Commission, individual nations have private incentives to resist common reforms, regardless of the negative effects on productivity, mobility, specialization, and trade.

During the 18th and 19th centuries, problems of institutional fragmentation within European states were solved through the establishment of uniform national laws by central governments (see Dincecco, 2006). Standardization of domestic systems of weights and measures in the 19th century provides a useful illustration of centralization efforts. Beforehand, spatial fragmentation of weights and measures across towns and provinces raised the costs of commerce, hindering competition, specialization, and trade. With the implementation of nation-wide decimal systems, transactions costs between locales were significantly reduced, stimulating economic growth.

This is not to suggest that what Europe need is greater government involvement in the regulation of health care markets. The market forces that ultimately drive innovation and efficiency, rather than the visible hand of the government, should be encouraged and coordinated. In parallel, the EU Commission should have greater control over the underlying "rules of the game," establishing the legal framework that sustain market integration and patient mobility.

At this final juncture, a caveat deserves mention. A distinction between the interests of the EU as a whole and those of individual states must be made. The establishment by the EU Commission of a uniform set of rules governing health care and pharmaceutical markets in Europe would reduce transactions costs and promote efficiency through competition and market integration. In the long run, Europe would benefit as a whole of the standardization of such rules, while rents accruing to individual countries and actors that had profited from the previous set of idiosyncratic institutional arrangement would be lost irrevocably. Hence, it is not surprising that states would resist institutional reforms with positive effects at the EU level if they were perceived to threaten traditional privileges (and associated revenue streams) at the national level.

It is precisely in this sort of situation, where the incentives of individual players diverge from the common interest, that a single centralizing authority such as the EU Commission should be granted the power to design an institutional framework that aligns the different sets of incentives of single member States.

## References

Abrantes-Metz R., C. Adams and A. Metz (2003), *Pharmaceutical Development Phases: a Duration Analysis*, Washington, D.C.: The Federal Trade Commission, Bureau of Economics Working Paper No. 274.

Amiti M. and Wei S.-J. (2004), *Fear of Service Outsourcing: Is It Justified?* Boston, Ma.: NBER Working Paper 10808.

Anderson G., Heyssel, R. and Dickler, R. (1993), "Competition vs regulation: its effect on hospitals," *Health Affairs*, 12: 70–80.

Armstrong, M. and Sappington E.M. (2006), "Regulation, Competition, and Liberalization," *Journal of Economic Literature*, XLIV: 325-366.

Bhagwati J., Panagariya A., Srinivasan T.N. (2004), The Muddles over Outsourcing, *The Journal of Economic Perspectives*, 18(4): 93-114.

Baldwin R. (2006), *Globalization: The Great Unbundling(s)*, paper prepared for the Secretariat of the Economic Council, mimeo.

Bertinato L., Busse R., Fahy N., Legido-Quigley H., McKee M., Palm W., Passamani I., Ronfini F. (2005), "Cross Border Health Care in Europe," *European Observatory on Health Systems and Policies Policy Brief*, World Health Organization.

Berg, O. (1999), "The organization of the Norwegian health care system: the rise and decline of a public iatrocracy," in O. Molven (ed.) *The Norwegian Health Care System*, Oslo: University of Oslo.

Caves R.E., (1998), Industrial Organization and New Findings on the Turnover and Mobility of Firms, *Journal of Economic Literature*, XXXVI: 1947-1982.

Caves R.E., Whinston M.D., Hurwitz M.A., Pakes A. and P. Temin (1991), Patent Expiration, Entry, and Competition in the U.S. Pharmaceutical Industry, *Brookings Papers on Economic Activity. Microeconomics*, Vol. 1991: 1-66.

Congressional Budget Office (1998), "How Increased Competition from Generic Drugs has Affected Prices and Returns in the Pharmaceutical Industry," Washington, D.C.: Congressional Budget Office.

Danzon P.M, and Chao L.W. (2000), "Cross-national price differences for pharmaceuticals: how large and why?" *Journal of Health Economics*, 19: 159-195.

Darby M. R. and Karmi E. (1973), "Free Competition and the Optimal Amount of Fraud," *Journal of Law and Economics*, 16(1): 67-88.

DiMasi J.A, Hansen R.W., Grabowski H.G. (2003), "The price of Innovation: New estimates of Drug Development Costs," *Journal of Health Economics*, 22(2): 151-185.

Domberger, S. and Jensen, P. (1997), "Contracting- out by the public sector: theory, evidence, prospects," *Oxford Review of Economic Policy*, 13: 67-78.

Dranove, D. (2000), *The Economic Evolution of American Health Care: From Marcus Welby to Managed Care*, Princeton: Princeton University Press.

Dulleck U. and Kerschbamer R. (2006), "On Doctors, Mechanics, and Computer Specialists: The Economics of Credence Goods," *Journal of Economic Literature*, 44(1): 5-22.

Ellis, R.P. (1998), "Creaming, skimping and dumping: provider competition on the intensive and extensive margins," *Journal of Health Economics*, 17: 537-555.

EPFIA (2006), *The Pharmaceutical Industry in Figures*, Brussels, Belgium.

European Commission (2006), *Consultation regarding the Community action on health services*, Communication from the Commission, Brussels.

Feldstein M. (1995), "The Economics of Health and Health Care. What Have we Learned? What have I learned?" *American Economic Review Papers and Proceedings*, 85(2): 28-31.

Freeman, R. (1998), "Competition in context: the politics of health care reforms in Europe," *International Journal for Quality in Health Care*, 10: 395-401.

Giaccotto C., Santerre R., and Vernon J. (2005), "Drug prices and research and development investment behavior in the pharmaceutical industry," *Journal of Law and Economics*, 48: 195-214.

Golek, J.H. and Vernon J. (2006), "European Pharmaceutical Price Regulation, Firm Profitability, and R&D Spending," Boston, Ma.: NBER Working Paper 12676.

Hamilton, D.S. and Quinlan J.P. (2005), *Deep Integration: How Transatlantic Markets are Leading Globalization*, Washington D.C.: Johns Hopkins University Center for Transatlantic Relations.

Hart O., Shleifer, A. and Vishny, R.W. (1997), "The proper scope of government: theory and an application to prisons," *Quarterly Journal of Economics*, 112: 1127–61.

Hollis, A. (2003) "The anti-competitive effects of brand-controlled 'pseudo-generics' in the Canadian pharmaceutical market," *Canadian Policy- Analyse de politiques*, 29: 22-32.

Hymer S. and P. Pashigian (1962), "Turnover of Firms As a Measure of Market Behavior," *The Review of Economics and Statistics*, 44: 82-87.

Kyle M. (2006), "Pharmaceutical Price Controls and Entry Strategies," *Review of Economics and Statistics*, forthcoming.

Jones C. (2002), "Why have health expenditures as a share of GDP risen so much?" Boston, Ma: *NBER Working Paper 9325.*

Levy F. and Yu K.-H. (2006), *Offshoring Radiology Services to India*, Cambridge, Ma.: MIT Working Paper Series MIT-IPC-06-005, September 2006.

Mervis J. (2005), "Productivity Counts—But the definition is key," *Science*, 309(29) July 2005.

Newhouse J.P. (1992), "Medical Care Costs: How Much Welfare Loss?" *Journal of Economic Perspectives*, 6(3): 3-21.

Newhouse J.P. (1996), Reimbursing health plans and health providers: efficiency in production versus selection, *Journal of Economic Literature*, 34: 1236-1263.

Owen-Smith J., Riccaboni M., Pammolli F., Powell W.W. (2002), "A Comparison of U.S. and European University-Industry Relations in the Life Sciences," *Management Sciences*, 48: 24-43.

Pammolli F., Riccaboni, M. (2007), "The institutional roots of industrial leadership. Lessons from pharmaceuticals," *mimeo.*

Reekie, W.D. (1998), "How competition lowers the costs of medicines," *Pharmacoeconomics*, 14: 107–113.

Rosenmoller M., McKee M, Baeten R. (2006), *Patient mobility in the European Union—Learning from Experience*, European Observatory on Health Systems and Policies, World Health Organization.

Saltman, R.B. (1997), "Balancing state and market in health system reform: editorial," *European Journal of Public Health*, 7: 119–120.

Saltman R.B., Busse R., Mossialos E. (2002), *Regulating Entrepreneurial Behavior in European Health Care Systems*, European Observatory on Health Care Systems Series, Buckingham, UK: Open University Press.

Sutton, J. (1998), *Technology and Market Structure*, Cambridge MA: MIT Press.

Thomas, L.G. (1994), "Implicit Industrial Policy: The Triumph of Britain and the Failure of France in Global Pharmaceuticals," *Industrial and Corporate Change*, 2: 451-489.

Vernon J. (1971), "Concentration, Promotion, and Market Share Stability in the Pharmaceutical Industry," *The Journal of Industrial Economics*, 19: 246-266.

Vernon, J. (2005), "Examining the link between price regulation and pharmaceutical R&D investment," *Health Economics* 14: 1-16.

Wallack S., Skalera, K.C. and Cai, J. (1996), "Redefining rate regulation in a competitive environment," *Journal of Health Politics, Policy and Law*, 21: 489–520.

Weill T.P., and Battistella R.M. (1998), "A blended strategy using competitive and regulatory models," *Health Care Management Review*, 23:37-45.

Weisbrod, B.A. (1991), "The Health Care Quadrilemma: An Essay on Technological Change, Insurance, Quality of Care, and Cost Containment," *Journal of Economic Literature*, 29: 523-552.

# *Chapter 5*

# Transatlantic Telecom Services: The Pros and Cons of Convergence

*Andrea Renda*

*Advocates of an open transatlantic economy often put emphasis on the need to eliminate barriers to entry and FDI in the communication services sector. However, despite broadly similar industry trends and a common need to encourage investment in Next Generation Networks, regulators on the two sides of the Atlantic are evidently dancing to "different drummers." In the U.S., industry consolidation at the infrastructure level was favored by 'access holidays' granted to firms investing in FTTx, DSL and BPL technologies, as well as the classification of VoIP as information service. In Europe, regulation is focused on facilitating wholesale access by new entrants at the infrastructure level. This chapter surveys industry and regulatory trends in the two regions and discusses the pros and cons of fully opening up the transatlantic market. It concludes that the main prospects lie in coordination of spectrum policy and frequencies allocation, cooperation on net neutrality issues and the removal of existing barriers to inward FDI. However, fully opening the market by restoring network sharing obligations would not contribute to a more prosperous transatlantic economy.*

## Introduction

The second half of 2006 saw growing interest in an intensification of transatlantic trade and regulatory cooperation: both the European Parliament's Mann Report, adopted on June 1, 2006, and a U.S. Senate Resolution of December 8, 2006, advocated for further opening of the transatlantic economy.[1] Such views were echoed also by industry players and by German Chancellor Angela Merkel, who made liberalization of transatlantic markets a key theme of Germany's EU Presidency

[1] See Senate Resolution n. 632, December 9, 2006.

in the spring of 2007.[2] The April 2007 EU-U.S. Summit unveiled a new initiative in this regard, with a specific emphasis on liberalizing services, including communication services. The Mann Report noted that the transatlantic telecommunications market is still hampered by "regulatory barriers and incompatible standards which translate into a situation whereby, despite the fact that nine out of the ten biggest telecom companies in the world are based in the EU or the U.S., no U.S. or European company is operating on both continents to any significant extent."[3] On the other hand, both the European Commission and the U.S. Trade Representative have listed a remarkable number of obstacles to transatlantic investment in communication services. Removing these obstacles would allegedly contribute to more competitive and integrated markets, thus benefiting end users and society as a whole. Strengthening transatlantic trade and investment would help the U.S. and EU face the growing competitive pressure exerted from the rest of the world; the transition to the knowledge economy exhibited a remarkable slowdown after the Internet bubble, leading the U.S. to surrender its leadership in the ICT sector to the benefit of China and other Asian countries.[4] 2005 was indeed the year in which China, after overtaking Japan and the EU in 2003, also surpassed the U.S. as global leader in the export of ICT goods.[5]

Few other sectors—if any—are facing a disruptive and breathtaking transformation as the one observed in this market. In many developed countries, the transition to all-IP networks will soon blur the boundaries between telecommunications and the Internet. This, in turn is creating unprecedented prospects for the proliferation of access platforms based on different technologies—including FTTx, 3G, WiMax, Broadband over Power Lines etc.—and for infrastructure-based competition to the full benefit of end users. Digital convergence is changing the way in which consumers gain access to applica-

---

[2] See Daniel Hamilton and Joseph Quinlan, "Merkel has posed right question in search for an Atlantic bridge," *Financial Times*, January 10, 2007. On the U.S.-EU Summit, see http://useu.usmission.gov/Dossiers/US_EU_Summits/Apr3007_Washington_Summit.asp.

[3] See European Parliament, *Resolution on EU-US transatlantic economic relations*, P6_TA(2006) 0239, June 1, 2006.

[4] See, e.g., Marcus, S. (2005), *Is the US Dancing to a Different Drummer?*, Communications & Strategies, no. 60, 4th quarter 2005, p. 39; and also Prestowitz, C. (2006), *America's Technology Future at Risk*, Economic Strategy Institute, March 2006.

[5] See OECD IT Outlook 2006. Japanese firm NTT DoCoMo is the largest provider of telecommunication services worldwide.

tions and content on broadband platforms, and operators are in turn changing their business models to match this transition in consumer preferences, engaging in the so-called 'competition for eyeballs' over a common information superhighway. Traditionally prominent services —e.g. PSTN telephony and broadcast TV—are increasingly being commoditized, and industry players seek to recover their margins by speeding up the launch of new value-added applications (such as VoIP and IPTV) that promise to revolutionise the customer's experience.

Would industry evolution and market competition be facilitated by an open transatlantic market for communications services? As a preliminary remark, there are several reasons to support this view. First, new digital services and applications need more scale, spectrum, technical standardization and high-speed connectivity than any legacy service ever required, leading to an increasingly global nature of the industry, especially as far as applications and content are concerned. An example is the WiMax technology, which promises high-speed wireless internet access over a range of 70 miles, but requires massive investment and the availability of suitable spectrum bands in the largest world markets to justify its deployment.

Secondly, persistence of incompatible standards hampers the maximization of network effects in many sectors, including 3G mobile telephony, digital terrestrial and satellite TV. Here too, the need to develop applications and services for more than one standard jeopardizes the business case for new risky investment in mobile platforms. Future 4G telephony will arguably be based on a single standard, but this requires cooperation between players and regulators.

Thirdly, strengthening the transatlantic market for communication services would have indirect virtuous effects on all ICT-enabled services, including financial services. The availability of suitable infrastructure and bandwidth for transatlantic exchanges would boost trade and growth in many other sectors: as "it takes two to tango," both sides of the Atlantic would have to improve their infrastructure endowment, by securing a smooth migration towards Next Generation Networks, protection of IPRs, interoperability of digital platforms and technology/service neutrality in spectrum allocation.

Finally, "legal rules do matter." As a matter of fact, faced with these unprecedented challenges, both the U.S. and EU are working to mod-

**Table 5.1 Top 10 Telecommunications Firms, 2000 and 2005 USD Millions, current prices**

| Firm | Country | Revenue 2000 | Revenue 2005 | Employees 2000 | Employees 2005 | Net income 2000 | Net income 2005 |
|---|---|---|---|---|---|---|---|
| NTT | Japan | 92,679 | 99,880 | 224,000 | 201,500 | -603 | 6,563 |
| Verizon | U.S. | 64,707 | 73,217 | 263,552 | 210,000 | 11,797 | 8,705 |
| Deutsche Telekom | Germany | 37,559 | 71,911 | 205,000 | 244,277 | 5,437 | 4,822 |
| France Telecom | France | 30,894 | 58,519 | 188,866 | 206,525 | 4,707 | 8,395 |
| Vodafone | UK | 11,929 | 54,249 | 29,465 | 57,378 | 838 | -25,058 |
| Telefonica | Spain | 27,306 | 42,864 | 145,730 | 173,554 | 1,693 | 4,531 |
| SBC | U.S. | 51,374 | 41,183 | 220,000 | 162,700 | 7,800 | 3,819 |
| TI/Olivetti | Italy | 27,516 | 36,277 | 107,171 | 82,397 | 3,231 | 5,380 |
| BT | UK | 28,356 | 33,860 | 132,000 | 102,100 | 2,111 | 3,309 |
| Sprint/Nextel | U.S. | 17,220 | 27,901 | 64,900 | 59,900 | 1,964 | -401 |
| Total | | 389,540 | 539,860 | 1,580,684 | 1,500,331 | 38,974 | 20,065 |

Source: OECD, IT Outlook 2006, at 54.

ernize their regulatory frameworks. The degree of market openness and the prospects for a more integrated transatlantic market for telecom services heavily depend on the results of such modernization efforts. As a preliminary remark, industry and regulatory developments seem to suggest that both the U.S. and Europe have made significant steps towards liberalization, thus facilitating entry by new players in their national markets; at the same time, however, remaining barriers to inward FDI and industry consolidation on both sides of the Atlantic may invert the trend in the next few years, further jeopardizing integration between the two markets.

This chapter illustrates the main industry developments and describes the main features of the regulatory models adopted in the two regions; it then assesses the prospects and the impact of achieving further integration between the two markets. Section one illustrates industry trends in the U.S. and EU, whereas section two describes the current regulatory challenges faced and the solutions identified by regulators in the U.S. and the EU. Section three contains an overview of existing data on barriers to trade and inward FDI from a transatlantic perspective, and comments on the potential for an open transatlantic market. Section four concludes.

## 1. Industry Trends: Technologies, Markets and Strategies

The market for communications services represented 44.5 percent of the total world ICT market in 2005, reaching a value of $1.2 trillion.[6] Europe and the U.S. hold a 55 percent share of this market, and —as shown in Table 5.1 below—nine of the top 10 firms worldwide belong to the "Sleeping Giant."[7] As shown in the table, many of the top 10 firms have reduced their number of employees since 2000, and the majority also had a lower net income in 2005.

Against this background, data on investment, productivity and trade patterns show a remarkable gap between most advanced countries—such as the Asian Tigers, but also the U.S. and some Northern European countries—and laggard countries that hardly keep the pace of technological innovation and services liberalization. The latter include also some Southern and most Eastern European countries. According to recent data by IDATE, large emerging markets such as new-entrant Romania exhibited a very high growth rate in telecom services in 2006 (over 20 percent), whereas countries where mobile telephony is still not fully mature—such as Greece, Spain, and most CEE countries—have reached growth rates between seven and 10 percent. On the contrary, a sharp decline in landline telephony has led to slower growth in Italy, Austria, Hungary and the Czech Republic; whereas most of Western European countries and Poland have exhibited growth rates below three percent due to market maturity, and Finland even showed a negative growth rate in 2006.[8]

Recent research in this field has shown that the percentage contribution of ICT to EU productivity growth—reaching 50 percent in 2006—increased mostly because productivity as a whole decreased overtime during the past five years; against this background, the largest single component of the U.S.-EU productivity growth differential is

---

6 Sources: EITO Annual Report 2006, and Infonetics (2005).

7 OECD IT Outlook, 2006, at 54.

8 Gassot, Y. (2006), presentation at the Transatlantic Telecom Dialogue, Columbia University, New York, October 20, 2006.

**Figure 5.1 Average annual per capita investments in telecommunications infrastructure, 1997-2003 (EUR per capita per year)**

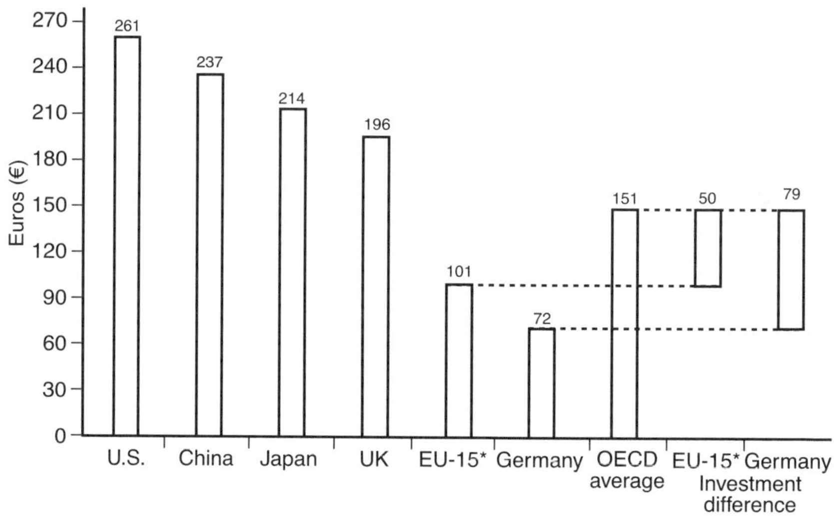


*Excluding UK. Source: OECD, McKinsey

the faster productivity growth rate in ICT-intensive industries in the U.S., where ICT accounts for 80 percent of productivity growth.[9]

## *1.1 Investment in Infrastructure: a Mixed Picture*

These trends are evident also when it comes to investment in telecom infrastructure. As shown below, in Figure 5.1, in the period 1997-2003 average annual per capita investment in telecommunications infrastructure in the EU15 (excluding the UK) totalled €101, well below the OECD average (€151). In Germany, the largest EU country, only €72 per capita was spent on telecoms infrastructure, less than half of the OECD average.[10] Against this backdrop, European ICT is projected to grow by 2.2 percent in 2006 and to slow down to 1.7 per-

[9] See Van Ark, B. and O. Mahony (2003), *EU Productivity and Competitiveness: An Industry Perspective. Can Europe Resume the Catching-up Process?* Office for Official Publications of the European Union, Luxembourg.

[10] Presentation by Luis Enriquez (McKinsey) at the CEPS Task Force on electronic communications, May 3, 2006.

**Figure 5.2 Telco's CAPEX, 2003-2005, billion USD**

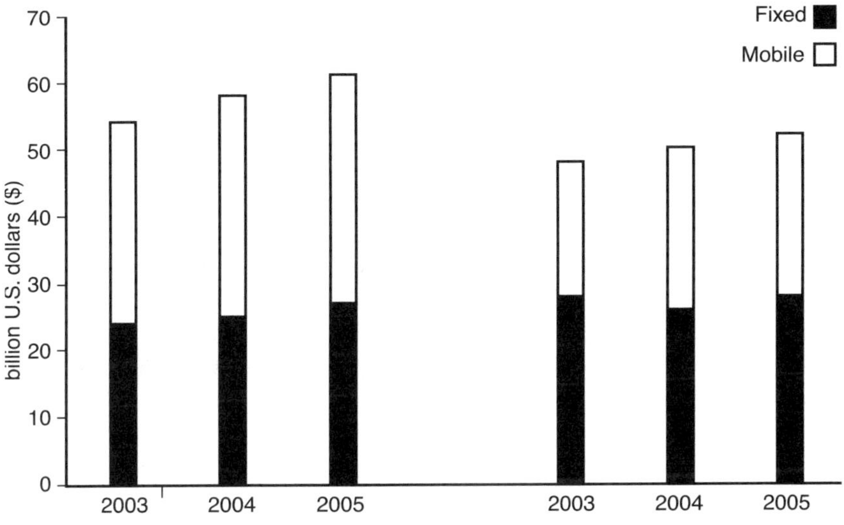


Source: IDATE

cent growth in 2007, whereas the U.S. will grow by 2.6 and 2.8 percent in 2006 and 2007, respectively.[11]

These figures hide a very different evolution, when broken down on a yearly basis: in 2003, after the bubble burst, the per capita investment in telecommunication infrastructure in the U.S. had fallen to €143.1, whereas Denmark was investing €157.6, Japan €170, the UK €184.1 and Switzerland €216.7. The OECD average was approximately €111.8 per capita by then.[12] Unfortunately, OECD figures only cover the 1997-2003 timeframe, and as such do not take adequate account of the huge investment in broadband technologies in the U.S. and in some EU member states (e.g. the UK).[13]

Against this background, data reported by Infonetics (2005), the European Commission (2006) and by IDATE (2006, shown in Figure 5.2) show that between 2003 and 2005 Europe outperformed the U.S. and even closed the gap with Far Eastern countries in terms of invest-

[11] EITO Report 2006.

[12] Source: OECD STAN Database. I owe this comment to Martin Wörter from Konjunkturforschungsstelle (KOF), Zurich.

[13] An example is Verizon's $18 billion investment in the FiOS network (see below, Section 2.1.1).

ment in telecommunications. Investments in the mobile sub-sector have overcome those in the fixed telephone sub-sector, and appear to have been the major element in the 2004 investment recovery observed in Europe. On the other hand, EU investment in the cable TV and broadcasting sub-sectors represent on average a combined 10 percent share of the total investment in e-communications. In addition, although incumbent firms still invest more than new entrants, the latter are investing more relative to their turnover.[14]

These data have been reported by the Commission as evidence that the 2002 regulatory framework for e-communications is actually achieving its goal of stimulating investment and growth in Europe.[15] However, contrasting signals were launched by the Commission in its recent First Annual Report on the implementation of the i2010 strategy.[16] There, Commission services reported that, although the ICT sector represented 5.6 percent of EU GDP between 2000 and 2003 and generated approximately 45 percent of EU productivity gains in the 2000-2004 timeframe, Europe's investment in R&D is still as low as 1.9 percent of GDP, and the contribution of ICT to productivity has remained about half that in the U.S. According to the UK Department of Trade and Industry, corporate R&D spending in Europe rose only 5.8 percent between 2005 and 2006, compared with 8.2 percent in the U.S., 10.7 percent in China and 25.1 percent in India.[17] As stated by the Commission, "[o]verall no indicator points to a change in the trend or an acceleration in ICT developments which would put the EU onto a sustainable path of growth and competitiveness.... The EU needs to shift up a gear if we are not to see a slowdown in the transition to the knowledge economy."[18]

Investment data in the U.S. also present a mixed picture. According to some commentators, the FCC decisions to lift regulatory obliga-

---

[14] Communication from the Commission to the Council, the European Parliament, the European Economic and Social Committee and the Committee of the Regions on the review of the EU Regulatory Framework for electronic communications networks and services (SEC(2006) 816) (SEC(2006) 817), June 29, 2006.

[15] See the Staff Working Document SEC(2006)816, June 29, 2006.

[16] See the Commission's First Annual Report of the i2010 Strategy, COM(2006)215, May 19, 2006; and the Second Annual Report, COM(2007)146, March 30, 2007.

[17] See the DTI R&D Scoreboard 2006 at http://www.innovation.gov.uk/rd_scoreboard/ (visited on April 25, 2007).

[18] COM(2006)215, May 19, 2006, at 4.

tions on new FTTx and DSL infrastructure have boosted investment by RBOCs between 2003 and 2005. On the other hand, available figures still do not show any significant change in the declining trend of investment that characterised the U.S. ICT sector after the Internet bubble. A study by Tom Hazlett (2005) concluded that access holidays led DSL subscribers to increase at a greater pace, and both SBC and Verizon have increased their investments in FTTH after regulatory obligations were lifted.[19] But to date, no convincing relation has been found between the U.S. regulatory approach and incentives to invest in new infrastructure in the U.S.

In summary, it is quite hard to draw any clear-cut conclusion on the relative performance of the U.S. and EU in the telecommunication sector. To be sure, some EU member states apparently outperformed the U.S. in many respects: these include Denmark, the Netherlands, Scandinavian countries and, to a certain extent, the UK. These trends must however be observed in light of the ongoing transformation of the industry, as well as differentiating per sub-sector.

## *1.2 Consolidation and Expansion*

The last two years have been characterized by a remarkable phase of consolidation and a resurgence of M&A activities both in the United States and in Europe. This trend was fuelled by declining wireline revenue growth, ongoing technological convergence, increased competitive pressure and the need to provide end users with multi-play offerings. Notable examples of "mammoth mergers" in the United States include, of course, the Verizon/MCI and SBC/AT&T mergers, cleared by U.S. authorities after the imposition of net neutrality conditions at the end of 2005. More recently, AT&T's $86 billion acquisition of BellSouth was approved by the FCC, although it will create a prominent player in the telecoms field, holding more than 50 percent of telephone and internet access lines in the U.S. Complementarities between the two firms' networks are expected to generate benefits as regards the deployment of broadband, increased competition in the market for advanced (IP-based) pay TV services,

[19] See Hazlett, T. (2005) *Rivalrous Telecommunications Networks With and Without Mandatory Sharing*, AEI-Brookings Joint Center for Regulatory Studies Working Paper No. 05-07, Washington, D.C..; and Wallsten, S. J. (2006), *Broadband and Unbundling Regulations in OECD Countries*, AEI-Brookings Joint Center Working Paper No. 06-16, Washington, D.C.

improvements in wireless products, services and reliability through the merged entity's unified management of Cingular Wireless; and even enhanced national security.[20] As a consequence, the communications infrastructure is now dominated by less than ten players in the U.S., with six major cable operators and three local phone companies. Together, these companies hold roughly 90 percent of the market.

In Europe, the situation is radically different. In line with the approach adopted already during the Open Network Provision (ONP) era, as improved and updated with the 1999 Communications review and the 2002 regulatory framework, competition policy tools have been embedded in the regulatory approach, and the role of *ex post* competition policy was maintained as a safeguard in case *ex ante* regulation failed to tackle a competitive problem.[21] The regulatory framework focuses mostly on ensuring new entrants' access at the wholesale level, and national regulators have broadly adopted the so-called "investment ladder" approach, which echoes the "stepping stones" model discarded long ago in the U.S., which puts strong emphasis on the gradual entry of new players in the many relevant markets that compose the telecoms sector.[22] As a result, as many as 2,000 operators are reportedly operating in Europe at different rungs of the 'ladder'. In many European countries, the share held by incumbents has fallen below 60 percent in broadband, whereas mobile markets are characterized by oligopolies, with three to seven players for each member state. Since 2005, M&A activity has resurged, and cross-border transactions—driven by the search for economies of scale and the implementation of pan-European strategies—were conservatively estimated by the European Commission at approximately €70 billion in both 2005 and 2006.[23] The list of recent mergers includes the following:

---

[20] See the FCC's Press Release, November 29, 2006, available at http://www.fcc.gov/ATT-BellSouth_Press_Release.pdf (visited on April 25, 2007).

[21] Where *ex ante* regulation under the 2002 framework failed to address a specific problem, in some cases further regulatory initiatives were undertaken. This is the case of international wholesale roaming charges, a market that was found to be competitive by regulators under the 2002 framework, but subject to a Commission proposed regulation, currently being debated at the European Parliament.

[22] See Cave, M., Majumdar, S., Rood, H., Valletti, T. and I. Vogelsang (2001), *The Relationship between Access Pricing and Infrastructure Competition*, Brunel University.

[23] According to an April 20 report from Standard & Poor's Equity Research, in the first quarter of 2006, M&A deals where the value was disclosed totaled €380 billion—almost triple the amount in the comparable period of 2005. See also European Commission, *European Electronic Communications Regulation and Markets*, 12th Report, COM(2007)155, March 29, 2007, Vol. 1, at 10.

- Spanish Telefonica acquired UK mobile operator $O_2$ for €24 billion;
- Wind (Italy) was acquired by Orascom (Egypt) for 12.1 billion euros;
- TDC, the Danish incumbent, was acquired by the U.S./UK firm NTC for 8.2 billion euros;
- France Telecom acquired the Spanish mobile operator Amena for €6.4 billion;
- In the UK, NTL acquired both Telewest (€5 billion) and Virgin Mobile (€1.3 billion);
- Cesky Telecom (Czech Republic) was acquired by Vodafone for €3.7 billion;
- The U.S.-based Blackstone Group invested 2.7 billion euros to buy a 4.5 percent stake of the German incumbent Deutsche Telekom;
- Deutsche Telekom, in turn, acquired Austrian Tele-ring for €1.3 billion.

On top of this, European players have started investing more heavily in non-EU operations. As shown in Figure 5.3 below, players such as Vodafone, Telefonica, Telenor, Portugal Telecom and Deutsche Telekom are very active outside the European borders. In addition, most of the larger players are now present in other national markets, and there has been a notable trend in investment in the new Member States by some of the more established players as well as by pan-European and local new entrants. In 2006, for example, France Telecom expanded its mobile phone network operations (under the Orange brand) in as many as ten EU member states, and challenges the position of truly global operators such as Vodafone.

As a matter of fact, European players are consolidating across platforms and attacking each other's market to an unprecedented extent. For such reason, the international exposure of EU players appears much greater than that of U.S. players, as shown in Figure 5.4 below. This has also led the European Commission to realize that a suitable future for EU telecoms would pass through the creation of a Euro-

**Figure 5.3 Geographical Breakdown of Sales for Leading EU Telcos in 2005**

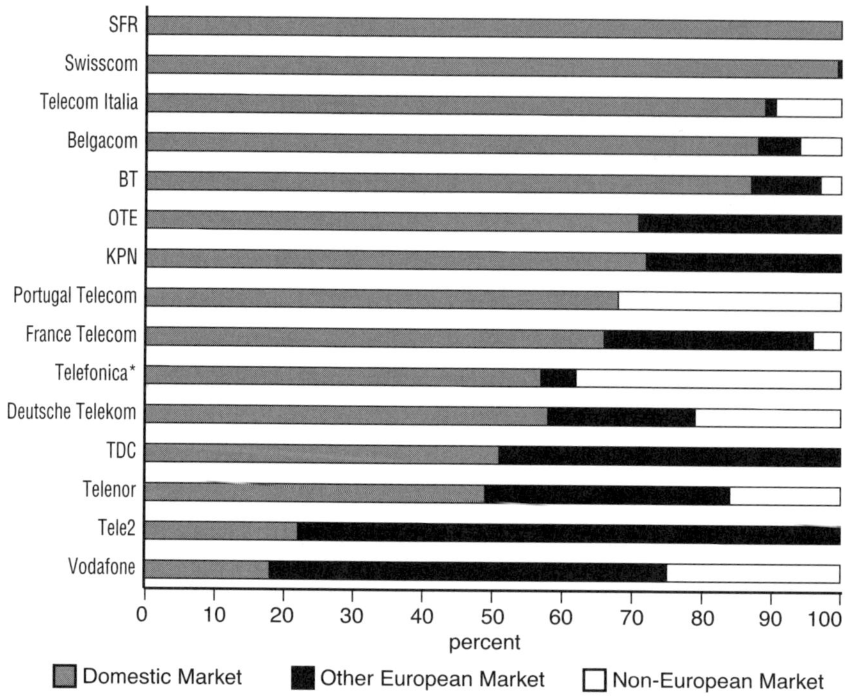


*Sales of O2 not consolidated with those of Telefonica at the end of 2005

Source: IDATE (2006)

pean single market in which large incumbents act as new entrants in a number of member states. This trend is also welcome as many of the new interactive services that should develop over future digital platforms need a pan-European scale, in order to ensure that investments are recovered. So to say, pan-European services also need, to a certain extent, pan-European players.

Investment, of course, is also spurred by current earnings. Players on both sides of the Atlantic are increasing recovering from the remarkable decrease observed in wireline revenues. In the U.S., in the second quarter of 2006 only BellSouth had increased revenues (+1 percent) in its wireline operations, whereas AT&T had a five percent decrease in revenues, and Verizon experienced a 6.2 percent fall. At the same time, however, the EBITDA/sales ratio decreased signifi-

**Figure 5.4 International Exposure of Selected Leading Telcos in the U.S. and EU**

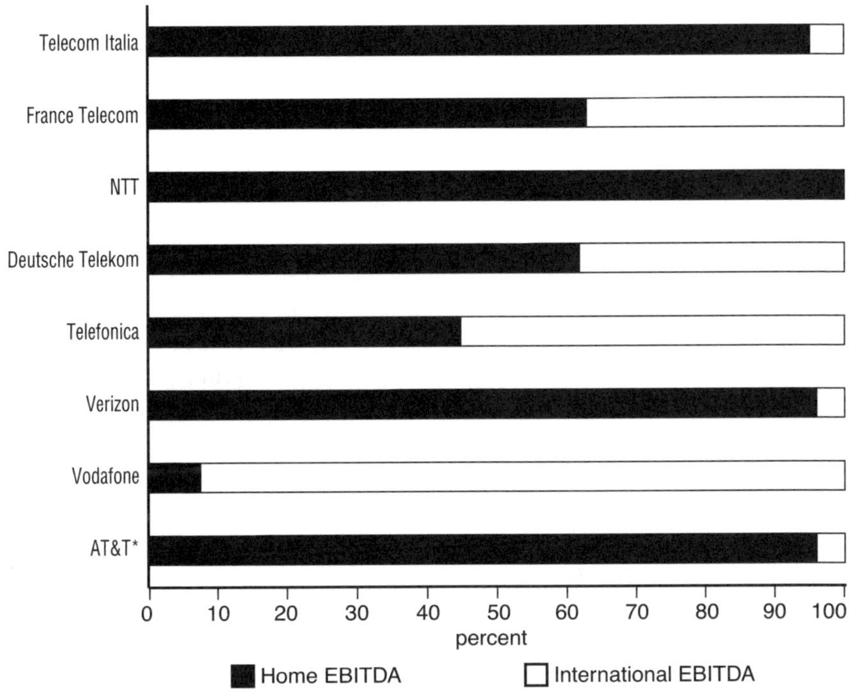


Estimate pro-forma by FT research for BellSouth
Source: FT (2006)

cantly for almost all major transatlantic players from 2005 to 2006 (with the exception of Cingular in the U.S.), showing an increased pressure on margins due to greater competition and—in the EU—also increased price regulation.[24]

## *1.3 Broadband Access and Penetration: Wireline and Wireless*

Broadband penetration is key to the ICT strategy both in the United States and in Europe. In the U.S., President George W. Bush launched the new U.S. broadband strategy already in March 2004, with the aim to achieve universal, affordable broadband availability not later

[24] Source: IDATE (2006).

than 2007. In Europe, broadband penetration is one of the pillars of the Lisbon strategy and of the more ICT-specific i2010 strategy launched in June 2005, which aims at realizing the "information society for all" by 2010. Such strategy heavily relies on the emergence of new digital platforms as a response to a strong demand for innovative interactive services by end users in the whole territory of the Union.

To be sure, over the past few years broadband penetration has been growing in all OECD countries. The OECD recently reported that broadband subscribers in its member countries increased 26 percent from 157 million in December 2005 to 197 million in December 2006. This growth increased broadband penetration rates in the OECD from 13.5 in December 2005 to 16.9 subscriptions per 100 inhabitants one year later.[25] Of these, subscribers in the U.S. totalled 56.5 million, whereas Commissioner Reding reported that Europe had "exceeded almost 70 million lines" in 2006.[26] With an average broadband density of 14.8 percent, Europe has now closed the gap with the U.S. and is close to Japan.[27] As shown in Figure 5.5 below, the leading countries in broadband penetration are northern European member states such as Denmark, the Netherlands and Scandinavian countries, and only Korea and Switzerland exhibit a similar penetration rate.

The United States lags behind these countries—due also to geographic features—whereas Southern European countries (e.g. Spain, Italy) remain below the OECD average. However, the OECD data reported above do not adequately take into account the degree of penetration in the business services market. In particular, as the price of special access (leased lines) in the U.S. is lower than in most of the EU-27, many U.S. businesses prefer to rely on leased lines to obtain their high-speed internet connection. But OECD data fail to capture this difference, and thus potentially underestimate the actual level of broadband penetration in the U.S. Finally, a recent studies show that, when compared with data expressed "by population", data "by household" lead to a higher ranking of the U.S. in terms of broadband penetration (42 percent) as opposed to the EU (23 percent). More in detail, the top

---

[25] See OECD Broadband Statistics to December 2006, available at www.oecd.org/sti/ict/broadband.

[26] Speech by Commissioner Viviane Reding at ECTA Conference, SPEECH/06/697, November 16, 2006.

[27] Source: IDATE (2006).

**Figure 5.5 OECD Broadband Subscribers per 100 Inhabitants, by Technology, June 2006**

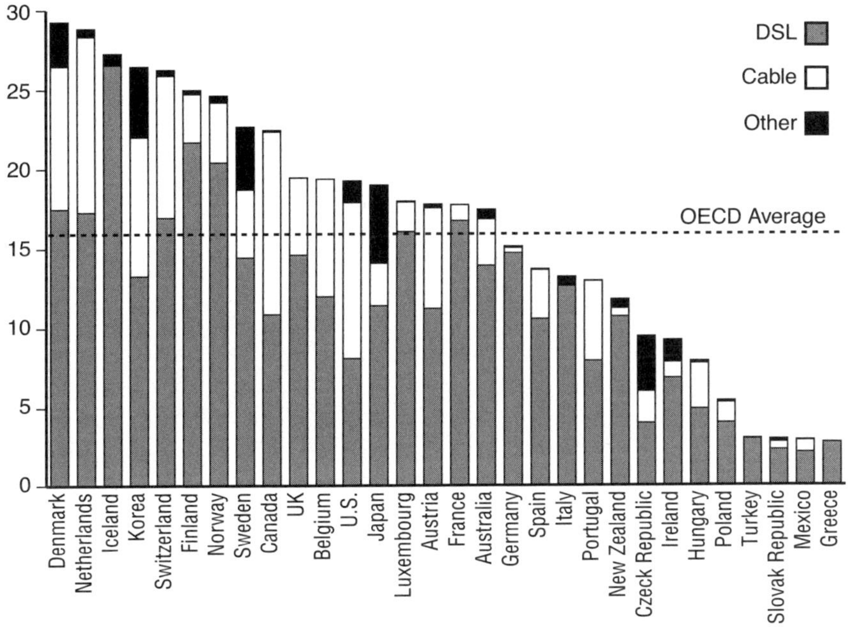


Source: OECD

six U.S. states would rank close to the top EU states (Denmark, the Netherlands), whereas the least penetrated U.S. states are significantly ahead of the least penetrated EU states, and only three U.S. states would fall below the EU average of 23 percent penetration.[28]

Figure 5.5 also shows that some Northern European countries have outperformed Korea since 2005 in terms of subscribers per 100 inhabitants. These countries have also managed to establish significant infrastructure-based competition over the past few years. As was noted also by Commissioner Reding, in all six EU countries that have exceeded 20 percent broadband penetration cable has an important market share, and this "regardless of the effectiveness of regulation".[29]

---

[28] Source: for the U.S., Leichtman Research Group, *Broadband Access and Services in the Home*, May 2006; and Pew Internet & American Life Project, *Home Broadband Adoption 2006*, May 28, 2006. For the EU, European Commission, *E-Communications Household Survey*, July 2006.

[29] Speech by Commissioner Viviane Reding at ECTA Conference, SPEECH/06/697, November 16, 2006.

**Figure 5.6 Average Cost of 1Mbps of Residential Bandwidth per Month**

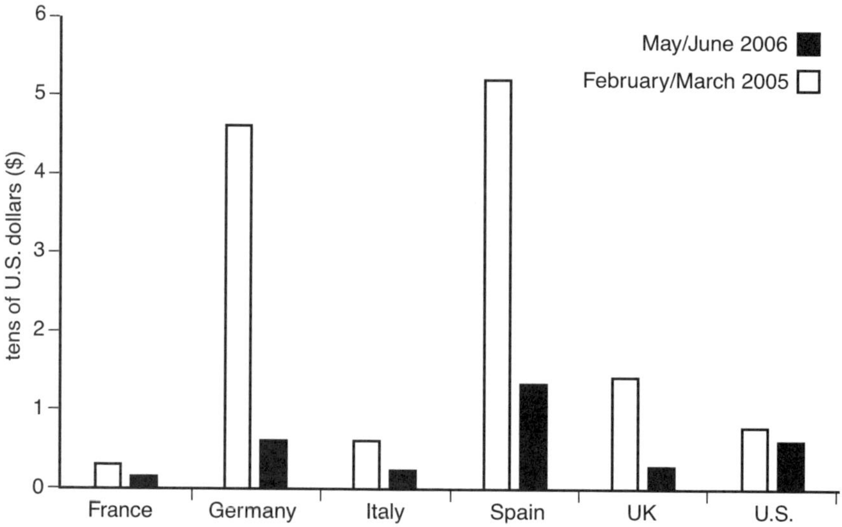


Source: elaboration from eMarketer data, 2006

Increased competition and innovation in many markets has also brought substantial benefits as regards the average cost of broadband subscriptions. Figure 5.6 below shows the enormous reduction in the average cost per 1Mps of residential bandwidth in selected countries between February 2005 and June 2006. As shown in the figure, countries like Spain and Germany have achieved huge reductions in the cost of broadband bandwidth. Such cost is now lower in UK, Italy and France than it is in the U.S.

### *1.3.1 Wireless Broadband: 3G Telephony and WiMax*

A growing feature of broadband in the U.S. and EU is the deployment of alternative, wireless access technologies. Wireless is expected to increase its share of the broadband market from two percent to around 17 percent in the early years of the next decade.[30] According to recent data, 29 percent of European Internet users had access to the Web on mobile devices in October 2006. This includes users in Germany (34

[30] See Rethink Research, *Operator Spending on WiMax*, September 2006.

**Figure 5.7 Mobile penetration and subscribers, 1990-2005**

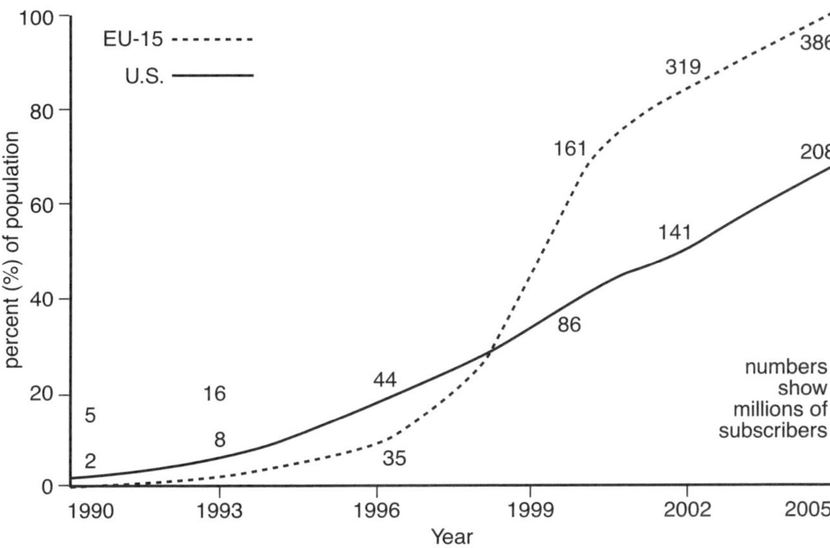


Source: UMTS Forum (2006)

percent); Italy (34 percent); France (28 percent); Spain (26 percent); and the U.K. (24 percent). In the U.S., to the contrary, only 19 percent of Internet users access the Internet on cell phones and other mobile devices.[31] This also depends on the relatively low penetration rate of mobile telephony in the U.S., as depicted in Figure 5.7 below.[32]

A similar trend is observable as far as fixed-mobile substitution is concerned. According to recent surveys, in Finland as many as 47 percent households have become mobile-only, followed by 38 percent in Portugal, 25 percent in Italy, 14 percent in France, 13 percent in the UK and 11 percent in Germany. The average figure for the EU-25 is already as high as 18 percent. On the other hand, only 10 percent of U.S. households are mobile only.[33]

---

[31] ComScore Mobile Tracking, available at http://www.clickz.com/showPage.html?page=3623758.

[32] Mobile penetration had reached 73.3 percent in the second quarter of 2006, according to Merrill Lynch, whereas the corresponding figure for Europe was 107 percent. See Campbell, G. (2006), *North American Telecom & Cable in Pictures*, presentation at the Transatlantic Telecom Dialogue, Columbia University, New York, October 20, 2006.

[33] Data updated at December 2006. Sources: for EU countries, Eurobarometer Special—eCommunications household survey, 2006; for the U.S., CTIA and FCC (adjusted).

**Figure 5.8 3G Penetration, 2006**

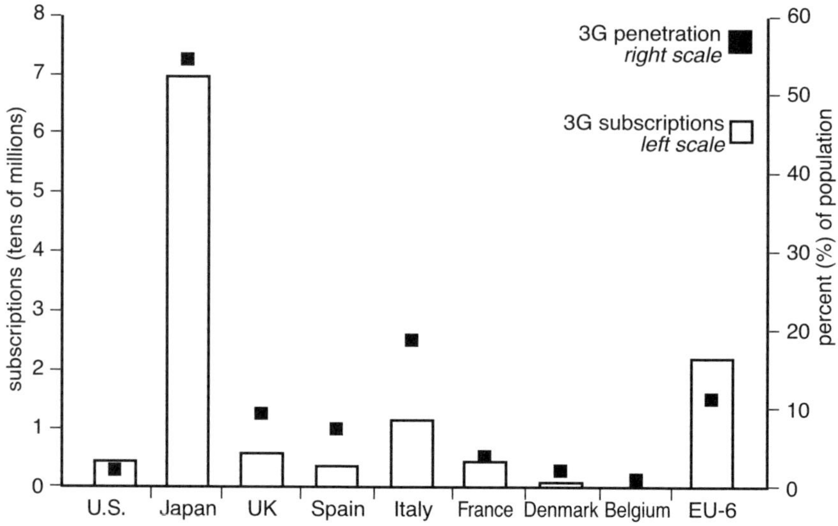


Source: Screen Digest

With penetration being already at 103.2 percent in Europe, however, revenue growth has declined below five percent in 2006, compared with double-digit figures in 2000-2003. On the other hand, since 2003 the average revenue growth in the U.S. has remained constantly above 10 percent, and declined below 10 percent only in the second half of 2006.

As regards 3G telephony, data reported by Ofcom for 2005 showed that the U.S. was lagging behind many European countries with as few as 2.7 million 3G connections, compared with Japan (29 million), Italy (10.8 million), Germany (5.5 million), UK (4.6 million) and France (3.4 million).[34]

Figure 5.8 below reports data by Screen Digest (2006) expressed as percentage of total population.[35]

---

[34] Ofcom, *The International Telecommunications Market 2006*, available at http://www.ofcom.org.uk/research/cm/icmr06/ (visited on April 25, 2007).

[35] For a comprehensive view, see the study for the European Commission by Screen Digest et al. (2006), *Interactive Content and Convergence. Implications for the Information Society*, available online at http://www.ec.europa.eu/information_society/eeurope/i2010/docs/studies/interactive_content_ec2006_final_report.pdf (last visit, April 25, 2007).

The prospects for infrastructure-based competition and the development of new digital platforms are also closely linked to investments in broadband wireless technologies. With WiFi being a rather limited technology due to very short-range coverage, the attention of operators and policymakers has recently shifted towards the WiMax technology, which promises to enable wireless access to fixed-line broadband at remarkable speed (up to 70 Mbps) and over a range of 30 miles.[36] WiMax is also particularly important for bridging the digital divide, especially as far as broadband coverage of rural areas is concerned.[37]

A recent report estimated that global WiMax infrastructure spending will rocket from $655 million today to $7.36 billion by 2009, rising from 22.5 percent of all broadband wireless spend in 2006 to be the dominant platform in the market, with a 63 percent share.[38] It is also expected that mobile operators, currently reluctant in investing in WiMax, will eventually exploit the potential for enhancing their handset with fixed-link technologies, then realising in full the convergence between fixed and wireless handsets.[39] This also implies that 802.16e is bound to become the dominant standard for WiMax, instead of the 802.16d.

Europe currently represents the bulk of investment in WiMax technologies, with a 56 percent share. In particular, Europe dominates the 3.5 GHz band in 2006 with over two-thirds of the world's licenses. This band will remain the key one for WiMax for the rest of the decade, and countries such as France, Germany and Italy already announced that they will offer additional 3.5 GHz licenses for the deployment of this technology.

On the other hand, in the U.S. the situation is more complex, as the 3.5 GHz band is not available for WiMax services.[40] The other band

---

[36] Morgan Stanley estimates that, as of mid-2006, there are about 60 million Wi-Fi users and 200,000 Wi-Fi hotspots worldwide, many of which are at Starbucks and McDonald's locations. See PFF, *The Digital Economy Factbook 2006*.

[37] See, e.g., OECD, *The Implications of WiMax for Competition and Regulation*, Working Party on Telecommunication and Information Services Policies, DSTI/ICCP/TISP(2005)4/FINAL, March 2, 2006.

[38] See Rethink Research (2006), *cit.*

[39] Though mobile operators still see WiMAX as being in the enemy camp, by 2009 mobile operators round the world will be the second largest spenders on WiMAX equipment, making up 17 percent of the total WiMAX equipment spend. The report shows that the market for WiMAX equipment will be larger than many have previously suggested and informs 802.16 vendors in which territories they should be making their biggest efforts.

[40] The 3,400-3,650 MHz range is allocated for use by the radiolocation service (radars) on a primary basis and does not contain provisions for use of fixed or mobile systems.

designated by the WiMax forum—the 2.5 GHz—is owned mostly by the third largest U.S. wireless carrier, Sprint, which committed to invest $1 billion in 2007 and $1.5 to $2 billion in 2008 to develop this promising technology as a complement and upgrade to its own cellular network, with the hope to reach 100 million U.S. citizens by 2008.[41] The other owner of spectrum in the 2.5 GHz band, Clearwire, has launched service based on a hybrid WiMax-WiFi technology in 29 metro areas, and recently started partnerships with municipalities to build privately operated public networks.[42] Finally, Valtech Communications deployed network in Northwest Ohio at beginning of 2006, and currently holds licenses for the Midwest and Florida; whereas NextWave Wireless holds licenses in the 1.7 GHz and 2.1 GHz band.

Although it is probably too early to judge on investments in WiMax technology, the need to secure adequate access to spectrum resources has already been stated with great emphasis. I will therefore come back to this issue later on in this paper, when dealing with spectrum policy issues.

### *1.3.2 Multiple Play Offers*

Ongoing technological convergence and digitization of voice services has spurred a number of changes in the industry both in the U.S. and the EU. In the all-IP value chain, value-added, low-cost applications such as VoIP threaten the sustainability of traditional business models, as traditional PSTN operators now face growing competition from nomadic players such as Skype, Vonage, Yahoo! and Microsoft. Available data on revenues from fixed voice services confirms the decline of the ARPU from wireline telephony in Western Europe, declining from €33.4 to €30.8 per access line per month in the 2001-2006 timeframe.[43]

At the same time, increased competition has led to a significant decrease in the broadband ARPU in many countries, including the largest EU member states and the U.S.[44] A similar trend is expected

---

[41] http://www.informationweek.com/story/showArticle.jhtml?articleID=191902091, August 14, 2006.

[42] See, e.g., http://www.grand-rapids.mi.us/index.pl?binobjid=4146.

[43] Source: IDATE (2006)

[44] See, e.g. Ofcom (2006), The International Telecommunications Markets, cit..

for mobile voice services in the near future, especially as handsets embed WiFi and WiMax functionality and 3G allows more intensive use of VoIP. As reported in a recent study by Analysys, by 2015 mobile VoIP will carry 28 percent of all fixed and mobile voice minutes in the U.S. and 23 percent in Western Europe.[45]

All these changes have led industry players to increasingly provide multiple-play offers to their customers, which range from triple-play bundles (fixed, mobile, Internet) to quadruple-play (fixed, mobile, Internet, TV). With the move to IP networks, PSTN are now offering their own Voice-over-Broadband (VoB) services to contrast the competition from nomadic players.

In the U.S., multiple-play offers have been launched by many players, which include SBC's quadruple-play on its ADSL/VDSL connections, Comcast on its cable network and MStar over the UTOPIA's fibre optic municipal network in Utah. TV services were also recently announced by Verizon on its FiOS network, which brings fibre to the premises.

In Europe, the Commission recently acknowledged that triple- and quadruple-play have become common ways of offering services to end users. European players have taken the lead in these types of offers and are currently changing their business models in search for new sources of revenue from bundling ancillary services and applications with the basic multi-play offer. A recent EU survey on the evolution of communication services in European households showed that 19 percent of EU households subscribed to at least one bundled service with higher percentages in Denmark (38 percent), Estonia (35 percent), the Netherlands (32 percent), Spain (29 percent) and Luxembourg (27 percent). As of early 2007, the most frequently purchased service package was a double play offer of fixed voice telephony and Internet access (eight percent of EU households), whereas triple play and quadruple play offers had been taken up by only three and one percent of EU households respectively.[46]

The development of multi-play offers also directly affects barriers to entry in a national market. In line with the economic theory of

[45] See Analysys, Forecasting the Commercial Impact of Wireless VoIP in the USA and Western Europe, August 2006.

[46] See European Commission, *European Electronic Communications Regulation and Markets*, 12th Report, COM(2007)155, March 29, 2007.

bundling, such offers can be seen at once as pro-competitive moves to conquer market share, but also as attempts to preserve and/or extend dominance across different relevant markets. In this respect, some competition authorities and national regulators have already had the temptation to define triple play as a distinct relevant market. Potential consequences of this market development for the entry of new players are the following:

- *Incumbent players are subject to increased competitive pressure from broadcasters, mobile operators, nomadic players, etc.* In order to replicate available multi-play offers and conquer customer base, every player needs to ensure that its customers have access not only to (commoditized) voice services, but also to mobile services, broadband services, killer applications, premium content and functionalities offered by operating systems, digital rights management technologies, etc. For such reason, players once operating in separate relevant markets now compete for the same customer, and have different competitive advantages.

- This inter-platform competition, in turn, spurs *cooperation between competitors (co-opetition) and industry consolidation.* Examples of recent M&A activity that confirms this trend are reported above, at section 1.2.

- *Barriers to entry are higher*, especially for foreign players, who need to gain access to a wide range of technologies, services, applications, content and spectrum if they want to play a role in a national market.

### 1.3.2.1 Broadcasting and Content

In the multi-play era, telecom services are increasingly linked to broadcast services and the delivery of digital content. Although a detailed description of developments in this segment would fall outside the scope of this paper, it is worth looking at some existing features of the U.S. and EU markets which may hinder entry by foreign players and create ambiguous regulatory regimes.

First, digital terrestrial television and cable television seem to have developed quite extensively in Europe over the past few years. Most of the EU27 today exhibit significant inter-platform competition, with some countries—notably, Austria, Belgium and the Netherlands—having almost replaced terrestrial TV.[47] This is also confirmed by the findings of the market analyses carried out by national regulators under the 2002 regulatory framework, which found the market (i.e. the so-called "market 18") to be fairly competitive in some member states due to platform-based competition. As a result, the share of terrestrial TV in households in the EU-27 decreased from 47.7 percent to as low as 29 percent from the end of 2004 to September 2005. The share of cable fell from 29.6 percent to 17 percent, whereas satellite TV increased its share from 22.4 percent to 52 percent and DSL conquered a two percent share of the market.[48]

In the United States, a similar situation is developing, with traditionally dominant cable companies now facing increased competition by Digital Broadcast Satellite (DBS) providers. The FCC, in its 12th annual report on the state of competition in the video market, acknowledged that "[c]ompetition in the delivery of video programming services has provided consumers with increased choice, better picture quality, and greater technological innovation". According to the FCC, almost all consumers have the choice between over-the-air (OTA) broadcast television, a cable service, and at least two DBS providers as well as "emerging technologies, such as digital broadcast spectrum, fiber to the home, or video over the Internet." Finally, video programming has become available over wireless handsets on networks operated by Sprint, Verizon Wireless, and Cingular.[49]

On both sides of the Atlantic, investments to upgrade the networks to migrate to NGNs are driven by expectations that digital content will provide the revenue source operators are missing after the decline in revenues from traditional voice services. In this segment, the United States still play a paramount role in the production and export of movies and formats, although the UK has outpaced the U.S. on this latter dimension in 2006.[50] But digital content is much more than this:

---

[47] Source: Dataxis (2006), *Digital Television Data*, Study for European Commission.

[48] *Ibid.*

[49] Verizon's V Cast service is available to more than 148 million people in 181 major metropolitan areas, while Cingular offers television programs from NBC, Fox, CNN, ESPN, Disney, The Weather Channel, and HBO.

[50] See Ofcom (2006), The International Telecommunications Market 2006, cit..

fast-growing markets include digital music and media stores (such as, e.g. Apple's iTunes), DRM-enabled peer-to-peer networks and super-distributors (e.g. Weedshare, Wippit, Napster, Virgin, etc.); user-created content mostly accessed through social networking websites—e.g. YouTube, Myspace, Friendster, etc.—and also instant messaging systems and blogs.[51] These services have become a source of economic power for their operators, as they ensure a high retention rate and thus a loyal customer base—a key asset in the converged world. It therefore came to no surprise that Microsoft and Yahoo! decided to make their own instant messaging systems interoperable, and that an Internet giant like Google spent no less than $900 million to Rupert Murdoch to power the Myspace search function in August 2007, and three months later decided to acquire Youtube in a $1.65 billion deal.

As many of the powerful Internet players strive to develop their own VoIP service, ensure the availability of killer applications and premium content, and even invest in network technologies (e.g. Google in BPL, Disney as MVNO) it becomes quite clear that the competitive landscape of telecommunications, particularly in the U.S., has become broader. From this perspective, the regulatory approach adopted by national policymakers at the higher layers of the NGN architecture becomes as important as the decision on whether to impose access obligations at the infrastructure layer, especially as far as the business case for investing in new technologies is concerned. I will come back to this issue below, in section two.

## 2. Policy Challenges: Getting Ready for NGNs

Most investments in the telecom sector today seek to ensure fast migration of legacy networks to all-IP Next Generation Networks (NGNs). NGNs are defined as "a packet-based network able to provide telecommunication services and able to make use of multiple broadband, QoS-enabled transport technologies and in which service-related functions are independent from underlying transport-related technologies."[52] NGNs enable unfettered access for users to networks and to competing service providers and/or services of their choice, and

[51] See FCC, Twelfth Annual Report, March 2006.

[52] See International Telecommunications Union, ITU-T NGN FG Proceedings, 2005, p. 53 (available at http://www.itu.int/ITU-T/ngn/files/NGN_FG-book_II.pdf).

**Figure 5.9 Layers of an IP-based Network Architecture**

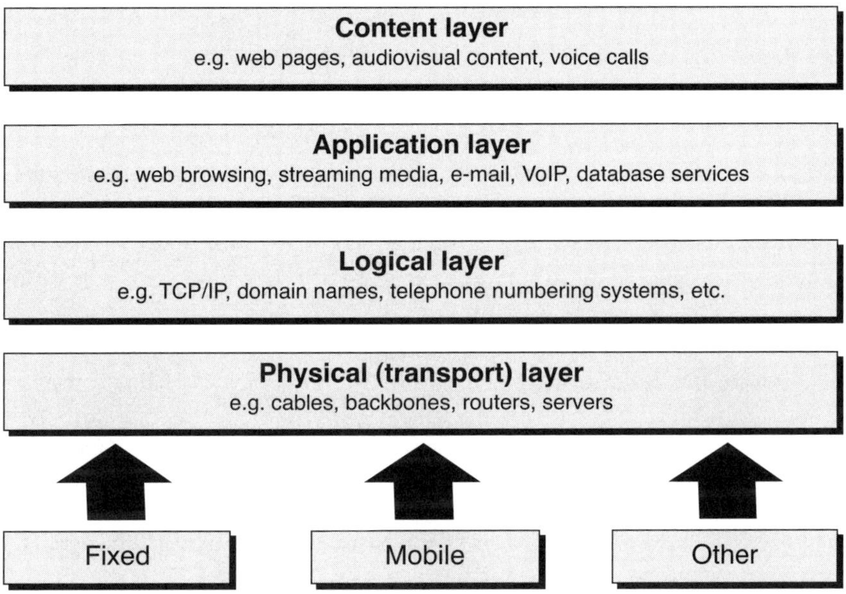


support generalized mobility which will allow consistent and ubiquitous provision of services to users.

NGNs are characterised by IP-based core networks that support the full range of services offered by operators. Depending on market development and regulatory strategy, countries rely on one or more core IP-based networks, and on securing that end users have different ways to access them. A prominent feature of IP-based networks is that they exhibit a layered end-to-end architecture, exactly as the internet does. As a result, a suitable way to observe the functioning and competitive dynamics of those networks is to look at the interactions that will take place between the different layers. Figure 5.9 below illustrates the main layers of an IP-based network architecture.

The migration to IP-based networks promises to unleash the potential for new services and applications to be delivered to end users at unprecedented speed, at the same time delivering Opex and Capex savings of hundreds of millions per operator.[53] Available data from

[53] For example, Verizon is on track to achieve in 2010 a total CAPEX per home of $1,350, a 22 percent cost saving over the next 4 years.

2005 showed that the global reshape in telecom services is more visible when one looks at future technologies: China was the leader with one third of all NGNs worldwide, followed by the U.S. with 26 percent, and the United Kingdom with 13 percent.[54]

Planned investments in NGNs in the U.S. and EU are of gigantic scale.[55] Such investments still face significant uncertainty, and many national regulators are realising that careful *ad hoc* policymaking is needed in order not to stifle incentives to build the infrastructure of the future. In particular, the business case for building an all-IP network is not only dependent on user demand, but also on the regulatory approach adopted by regulators as regards spectrum availability/trading, unbundling obligations at the infrastructure layer, and net neutrality at higher layers. For such reason, in order to understand the potential for infrastructure deployment in the U.S. and EU, all these policy developments must be duly considered.

As acknowledged by scholars, practitioners and policymakers, the migration to Next Generation Networks will radically change the industry structure and—accordingly—the challenges faced by regulators. This change will affect more the EU regulatory approach than the U.S. one. For example, the current list of 18 relevant markets included in the 2003 Commission Recommendation—which forms the basis for the market analyses performed by NRAs and reviewed by the Commission—will become obsolete and will have to be significantly reshaped. More importantly, the assessment of market power by NRAs will have to take into account the broader competitive landscape in which once-dominant operators will end up after convergence will be fully realized. Given that competition policy tools are so deeply embedded in the EU framework, new tools for market analysis will have to be developed: these include two-sided markets and cluster market concepts.

---

[54] See Worldwide NGN Migration Status and Vendors Opportunity Analysis Report, Dittberner Associates, November 2005.

[55] In Europe, investment in NGN by the top 5 players is in the magnitude of 100 billion. For example, BT has announced it will have invested £10 billion by the end of the decade on its 21CN initiative, and expect savings of around one billion pounds a year by September, 2008. In the U.S., Verizon believes that in the 2004-2010 timeframe it will have spent $18 billion passing 18 million households, according to Ovum-RHK.

In this section, I briefly describe the current regulatory frameworks in the U.S. and EU and then address the current approaches to encouraging investment in NGN and their likely effects on market openness and entry of new players.

## *2.1 The United States: the Long Way Out from the 1996 Telecommunications Act*

Since the 1980s, the U.S. telecom industry has been characterized by an artificial regulatory segregation of local exchange telephony from long-distance telephony that arose principally from the consent decree signed by the U.S. Department of Justice and AT&T in 1984.[56] The 1996 Telecommunications Act deregulated long-distance telephone services, local exchange telephone services, and local cable television services. As a result, the RBOCs were finally allowed to enter lucrative long-distance markets under the condition that they provided unbundled access to any entrant that wished to use part of their networks (the so-called Unbundled Network Elements or UNE) at fair, reasonable and non-discriminatory conditions, based on the so-called TELRIC pricing.[57]

The 1996 Act, initially welcomed with enthusiasm as a "Camelot moment," soon proved to be inadequate to efficiently regulate the fast-changing U.S. telecom industry.[58] Two main problems emerged:

- mandatory unbundling obligations have been increasingly considered as an insurmountable hurdle for investments in (DSL) broadband deployment by RBOCs. In this respect, many economists have highlighted that charges to access the incumbents' UNE were insufficient to reward investments in infrastructure.[59]
- the so-called "silos" approach adopted by the Act—in which each type of telecommunication service (broadcasting, telephony, cable television, information services) is subject to its own regulatory structure—seems to have hampered the level-playing field, by creating an artificial "regulatory apartheid"

---

[56] Modification of Final Judgment, reprinted in United States v. AT&T Co., 552 F. Supp. 131, 226-34 (D.D.C. 1982), *aff'd sub nom.* Maryland v. United States, 460 U.S. 1001 (1983).

[57] TELRIC stands for Total Element Long-Run Incremental Cost.

**Figure 5.10 High Speed Line Growth in the U.S., 1999-2005**

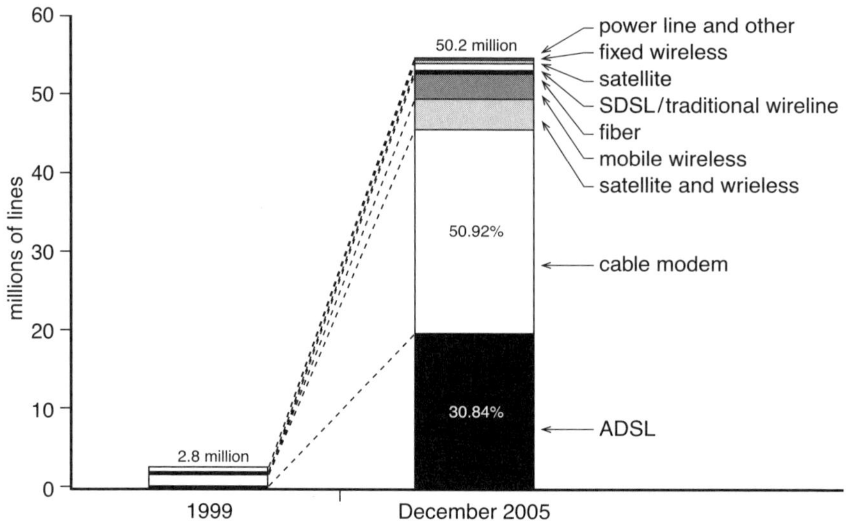


between sectors subject to common carriage obligations under Title II of the 1934 Act (the wireline companies); sectors falling under Title III (which include satellite and wireless) and under Title VI (cable), which were generally exempted from common carriage obligations.[60]

The UNE regime collapsed after the *USTA II* case in 2004, especially after the decision by the FCC not to appeal.

### *2.1.1 Focus on Broadband Deployment*

Cable operators have had the first move in deploying U.S. broadband. The legacy of the 1996 Telecommunications Act is the main explanation for the cable-intensive nature of broadband connection in

[58] Senate Commerce Committee Hearing, Voice over Internet Protocol, Feb. 24, 2004.

[59] See, e.g., Hausman, J.A. and J.G. Sidak (2005), *Did Mandatory Unbundling Achieve Its Purpose? Empirical Evidence from Five Countries*, Journal of Competition Law and Economics, Vol. 1, pp. 173-245.

[60] The definition of "regulatory apartheid" was given by Peter Huber, quoted in Thomas W. Hazlett, *Explaining the Telecommunications Act of 1996: Comment on Thomas G. Krattenmaker*, 29 Conn. L. Rev. 217 (1996).

the U.S.[61] Figure 5.10 below shows the enormous increase in high-speed lines that occurred in the U.S. between 1999 and 2005, with cable broadband rising from 1.4 million lines in 1999 to 25.6 million in December 2005, and DSL climbing up to 19.5 million lines, with a growth of almost 20 percent in the second half of 2005 only.[62] Of these, 82.2 percent was provided by RBOCs, whereas ILECs and non-ILECs were providing 14.1 and 3.7 percent, respectively.

Like incumbents in Europe, RBOCs have been facing decreasing margins from traditional voice services. The most (if not only) relevant source of profits is today provided by wireless services and by triple-play offers. Faced with the prominent position of cable operators in the broadband market, the FCC attempted to restore the level-playing field. The FCC approach, however, was very different from the European one: as a matter of fact, a degree of technological neutrality was achieved in the U.S. not by regulating all services regardless of the underlying technologies, but by lifting up regulation on both FTTx and DSL investments. The FCC decided to declare cable modem broadband services as an 'information service' back in 2002; later, it decided to forbear from imposing mandatory unbundling and pricing of FTTH in August 2003, and extended its decision to FTTC in October 2004 and to DSL in September 2005. The FCC decision to forbear from imposing mandatory unbundling and price regulation on FTTC, FTTH and DSL reportedly provided a tremendous stimulus to investment in the U.S.[63]

Today, cable companies still hold the largest share of high-speed connections (51 percent), but market analysts expect DSL to conquer 55 percent of new subscribers in 2007. Since 2004 telcos outpaced cable operators in subscriber growth for the first time, by focusing on price instead of speed. The price for DSL broadband services is

---

[61] Another explanation is that DSL is constrained by the distance between the subscriber and the central office. DSL over a copper wire only works within 18,000 feet of a central office facility. See, *i.a.*, A. A. Gilroy and L. G. Kruger, *Broadband Internet Access: Background and Issues*, CRS Issue Brief for Congress, updated April 4, 2005.

[62] See FCC High-Speed Services for Internet Access Report, July 2006.

[63] SBC Communications announced investments of $4-6 billion, Verizon planned investments totalling $15 to 20 billion and other providers, including incumbents like BellSouth, followed a similar strategy by announcing investments of $3 to 4 billion. Some commentators have argued that investments by regional incumbents (RBOCs) would have taken place anyway, given the intense competitive pressure exerted by cable operators, and were not significantly affected by the FCC announcements.

reported to have fallen down substantially from February 2002 to January 2005. In 2002, SBC and Verizon both priced their monthly DSL subscription at $49.95; at the end of 2006, AT&T introduced a new low-speed service (768 Kbps) at $14.99 per month, whereas BellSouth lowered 3 Mbps service to $37.95 and 6 Mbps service at $42.95. Verizon offers low speed service at $19.99 and its high-speed FiOS service (50 Mbps in NY, NJ, and CT) at $89.95.

### *2.1.2 A (Deregulated) Level Playing Field?*

In order to encourage investment in new infrastructure, the FCC has decided to exempt also other high-speed technologies from heavy-handed regulatory obligations. Broadband over Power Lines is considered as an information service, and as such exempted from state regulation and from common carriage obligations.[64] This approach is consistent with the framework that the Commission has established for cable and DSL broadband Internet access services, and could encourage investment by large players. One early example is the $100 billion investment by Google and Goldman Sachs in the BPL provider Current Communications Group in 2005.

A 'hands-off' approach to regulation was also applied to IP-enabled services such as VoIP. The FCC has taken advantage of its legacy "silos approach" by classifying VoIP as an "interstate information service" back in November 2004, therefore exempting it from state regulation just as cable modem services. More recently, the FCC started its IP-Enabled Services Proceeding in order to assess whether VoIP is to be considered a telecom or an information service.[65] Meanwhile, VoIP already became a reality in the U.S. According to a recent report by Infonetics, North American VoIP service revenue is poised to grow eighteen-fold between 2004 and 2009, from $1.24 to $23.4 billion. More than $62 billion will be spent on VoIP services over the five year

[64] Specifically, the FCC 06-165 Order classifies the transmission component underlying BPL-enabled Internet access service as "telecommunications," and the provision of this transmission component as part of a functionally integrated, finished BPL-enabled Internet access service offering as an information service.

[65] An example is the order issued by the FCC on May 19, 2005, requiring VoIP providers to "supply enhanced 911 (E911) emergency calling capabilities to their customers as a mandatory feature of the service". In that occasion, the FCC also clarified that "[t]he IP-enabled services marketplace is the latest new frontier of our nation's communications landscape, and the Commission is committed to allowing IP-enabled services to evolve without undue regulation". WC Docket Nos. 04-36, 05-196, May 19, 2005.

forecast period. At the end of 2006, the number of VoIP subscribers in the U.S. was estimated at more than 9 million.[66] Forecasts that cable operators would dominate the market already in 2006 were not confirmed by market evidence. Vonage still leads this segment with more than 1.8 million subscribers, with Time Warner following closely at almost 1.6 million. Other big players are Cablevision (988,000) and Comcast (721,000).

In summary, the U.S. has reached a greater degree of technological neutrality than initially achieved with the 1996 Act. Such neutrality comes close to creating the level-playing field that is needed for infrastructure-based competition and fast, almost universal broadband coverage. As a result, although lifting up regulation for investments in high-speed technologies might hamper access and investment by foreign players, such an approach appears to fit the U.S. telecoms sector, due to legacy infrastructure–based competition.

### *2.1.3 The "Net Neutrality Thicket"*

The extent to which investment will be driven by expected profits as well as by end user demand is also significantly affected by the "net neutrality" debate. Especially as telecom services migrate on all-IP networks, the risk of congestion and the need to customize platforms and prioritize packets for some bandwidth-intensive services such as IPTV or VoIP has led some industry players to claim the possibility to abandon the TCP/IP protocol and, where appropriate, also charge application and content providers for use of their bandwidth. The so-called "net diversity" advocates suggest that application and customer tiering are the only ways in which operators can provide enhanced customer experience on all-IP communication networks.[67]

---

[66] Source: In-Stat (2006). Cable VoIP subscriber are expected to reach six million at the end of 2006 due to aggressive cable VoIP deployments by Comcast and Charter, and will reach 9.9 million customers at the end of 2007. In 2006, independent VoIP subscribers are expected to reach 2.8 million.

[67] Net diversity should allow for optimisation of service quality for different uses: for example, Yoo (2006) advocates for three different types of networks: one optimized for traditional Internet applications such as e-mail and website access; another incorporating security features to facilitate e-commerce and to guard against viruses, spam, and other undesirable aspects of life on the Internet; and a third that prioritizes packets in the manner needed to facilitate time-sensitive applications such as streaming media and VoIP. Likewise, different networks also allow for different degrees of control and anonymity, which may be needed if connections serve different purposes and are consequently optimised. Some services would not even take-up without more secure network systems.

On the other hand, net neutrality was defined by the FCC as the right for internet users to access any content and run any application as they see fit. Under full-fledged net neutrality provisions, broadband network operators should not be allowed to discriminate between content or applications when offering access to end users—i.e., they should not be able to adopt a proprietary architecture for their platform, by departing from the TCP/IP protocol. Advocates of network neutrality basically fear that players holding market power in the infrastructure layer should not be given the chance to leverage such power into the logical layer to discriminate between players in the application and content layers of the IP architecture. The main concern expressed by these commentators is that "deviating from the universal interoperability that currently characterizes the Internet would inflict irreparable harm to the market for Internet content and applications."[68]

As a result, network owners should be forced to adhere to the TCP/IP protocol and preserve an end-to-end (e2e) architecture.[69] In addition, they should refrain from vertically integrating from the physical and logical to the application and content layer, unless they grant access and interoperability to all application developers and content providers, be they welcome or not.[70] Finally, Network operators should also refrain from entering any exclusivity agreement with content and application providers, as well as from imposing any use restrictions on end users.[71]

---

[68] See Yoo, C. (2006), *Promoting Broadband Through Network Diversity*, NCTA Expert Study, June 2, 2006.

[69] A good example of an attempt to change the e2e architecture is the launch by AOL/Time Warner and AT&T of broadband TV services @Home and Roadrunner in the late 1990s, which authoritative commentators saw as the imminent "end of end-to-end". See Lemley, M. A. and L. Lessig (2001), "The End of End-to-End: Preserving the Architecture of the Internet in the Broadband Era", *UCLA Law Review*, Vol. 48, at 925.

[70] This also means that network operators will not be able to recover any lost revenue in providing access service by charging higher rates on applications and content.

[71] In other words, network operators will not be able to ban certain uses on their networks. Evidence of attempts to impose usage restrictions is abundant in the U.S. since the famous 2005 Settlement between Vonage and Madison River Telephone Company, in which the FCC's Enforcement Bureau prohibited Madison River from blocking the "ports" for VoIP traffic, and Madison River agreed to pay $15,000. Other examples include cases in which cable operators, DSL operators and wireless operators wilfully blocked VoIP applications, and one case in which AT&T imposed VPN restrictions. Such a requirement, however, also means that, in case of congestion on a given network, cable and DSL operators will not be able to respond by imposing use restrictions for more bandwidth-consuming uses. This also implies that the only possible way to contrast congestion is through higher prices for all users (and cross-subsidies).

The network neutrality v. network diversity dilemma is far from its final word in the U.S., although the FCC seems to have taken a decisive stance in favor of internet freedom. Network neutrality proposals include provisions relating to consumer access similar to those found in the FCC principles and Internet Bill of Rights, but also provisions relating to non-discriminatory or neutral access to broadband networks or the internet by independent applications providers.[72] Three such proposals have been incorporated in legislation introduced in the 109th Congress—the *Network Neutrality Act of 2006* (H.R. 5273), the *Internet Non-Discrimination Act of 2006* (S. 2360), and the *Internet Freedom Preservation Act* (S. 2917).

Finally, during the FCC proceeding related to its acquisition of BellSouth, AT&T recently committed to refrain from charging companies such as Google premium fees for faster subscriber access.[73] Such net neutrality commitment provides a clearer view of the current development of communication services in the U.S.: a more lenient approach to investments in new high-speed infrastructure is coupled with neutrality principles at higher layers, thus leaving more room for competition and entry in application and content provision, at the same time ensuring fast broadband deployment in the years to come. Such approach, as will be made clear in the next section, appears quite different from that of the European Commission, and has raised concerns in Brussels over the potential for EU companies to invest in infrastructure in the U.S.[74]

## 2.2 *European Telecoms Regulation and NGNs*

In 2006, the European Commission launched the review of its 2002 regulatory framework for electronic communications.[75] The 2002 framework was highly praised for its reliance on a decentralised appli-

[72] See Kilroy, A. A. and Kruger, L. G. (2006), *Broadband Internet Regulation and Access*, CRS Report for Congress, September 28, 2006.

[73] See "AT&T Wins Backing on BellSouth Merger," *Financial Times*, December 30, 2006, available at http://www.ft.com/cms/s/b047c064-97a5-11db-a680-0000779e2340.html.

[74] See below, section 4.

[75] The new regulatory package consists of the Framework Directive (2002/21/EC, OJ/L 24/04/2002, P.33), the Access Directive (2002/19/EC, OJ/L 108, 24/04/2002, P.7), the Authorisation Directive (2002/20/EC, OJ/L 108, 24/04/2002, P.21), the Universal Service Directive (2002/22/EC, OJ/L 108, 24/04/2002, P.51), the Radio Spectrum Decision (676/2002/EC, OJ/L 108, 24/04/2002, P.1), the Directive on (continues on next page)

cation of tools mostly borrowed from competition policy practice, as well as for its thorough implementation of technological neutrality principles. As a matter of fact, no 'silos' approach was adopted in Europe: National Regulatory Authorities (NRAs), in charge of enforcing the framework, were called to perform detailed market analyses in order to identify (and notify) operators with Significant Market Power (SMP) in a given set of markets.

The 2002 framework was implemented by most NRAs with strong reliance on the "investment ladder" model, aimed at achieving long-term infrastructure-based competition through short-term service-based competition.[76] However, delays in the implementation of the framework at national level—with one member state (Greece) adopting the directives only in January 2006—and difficulties in market analyses and in implementing the 'ladder' approach have led to slow liberalization of most national markets, as well as regulatory uncertainty for industry players. Accordingly, real infrastructure-based competition is missing in many EU member states.[77] As recalled by Commissioner Reding in a recent speech, Europe has moved to "a competitive environment where a large number of telecom service providers thrive. This is based to a good part on service-based competition but whenever possible we should increasingly seek more infrastructure-based competition which is sustainable in the long term".[78] As an example, only in a few European countries cable holds a significant share of the broadband market, whereas DSL dominates the scene and 3G still offers a barely comparable customer experience.

In 2006, the Commission decided to propose a substantial simplification of the list of relevant markets that are presumed to warrant *ex ante* regulation, by repealing most of the retail markets included in the

([79] cont.) Privacy and Electronic Communications (2002/58/EC, OJ/L 201, 31/07/2002, P37) and the Regulation on Unbundling of the Local Loop (2887/2000/EC, OJ/L 336, 30/12/2000, P.4). The application of competition rules to the telecommunications sector was also clarified in a 1998 Notice, and the terms of ULL obligations by incumbent operators were anticipated by a Communication issued by the Commission in 2000. See Communication from the Commission of April 26, 2000 on the Unbundled access to the local loop, OJ 23.9.2000 C272/55.

[76] Cave et al. (2002), *cit.*

[77] See the survey by London Economics and PwC for the European Commission, An assessment of the regulatory framework for electronic communications: growth and investment in the EU e-Communications sector, July 2006.

[78] Viviane Reding, SPEECH/06/697, November 16, 2006.

2003 Recommendation.[79] Other two markets, wholesale mobile origination (former market 15) and broadcasting transmission services (former market 18) have been subject to consultation, in order to assess the merit of retaining them in the list of markets warranting *ex ante* regulation. Another market, that for wholesale international roaming (former market 17), was dealt with separately by the Commission, which issues a proposal to regulate roaming charges at the retail and wholesale level and impose transparency obligations on mobile operators to the benefit of roaming customers.[80] In addition, currently proposed changes include a more coordinated approach to spectrum policy, restrictions on appeals process for NRA decisions, and the extension of the Commission veto power—currently covering only market analysis and SMP assessment—also to remedies proposed by NRAs, in the attempt to achieve greater harmonisation in the implementation of EU rules in the 27 member states.[81]

Interestingly, the Commission did not take any stance as regards the encouragement of investments in NGNs in its proposed review. This was motivated by the technologically neutral features embedded in the current framework, which allegedly make it perfectly fit to regulate also new technologies. However, many industry players and some national regulators disagree with the Commission's view. As a result, the issue of encouraging investments in all-IP networks is entirely dealt with at national level, with widely different approaches.

Some industry players—e.g. Deutsche Telekom—advocate for a 'regulatory forbearance' approach, similar to that adopted in the United States since 2003 to stimulate investments in FTTH, FTTC and DSL technologies. However, Commissioner Reding has in several occasions clarified that regulatory forbearance for investments in NGNs is "not a policy option" for the review of the 2002 framework.[82] Other players, such as British Telecom, rejected this approach and

---

[79] Markets warranting *ex ante* regulation are those that fulfil three basic criteria: a) existence of significant barriers to entry; b) absence of a tendency towards effective competition; and c) the insufficiency of competition law to address the market failure.

[80] See the Commission's proposed regulation, COM(2006)382, July 12, 2006.

[81] See Communication from the Commission to the Council, the European Parliament, the European Economic and Social Committee and the Committee of the Regions on the review of the EU Regulatory Framework for electronic communications networks and services (SEC(2006) 816) (SEC(2006) 817), June 29, 2006.

[82] Viviane Reding, SPEECH/06/697, November 16, 2006.

chose to focus on the deployment of one core NGN and on access to such networks by alternative operators. This, in turn, led to a more extensive consideration of the incumbent's investments when determining access charges for new entrants.

As a result, at least two extremely different regulatory approaches emerged in largest EU countries:

- The UK regulator Ofcom chose to initially rely on a single core NGN (the 21st Century Network being deployed by British Telecom) to be made available for access to all industry players. Ofcom has reached an agreement with BT, which imposes a comprehensive range of undertakings, under which BT commits not to foreclose network access, to ensure equivalence of inputs (EoI) between its downstream operations and competing players; and to make access available to all operators wishing to launch services at higher layers, with reasonable timing to allow for the simultaneous launch of competing products.
- In Germany, concerns have emerged that unbundling obligations could jeopardise the business case for Deutsche Telekom's new high-speed VDSL infrastructure—which currently covers 10 German metropolitan areas. As a result, the government recently approved a bill exempting Deutsche Telekom from mandatory unbundling of the new network, provided that the German incumbent proves that it offers innovative services, such as IPTV and VOD. Such move was heavily criticised by the European Commission, which reacted by starting a "fast track" infringement proceeding in February 2007.[83]

Of these two emerging models, the former seems to have been endorsed by the European Commission, which is currently working on including "functional separation" as a possible remedy available to NRAs under the EU regulatory framework.[84] In other large European countries—e.g., Italy—the sectoral regulator has already declared that it intends to pursue vertical separation and equivalence of inputs along with the UK model.

[83] See Press Release, Commission launches "fast track" infringement proceedings against Germany for "regulatory holidays" for Deutsche Telekom, February 26, 2007, IP/07/237.

[84] Viviane Reding, SPEECH/06/697, *cit.*

### 2.2.1 *Europe and Net Neutrality*

The ongoing tendency toward functional separation of infrastructures in Europe calls for a thorough assessment of the current business case for deploying NGNs in the years to come. As a matter of fact, the enormous size of investment plans must be justified by a reasonable expectation that costs will be recovered through efficiency gains in the networks, but also through revenues from subscribers, advertisers and application providers within a reasonable timeframe. For such reasons, firms wishing to deploy NGNs have called for regulatory certainty over the future approach that will be adopted by regulators and the European Commission at all layers of the value chain. Hence, not surprisingly, a net neutrality debate has emerged also in Europe: in particular, the current debate is focusing on whether access providers should be able to charge application providers premium fees for using their bandwidth, or whether full neutrality conditions should apply just as those imposed in the U.S. in occasion of the "mammoth mergers."

The debate is way more complex than it may seem at first blush. For example, the most influential sectoral regulator in Europe, Ofcom, recently acknowledged that "[o]ne way that operators may plan to monetise investments in next generation access is through offering content providers different levels of quality of service to deliver their applications to consumers.... This could make a substantial difference to the business case for such infrastructure investments.... Were regulation introduced in Europe which restricted service providers from acting in this way, it could affect their incentives for investing in next generation access networks."[85]

Dougal Scott, the Director of Policy Development at Ofcom, recently addressed the business case for investing in fibre networks, by identifying a sort of "incumbent's curse", in which players wishing to invest in an access NGN have two main ways to monetise their investment: a) by offering premium delivery services to application and content providers; and b) by closing down the copper network in time, or by selling exchange buildings. But in both cases, the road is blocked by regulation. Premium delivery services must confront the net neutrality debate, and assets such as exchange buildings are being used by LLU and other operators in line with the EU 2002 regulatory framework.

---

[85] Ofcom (2006), *Next Generation Access*, Discussion Paper, November 23, 2006.

The European Commission has not taken any decisive stance on net neutrality issues to date, perhaps underestimating its importance for future investments in access NGN. The only statement on net neutrality is found in the Staff Working Document accompanying the proposed review of the 2002 framework.[86] According to the Commission, the current framework "allows operators to offer different services to different customer groups, but does not allow those who are in a dominant position to *discriminate* between customers in similar circumstances". However, if there is a risk that QoS degrades to unacceptably low levels, the Commission is proposing to give NRAs the power "to set minimum quality levels for network transmission services in an NGN environment based on technical standards identified at EU level"; "to prevent any blocking of information society services, or degradation in the quality of transmission of electronic communication services for third parties"; and "to impose appropriate interoperability requirements". The issue was further raised by industry players in the consultation on online content closed by the Commission in October 2006; and greater clarity on the net neutrality issue was also invoked by ERG.[87]

As a result, uncertainty over net neutrality issues still remains in Europe, and too much discretion seems to have been awarded to national regulators, which will inevitably result in regulatory uncertainty. Industry players and investors, while waiting for further certainty on the outcome of the EU (and national) debate, might then reconsider their willingness to invest in such a risky venture. Meanwhile, some mobile operators are reportedly considering to adopt a "walled garden" business model similar to that of most U.S. players, by blocking peer-to-peer and nomadic VoIP applications on their networks.[88]

## 2.2 *Summary: Two Worlds Apart?*

Just as technologies, markets and services converge into the 'information superhighway', the U.S. and the EU seem to be diverging substantially in terms of industry structure, market trends, growth speed and the regulatory approach. On the one hand, the U.S.

[86] See the Staff Working Document SEC(2006)816, June 29, 2006.

[87] See Kip Meek in http://erg.eu.int/doc/meeting/erg_18_plenary_oct06_chair_presentation.ppt.

[88] These include Vodafone Germany, T-Mobile and the French operator SFR. See OECD (2007), *Mobile Multiple Play: New Service Pricing and Policy Implications*, January 15, 2007.

telecommunications industry is almost going back to the old "Ma' Bell," with six of the eight RBOCs regrouped under the AT&T brand. U.S. authorities are pursuing ambitious universal broadband penetration objectives by protecting investment in infrastructure and NGN by incumbent telcos and cable companies, to the (temporary) disadvantage of new entrants. This is certainly due to the U.S. infrastructural endowment, characterized by facilities-based competition due to the widespread availability of cable: once wireless platforms develop their own broadband offerings through 3G technologies and WiMax functionality, U.S. citizens will have at least three alternative platforms to access the information superhighway for each zip code. The U.S. preference for investment over competition is found in FCC decisions, in Supreme Court judgments such as *Trinko*, and even in the more recent developments of the U.S. Microsoft case. The market reaction has been mixed: productivity is high, investment is resurging, but U.S. firms are losing competitiveness *vis-à-vis* "Chindian" players in the production and trade of communication services.

On the other hand, Europe leads in 3G penetration and in the development of multi-play digital platforms, and the share of incumbents in fixed-line voice services and broadband access has been slowly declining also due to the delayed implementation of the 2002 regulatory framework. Overall, however, the current regulatory framework seems to have created uncertainty for industry players: such uncertainty may ultimately result in a lack of investment and a consequent absence of facilities-based competition.

The relative strengths of the two regions—investment and productivity in the U.S., platform-building and fixed-mobile convergence in Europe—suggest that the U.S. and the EU can learn a lot from each other. As a matter of fact, many industry players in Europe have advocated for a more U.S.-like approach during the recent consultation on the review of the 2002 regulatory framework, but also some U.S. scholars have suggested that the U.S. pay more attention to the EU regulatory model as an example of almost-perfect technological neutrality.[89]

[89] Including Speta, J. B. (2004), *Rewriting US Telecommunications Law with an Eye on Europe*. preliminary draft, available online at http://web.si.umich.edu/tprc/papers/2004/322/Speta%20TPRC%202004.pdf; and Weisman, M. (2005), *You Pick Up The Phone And It Works: An Examination Of Real World Telecom Reform In The European Union*, Available at SSRN: http://ssrn.com/abstract=940705.

Differences between the two approaches, however, do not necessarily suggest that creating an open transatlantic market would prove beneficial for end users in a long-term perspective. Creating a fertile business environment that proves conducive to innovation and competition is a very delicate task in this sector, and is being dealt with by national policymakers with a mix of deregulation and access policy. As a result, promoting investment in infrastructure by transatlantic players is not a priority for most countries in the EU, nor it is in the U.S. The potential for transatlantic investment in communication services is then mostly confined to the three following options:

- EU firms may invest in new access infrastructure in the U.S., such a BPL or wireless broadband. Of course, this requires massive resources and scale.
- As the regulatory framework is being implemented more fully in European member states, U.S. firms may consider investing in wholesale access to legacy networks and NGNs, and gradually build their platforms by achieving customer base and scale.
- Entering at higher layers with global applications/services/content is possible in both areas, due to current net neutrality provisions in the U.S. and EU.

In summary, the U.S. and EU, as was authoritatively stated in a recent paper, are each "dancing to a different drummer."[90] Since such differences are due to peculiar industrial and sectoral policy, removing them may well create more distortions than the ones it seeks to solve —in other words, the cure would be worse than the disease. To be sure, regulatory cooperation between the EU and the U.S. can help remove some of the obstacles to entry and inward FDI in both areas; but a 'holistic' approach has to be maintained—solving, e.g., the net neutrality issue without harmonizing the regulation of infrastructure would inevitably hamper the sustainability of market operations or the prospects for consumer welfare in one of the two regions.

---

[90] Scott Marcus (2005), *cit.*.

## 3. An Open Transatlantic Market?

As recalled in the introductory section, late 2006 and early 2007 were marked by announcements on the need to intensify U.S.-EU regulatory cooperation to create an open transatlantic market and remove all barriers to transatlantic investment by 2015. In the case of telecoms, as explained in the previous section, the issue is particularly delicate. To be sure, there are remaining barriers to inward FDI on both sides of the Atlantic, ranging from incompatible standards to ownership restrictions, to delays in liberalization and persistence of high wholesale access charges. These barriers are surveyed in section 3.1.

However, removing those barriers does not mean opening up the transatlantic market fully. A real transatlantic market in telecom services must still be created, and examples of substantial investment ventures across the Atlantic are still very few. Thus, section 3.2 discusses in detail the prospects for an open transatlantic market, by identifying areas for cooperation/mutual learning and areas where national/community policies should not be harmonised.

### *3.1 Trade and Investment*

Trade in communication services represented approximately 2.5 percent of overall trade in services between the EU and U.S. in 2003-2004.[91] As reported by the OECD, the leading exporters of communications services worldwide are currently the U.S., the UK, the Netherlands, Germany and France. Data comparing the situation in 1996 and 2004 show, however, that U.S. imports of communication services have fallen by approximately 44 percent, from $8.8 to $4.9 billion. Meanwhile, Japan has drastically reduced its trade, whereas the Netherlands and Sweden have enormously expanded their trade. Figure 5.11 below shows imports and exports of communication services for selected EU countries and the U.S.

Data on trade in communication services are quite difficult to read and sometimes hardly meaningful, due to their strong dependence on regulatory trends and to the often observed inverse relationship with global trade trends in manufactured goods and other services.[92] To the

---

[91] Last data available from Eurostat.

[92] See OECD IT Outlook 2006.

**Figure 5.11 Trade in Communication Services, 2004**

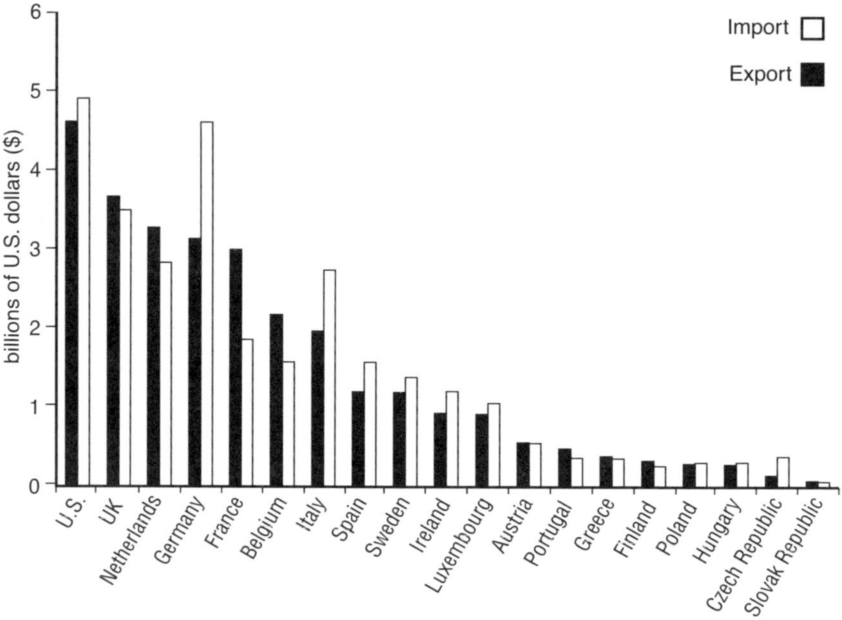


Source: OECD IT Outlook 2006

contrary, data on cross-border M&A activities are normally used as a proxy for FDI activity. In this respect, as already recalled, the two areas have witnessed a common wave of consolidation: but such consolidation most often involved the internal U.S. and EU markets. In addition, EU firms have increased their investment in Latin America and Southern Mediterranean countries, but very few EU-U.S. transactions took place in the communications services field.

On the other hand, global players have been very active at the physical layer—mostly in the field of networking equipment—and at higher layers of the IP architecture, especially in the application layer. Such trends are spurred by the need to invest in next generation infrastructure, on the one hand, and by the emergence of the IP era, on the other.

The most notable example of a transatlantic merger taking place in the physical layer is the acquisition of U.S. networking equipment company Lucent (formerly AT&T Network Systems) by French com-

**Figure 5.12 Restriction of Inward FDI in Specific Sectors, OECD, 2003**

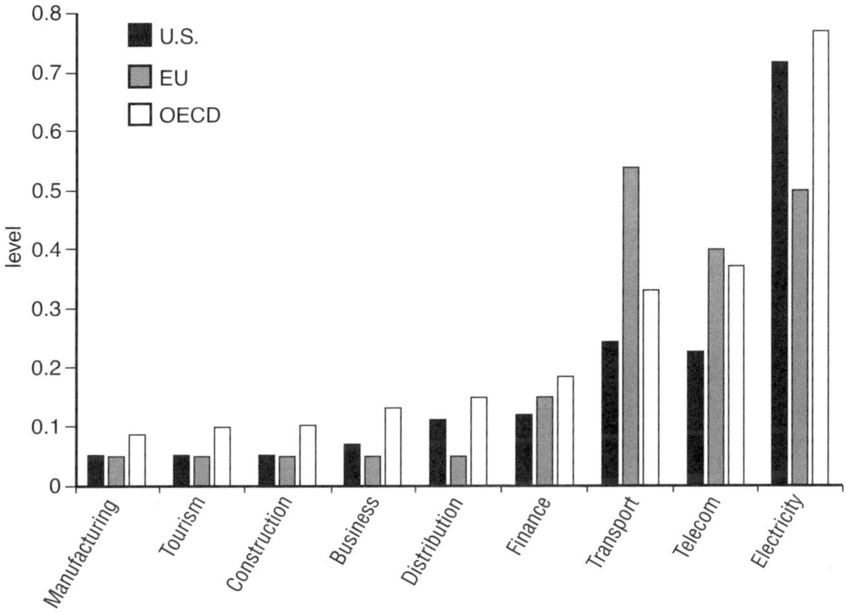


The indicator ranges from 0 (least restrictive) to 1 (most restrictive)

Source: OECD IT Outlook 2006

pany Alcatel in a €11.6 billion deal, which created the world's largest producer of communication equipment. The transatlantic giant company will top $25 billion of revenues in as many as 130 markets, reaching a 20 percent market share worldwide and overcoming Cisco Systems and Ericsson as world leader. The transaction was completed on December 4, 2006, after the approval of the Committee on Foreign Investment in the U.S., i.e. the inter-agency panel that reviews foreign takeovers of U.S. assets (see below, section 3.2, for further details on the procedure). The new global player has equally distributed revenues on the two sides of the Atlantic (35 percent in Europe, 34 percent in the U.S., 15 percent Asia and Pacific, 16 percent in the rest of the world). The merged entity immediately decided to acquire Nortel's UMTS radio access business and related assets for $320 million, completing the acquisition on December 31, 2006. This acquisition will lead, *i.a.*, Alcatel-Lucent UMTS solutions to serve around 40 UMTS providers in the world. The Alcatel deal is a major step towards the intensification of commercial relationship and technological cooperation by transatlantic players.[93]

At higher layers, competition 'for eyeballs' is driving also cross-border M&A activity, with many companies active in the search for preserving and increasing their customer base. For example, eBay's acquisition of Luxembourg-based company Skype in 2005 created a powerful player with killer applications and a strong customer base. The a-territorial nature of the Internet will increasingly facilitate these transactions in the future.

The issue of cross-border investment, as was already mentioned, is way more complex in the market for telecommunication services. A survey conducted by London Economics and PwC for the European Commission in July 2006 revealed that only 26 European telecom operators were investing in non-EU countries, and investments are mostly directed to developing countries with high market growth prospects. Cases of European telcos operating in the U.S. are limited, and include Deutsche Telekom's T-Mobile U.S., currently the fourth-largest wireless carrier in the U.S. market with 27.5 million customers; and Vodafone's 45 percent stake of Verizon Wireless, which serves 57 million customers in the U.S.

### *3.1.1 Barriers to Inward FDI in the U.S.*

Every year, the European Commission publishes a list of obstacles to FDI by European firms in the U.S., covering also communication services. In 2006, some of the traditionally mentioned obstacles have been lifted or alleviated. For example, the rigid taxonomy of services ('silos' approach) traditionally hampered the competitive level-playing field from 1996 until 2004 in the U.S.[94] Such classification arrangements, according to the European Commission, affected the ability of new players to enter the U.S. market in the near future. As the 'silos' approach was set aside for new high-speed technologies, such obstacle should not be considered as insurmountable anymore.

---

[93] For example, Alcatel advanced triple-play solutions will be the basis of a $1.7 billion investment by SBC to implement Project Lightspeed and deliver integrated IPTV, high-speed broadband, IP voice and wireless services to 18 million households by the end of 2007.

[94] See Renda, A. (2005), "Telecom Services: a Transatlantic Perspective", in Daniel S. Hamilton and Joseph P. Quinlan, *Deep Integration. How Transatlantic Markets are Leading Globalization*, Center for Transatlantic Relations and CEPS, Chapter 11.

On the other hand, the wave of industry consolidation that has characterized the U.S. in the past few years, resulting in the almost-complete resurgence of the old AT&T, could significantly reduce the degree of market openness in the U.S.; on top of this, the need to develop triple- or quadruple-play bundles and negotiate arrangements with content and application providers—when not with state authorities and municipalities—further jeopardises the business case for entering the U.S. market. New entrants, as of today, should possess remarkable scale and economic resources to profitably enter the market (like in the case of Alcatel), and even in this case—at least, at the infrastructure layer—the success of such venture is not at all guaranteed.

The European Commission has identified a number of remaining U.S. practices that substantially hamper EU firms trying to enter the U.S. market.[95] The main concerns expressed were related to the satellite and mobile sectors, as well as to spectrum availability and diverging standards. Existing barriers are listed in more detail in the next sections.

#### 3.1.1.1 The ECO-Test

Since November 1995, the FCC adopted a rule on entry of foreign-affiliated carriers into the U.S. market, by introducing the so-called "Effective Competitive Opportunity test" (ECO-test). In the aftermath of the *WTO Basic Telecommunications Agreement*, then, the FCC replaced such test with a "rebuttable presumption" that entry by a foreign-affiliated competitor is pro-competitive, but retained a "public interest" criterion which can still be invoked to deny a license to a foreign operator in cases of trade concerns, foreign policy concerns and very high risk to competition. These rules are said to create uncertainty for foreign operators wishing to invest in the United States. Such system has later been extended to satellites licensed by WTO countries.[96] Although the FCC expressed its intention to only deny

---

[95] See the European Commission's Report on U.S. Barriers to Trade and Investment, March 2006, stating that: "[t]he reduction in the number of competitors in the wire line sector raises some concerns, in particular, regarding the provision of local connectivity (namely special access lines for businesses requiring dedicated, non-switched connections to external networks), as well as Internet connectivity services. On the one hand, special access lines are key inputs for the provision of global telecoms services and particular attention will be required to ensure a fair and non-discriminatory special access offer. On the other hand, several submissions to the Federal Communications Commission (FCC) in the above mentioned proceedings have also expressed concerns about a reduction of competition in the internet backbone market leading to "de-peering", dominance and packet-discrimination concerns."

[96] See 2005 Report on U.S. Barriers to Trade and Investment, European Commission, December 2004.

market access on this basis in exceptional circumstances (which are not well defined) the discretion retained by the FCC remains of concern to the EU and raises questions as to the compatibility of the FCC rules with U.S. WTO commitments.

#### 3.1.1.2 Direct Limitation of Ownership of Common Carrier Radio Licenses and Broadcast Licenses

Direct investment in U.S. companies holding common carriers radio licenses is still limited to 20 percent by section 310 of the 1934 Communications Act. This rule—which applies also to companies holding broadcast licenses—seems to run counter to the commitments undertaken by the U.S. within the WTO Basic Telecommunications Agreement, and inevitably limits the freedom for EU firms to invest in U.S. companies. The European Union expressly stated that "the U.S. broadcasting market today is hardly accessible to foreign media companies".[97] The U.S. Administration holds the view that it is not necessary to adopt specific legislation to abolish such investment restrictions, since the FCC may waive these restrictions under the current law by invoking the "public interest." In light of the ongoing technological convergence and consolidation between telecoms and media in the U.S., ownership restrictions may hamper attempts by EU companies to enter a dynamic and profitable market.

#### 3.1.1.3 Satellite Operators

After the Basic Telecommunications Agreement, the U.S. has kept a market access restriction on satellite-based services—*i.e.* protecting the monopoly of Comsat although formally abolished by the 2000 ORBIT Act. European satellite operators such as Intelsat, Inmarsat Ventures plc and New Skies N.V. have experienced substantial barriers to entry and suffered from complex and lengthy proceedings in their attempt to enter the U.S. satellite market. In addition, the U.S. has taken an exemption to the MFN principle for one-way satellite transmission of Direct-to-Home, Direct-Broadcast-Satellite and digital audio services. Such exemption was considered by the European Commission as a measure that "may impair European interests".[98]

---

[97] *Ibid.*

[98] *Ibid.*

The initial U.S. offer in the current WTO round of negotiations proposes to eliminate these exceptions.

### 3.1.1.4 Spectrum Availability for 3G

An obstacle to entry in the U.S. telecommunications sector traditionally identified by the European Commission is the limited availability of spectrum licenses, especially for 3G and wireless broadband services. In particular, the unavailability of 3.5 GHz bands in the U.S. is considered as a limit to the deployment of WiMax, typically implemented in that band in the rest of the world. In November 2006, the FCC granted 550 of the 1,087 new licenses won in the AWS (Advanced Wireless Services) auction run on September 18, 2006.[99] These licenses are worth $12.2 billion and are located in the 1710-1755 MHz and 2110-2155 MHz band. One of the top bidders was T-Mobile U.S., the U.S. wireless carrier owned by Deutsche Telekom. Despite this encouraging result, further moves towards the compatibility of 3G frequency bands used in the U.S. and the EU would facilitate roaming between the U.S. and the EU via multi-mode terminals, thus boosting the provision of transatlantic communication services.

### 3.1.1.5 Incompatible Standards

The U.S. is normally praised for its bottom-up, market-based approach to standard-setting. However, whenever incompatible standards are chosen or exclusive standards are selected in the U.S., entry of European companies in the U.S. market can be strongly hampered. This of course mostly applies where the EU already holds widely adopted standards, as is the case for mobile telephony and digital terrestrial television. As regards the former, U.S. wireless carriers still rely on a number of incompatible technologies—Cingular and T-Mobile use GSM, GPRS, EGDE, UMTS and TDMA; Verizon and Sprint rely on CDMA, 1xRTT and EV-DO. For what concerns digital terrestrial TV, the ATSC technology is incompatible with the established DVB-T standard adopted in the EU.

Incompatible standards in 3G telephony are also an important obstacle to international data roaming services. A recent report by the

[99] Auction No. 66. the 1,087 licenses were won by 104 bidders for a total revenue of $13,700,267,150.

OECD shows that almost all 3G operators provide international data roaming services based on 3G technologies, but European operators only covered EU countries, whereas North American operators tended to cover mainly North America.[100]

#### 3.1.1.6 Cable Franchises

Municipalities in the United States require cable companies to offer services to everyone in a given area in exchange for a license. This could potentially create an uneven playing field for telecommunication and cable operators offering multiple-play services, creating further barriers to entry by foreign players in the U.S. The FCC has taken action on December 20, 2006 to streamline cable franchise procedures, in its attempt to create a level-playing field between cable operators and telecom players such as AT&T and Verizon. This may lift up barriers to entry also for foreign players in the medium term.

### *3.2.2 Non-tariff Barriers in the EU*

Similarly, the U.S. Trade Representative (USTR), in reviewing the operation and effectiveness of U.S. telecommunications trade agreements, pursuant to Section 1377 of the Omnibus Trade and Competitiveness Act of 1988, recently identified remaining barriers to investment in EU member states and at community level.[101] Here too, significant steps forward have been made, most notably in the liberalization of markets pursuant to the 2002 regulatory framework. The most relevant barriers identified are listed below.

#### 3.2.1.1 Slow Market Liberalization, Especially in the Fixed-line Sector

The observed delays in the implementation of the 2002 framework have hampered the effective ability of U.S. firms to successfully enter the EU market. Primary legislation was adopted only recently by five Member States (Belgium, Czech Republic, Estonia, Luxembourg and

[100] See OECD (2007), Mobile Multiple Play: New Service Pricing and Policy Implications, January 15, 2007.

[101] See USTR, 2007 National Trade Estimate Report on Foreign Trade Barriers (NTE), April 2, 2007.

especially Greece), and market analyses by NRAs have taken too long and were completed only in 2006, when the 2002 framework was already being reviewed. Moreover, appeals procedures have slowed down the implementation of the 2002 framework, creating problems in at least 17 of the 25 (now 27) member states. A timely implementation of the new package in laggard States would certainly contribute to further boosting the telecom sector in the EU and open up the market to U.S. firms. As recently showed by recent data, the market share held by incumbent firms in the fixed-line sector has fallen in many countries; at the end of 2005, the incumbent's share was 47.2 percent in Germany, 51.8 percent in the UK, 65.2 percent in France, 66.5 percent in Spain and 72.2 percent in Italy.[102]

Recent attempts by the Commission to achieve further consistency in the national application of the regulatory framework for e-communications should bring more legal certainty for U.S. operators. Implementation of the framework should also bring relief to U.S. companies currently denouncing unfair practices by national incumbents, such as Vega in Slovenia.[103]

#### 3.2.1.2 Excessively High Interconnection Prices

Telecom liberalization in Europe is also leading to increased price regulation of mobile termination rates. The U.S. Trade Representative has recalled in several occasions that mobile termination is still too expensive in many EU countries, and particularly in Germany, Belgium and France. The different interconnection models used in the U.S. and EU (the mobile-party-pays to the U.S., the calling-party-pays in Europe) also determines the different levels of termination charges. Over the past few months, the situation has improved, after market 16 (wholesale mobile termination) has been found to be anti-competitive and subsequently regulated in all member states. Figure 5.13 below shows the average mobile termination rates in the EU-27 in January 2006. A comparison with 2004 shows that significant reductions have been achieved in most countries.[104]

---

102 Ofcom Discussion Paper on Next Generation Access (2006).

103 USTR, 2006 National Trade Estimate Report on Foreign Trade Barriers (NTE), March 31, 2007.

104 See, e.g., Renda, in *Deep Integration* (2005), cit.

**Figure 5.13 Average Mobile Termination Rates in the EU-27, January 2006**

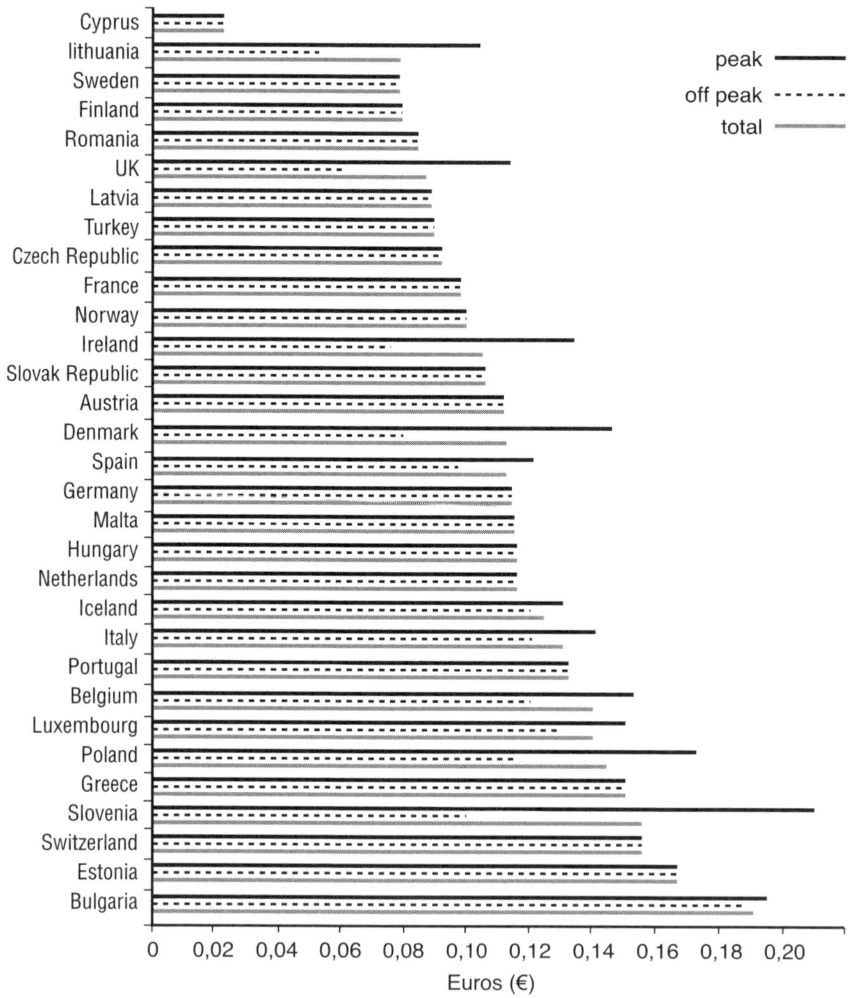


### 3.2.1.3 Spectrum Policy

A potentially significant barrier to entry in the EU telecoms market is the rigidity of spectrum policies in most member states. In this respect, the European Commission has paved the way for a more coordinated approach to spectrum policy in its proposal to review to 2002 regulatory framework. Current proposals include the endorsement of principles of technology and service neutrality, and the identification of certain bands for spectrum trading/liberalization, as well as bands for unlicensed uses of spectrum. However, the future of spectrum liberalization in Europe is still uncertain, and the 'command and control' method of spectrum allocation will dominate the scene in most of the EU27 in the next few years. Some countries have taken action to liberalize uses of spectrum in certain bands, although the Commission's project to reach agreement with member states on a number of selected bands for wireless access services is currently stalled.[105] A notable example of progress in spectrum policy is the upcoming 'digital dividend' auction of spectrum for mobile television and wireless broadband in the UK, expected by late 2008. Ofcom estimates the value for consumers and businesses over 20 years to be between 5 and 10 billion pounds.

In subsequent years, the switch-off of analog TV will free valuable frequencies in most member states. If frequencies will be auctioned or traded under technology and service neutrality conditions, this will represent a major occasion for investment in EU communication services also by non-EU firms.

### 3.2.1.4 The TVWF Directive

The 1989 Television Without Frontiers Directive (TVWF) contains provisions related to the protection of European-origin programs; such provisions were not changed by the review launched on December 13, 2005, and were confirmed also in the European Parliament's first reading in December 2006. Article four of the TVWF Directive stipulates that a majority of television transmission time must be reserved for European-origin programs "where practicable and by appropriate means", excluding the time appointed to news, sports events, games, advertising and teletext services. According to the latest report published by the European Commission, the EU-average transmission time reserved for European works by all covered channels in all member states was 65.18 percent in 2003 and 63.32 percent in 2004. In addition, some member states have decided to implement the TVWF directive by reserving even more space for EU or national programs. This is the case for France, Italy and Spain.

[105] The so-called WAPECS project. On this, see the final report by the Radio Spectrum Policy Group, at http://rspg.groups.eu.int/doc/documents/meeting/rspg8/rspg_05_102.pdf.

## 3.3. The Pros and Cons of an Open Transatlantic Market

Evidence reported in the previous section portraits a mixed picture as far as the prospects for an open transatlantic market for communications services is concerned. No doubt, the U.S. and EU can work together to reduce the impact of existing non-tariff barriers to entry and investment, such as those identified above in section 3.1. However, there are other ways in which transatlantic trade might be boosted—e.g. by facilitating wholesale access of new players to the incumbents' infrastructure, and by improving the regulatory environment through regulatory cooperation. These aspects must be kept separate in the assessment of the prospects for an open transatlantic market.

Available estimates on the costs and benefits of changes in the regulatory environment in the U.S. and EU show the following expected gains:

- **Liberalization efforts**
    - Restoring mandatory network sharing rules in the U.S. may lead to significant welfare decreases.[106] A study by Hazlett *et al.* (2004) calculated that the phasing out of network sharing rules—together with greater availability of spectrum and measures aimed at exempting DSL and internet services from state regulation, would have led to incremental investment of $58 billion and a combined effect of both supply and demand channels totaling $634 billion of additional goods and services, including $113 billion in new tax revenues over five years.
    - Further liberalization of communications services in the EU would increase growth. In 2003, The Commission estimated that the liberalization of the telecommunication and electricity markets would lead to GDP and employment levels increase of 0.4 and 0.6 percent respectively, four years after the liberalization, and a GDP level increase of 0.6 percent, ten years after liberalization.[107]

---

[106] See Hazlett *et al.* (2004), *Sending the Right Signals: Promoting Competition through Telecommunications Reform*, a Report to the U.S. Chamber of Commerce, September 22, 2004.

[107] European Commission, Chapter 2—Structural reforms in labour and product markets and macroeconomic performance in the EU, in: The EU Economy: 2002 Review. In a more recent study, Kox and Lejour (2006) estimate that the trade and FDI effects of the

- **Spectrum liberalization and trading**
  - In Europe, spectrum trading and liberalization is expected to generate benefits of as much as €900 billion yearly, whereas trading without liberalization would yield much lower welfare gains, at around €900 million yearly. A recent study by Mott McDonald *et al.* (2006) estimated the net present value of the harmonisation of collective uses of spectrum in the EU in a range between €463 and €898 billion; this means a yearly contribution to GDP of up to 0.17 percent.
  - Estimates put the value of U.S. spectrum at $771 billion, and U.S. consumer welfare gains associated with introducing a suitable system of issuing spectrum usage rights at $77 billion/year.[108]
  - In the UK, Ofcom estimated that the benefits of introducing spectrum trading will substantially exceed costs with net economic benefits ranging from £67 to £144 million if the impact of increased competition is taken into account.[109]

These estimates are of course quite conservative: harmonized spectrum bands would boost the deployment of new technologies that need almost global scale to be developed. Potential benefits that would accrue to the transatlantic economy from cooperation on spectrum allocation are related to economies of scale in manufacturing of equipment, more competition for equipment procurement, increased spectrum efficiency, greater stability in band planning, and even increased response to disaster relief.[110] Notable examples of technolo-

EU services market liberalization could lead to an increase in GDP by 0.5 to 1.5 percent. However, such increases are only marginally related to communication services, as liberalisation is well on its way in most European countries. See Dynamic effects of European services liberalisation: more to be gained, in Global challenges for Europe, Report by the Secretariat of the Economic council, PART 1, Prime Minister's Office Publications 18/2006, 2006, p. 313-142.

108 See European Commission, *A New EU Radio Spectrum Strategy*, MEMO/05/345.

109 A study for Ofcom by Analysys, DotEcon and Hogan & Hartson estimated that benefits due to the additional competition that would result from spectrum trading on its own would be roughly equal to the direct benefits of spectrum trading. This would increase the Net Present Value of the benefits to the United Kingdom to £154 million.

110 See the ITU Background paper, *Issues Related to Spectrum*, 2004, available at http://www.itu.int/ITU-D/partners/Events/2004/New-Delhi_Apr04/Backgrounds/Spectrum.pdf.

gies that would enormously profit from global harmonisation are RFID and WiMAX.

- **Tackling net neutrality**
  - A recent study by Darby in the U.S. found that solving the 'net neutrality thicket' by allowing carriers are to recover 10 percent of the common costs of building a new FTTH network from content providers would generate direct consumer welfare gains of $8 billion over a ten-year period.
  - Starting from Darby's calculation, Sidak (2007) finds that allowing broadband access providers to reduce their monthly access prices by $5 to $10 and assuming a demand elasticity of -2.0 would produce yearly welfare gains from $3.441 billion (in response to a $5 per month subsidy) to $7.740 billion (in response to a $10 per month subsidy).[111] These estimates, however, do not take into account potential dynamic losses in product variety, and welfare losses from reduced internet freedom and enhanced barriers to entry for nomadic application providers.
  - In Europe, the issue still has to be tackled. As already recalled, Ofcom has recently stated that full net neutrality provision would undermine incentives to invest in NGNs by depriving access providers of one possible source of revenue. Accordingly, finding a suitable compromise at EU level would improve regulatory certainty for increasingly pan-European players both at the infrastructure and the application layers, and thus seems to be highly advisable in Europe.

As a result, the prospects for transatlantic communications services seem to lie more in achieving spectrum harmonization and certainty on net neutrality, whereas pursuing further market opening at the infrastructure layer seems to be a solution to a rather obscure problem. To the contrary, the current development of U.S. and EU markets suggests that encouraging investment in new enabling technologies is an absolute priority for the transatlantic economy, and this may require lifting up regulation in some cases, especially when infrastruc-

[111] See Sidak, J. G. (2006), A Consumer-Welfare Approach to Network Neutrality Regulation of the Internet, 2 Journal of Competition Law & Economics.

ture-based competition already exists. In Europe, this is the case of the Scandinavian countries, the Netherlands and Belgium. The area in which transatlantic activities seem to have the greatest potential to improve welfare is spectrum allocation.

### *3.3.1 Enhancing regulatory cooperation*

Creating a fertile business environment for industry players is essential on both sides of the Atlantic. In this respect, regulatory cooperation can boost the transatlantic economy in many ways, including arrangements that are more indirectly related to the telecom sector. The most important are the following:

- ***Regulatory certainty on DRM and interoperability issues:*** the development of new global platforms highly depends on the availability of DRM solutions and access to them by new entrants wishing to market new products. There is a clear trade-off between the need to protect valuable investment in new technologies and the need to avoid the crystallization of market power on *de facto* standards in the industry. In this respect, the U.S. demise of the essential facility doctrine (after *Trinko*), the "deferential approach" to system design in antitrust (after *IBM v. Telex*), the absence of overlaps between antitrust and sector-specific regulation and the ongoing deregulation of most communications services add regulatory certainty to firms' investment decisions. In Europe, on the other hand, regulatory certainty is still undermined by differences in national approaches to market analysis and remedies, by the upcoming review of Article 82 of the Treaty, and by the approach to system design and interoperability adopted by the Commission in *Microsoft* and soon to be judged by the CFI.

- ***Cooperation on better regulation issues.*** Recent developments in the debate on better regulation include discussions on whether it would be appropriate to include competition assessments and trade impact assessments in the standard RIA process. This would of course help policymakers raise their awareness of the consequences of their actions for entry of foreign players and trade openness. Some countries, e.g. the

UK have already mainstreamed competition assessment into the RIA process.

- ***Cooperation on competition issues.*** The work of the Antitrust Modernization Commission in the U.S. and the review of the application of Article 82 to exclusionary abuses in the EU will exert a significant impact on the future trends of competition in the telecoms sector. In this respect, transatlantic cooperation is taking place, and could be further strengthened to become transatlantic coordination.

## 4. Conclusions: Should the Giant be Awakened?

There is little doubt that future developments of telecommunications services will result in increased globalization. Available studies show that full liberalization of communication services worldwide would bring at least some short-term benefits to the world economy, although these benefits would not be reaped by the transatlantic economy.[112] In light of these findings, the U.S. and EU can profitably work together to achieve further harmonization in spectrum allocation and in tackling multi-layer trade-offs such as the net neutrality issue. Harmonized conditions of competition can lead to substantial welfare increases in a dynamic sector such as telecoms. In a word, diverging regulations in a converging world are hardly conducive to dynamic welfare gains.

However, current trends towards a more lenient approach to network sharing obligations at the infrastructure layer should no be considered as harming social welfare in the U.S. and EU. Policymakers are currently prioritizing investment in enabling infrastructures to accelerate the transition towards the information society for all and bridging the digital divide. In this respect, competition and openness are likely to flourish in the application and content layer, just as the do on the Internet today.

---

[112] Dee and Hanslow, Verikios and Zhang (2000) simulate multilateral liberalization of trade in communication services and financial services in a post-Uruguay Round environment and finds positive welfare effects for the world as a whole in both cases. According to this study, when liberalizing trade in communication services, the world as a whole is projected to gain about $13 billion or 0.05 percent in terms of real income with China capturing 4.4 billion. See also Verikios and Zhang, at http://www.monash.edu.au/policy/conf/53Verikios.pdf, Table 5.

Finally, barriers to FDI in the transatlantic economy have been substantially reduced over the past few years, especially in Europe, thanks to the liberalization process spurred by the 2002 framework. Further improvements depend on the removal of ownership restrictions in the U.S., and on the free circulation of content and non-linear services in the EU.

# Part III

# Opening the Transatlantic Services Economy: Global and Transatlantic Implications

# *Chapter 6*

# Transatlantic Cooperation to Open Services Markets: Implications for Multilateralism

*Bernard Hoekman*[1]

## Introduction

Technological changes and the demise of "natural monopoly" arguments for state-provision or control of major service industries have allowed an increasing number of services markets to be contested internationally through telecommunications networks and foreign direct investment (FDI). While the policy reforms—liberalization, privatization—that have allowed the expansion of trade in services have mostly been implemented by governments autonomously, countries have also sought to negotiate better access to foreign markets for both FDI and cross-border trade in services. One of the major results of the Uruguay Round (1986-93) was the creation of the General Agreement on Trade in Services (GATS),[2] and almost all recent preferential trade agreements include provisions on services.

An important policy question is what international cooperation and trade agreements can/should do to support domestic regulatory reform. In principle, trade agreements can provide a focal point for policy reforms ("good regulatory practices") as well as a mechanism to enhance access to export markets. The stylized fact that looms large here is that very little progress has been made to date in using the GATS to lock in unilateral reforms that have already been imple-

[1] An earlier version of this paper was presented at the conference "Sleeping Giant: The Transatlantic Services Market," Center for Transatlantic Relations, Paul Nitze School of Advanced International Studies, Washington D.C., February 8, 2007. I am grateful to Bruce Stokes and conference participants for helpful comments on the conference draft of this paper. The views expressed are personal and should not be attributed to the World Bank.

[2] The original GATT-1947 did not cover services for a simple reason: at the time the GATT was negotiated services were mostly nontradable.

mented, let alone in inducing new liberalization. At the same time, an increasing number of countries are pursuing or have signed bilateral or regional trade agreements that include service sector commitments, and bilateral investment treaties that include services investment. It is rather unclear what implications this has for the multilateral trading system (the WTO): are these building blocks or stumbling blocks for a more integrated world in which the most efficient and competitive firms will be able to supply markets?

The question that motivates this chapter is what a possible bilateral agreement or set of agreements on services between the EU and the U.S. might imply for the rest of the world, more specifically, the multilateral trading system. The issue is of particular importance given that the EU and the U.S. have been the anchors of the GATS: the WTO has been the primary forum for the parties to negotiate binding disciplines on services trade policies. Although both the EU and the U.S. have been active proponents of bilateral and regional trade agreements with third countries, a new transatlantic framework for economic integration between the EU and the U.S. would imply a shift in focus and emphasis for both parties that could have major implications for the multilateral trading system.

The chapter begins in section one with a brief discussion of why services liberalization and regulatory reform matters for the trading system and the world economy. Section two reviews the status quo in the WTO on services liberalization commitments and suggests a number of possible explanations for the rather limited progress that has been made to date. Section three discusses whether the factors that appear to impede multilateral progress might be easier to overcome in a bilateral or regional setting. Section four turns to the possible content and implications of closer EU-U.S. cooperation on services for the rest of the world. In Section five some proposals are made that aim to increase the payoffs of bilateral EU-U.S. cooperation for the rest of the world, in particular developing countries. Section six concludes.

## 1. Why Services Liberalization Matters

Services have unique characteristics that affect their tradability. Typical characteristics include:

1. intangibility—so that international transactions in services are often difficult to monitor, measure and tax;
2. nonstorability—so that production and consumption often must occur at the same place and time;
3. differentiation—services are often tailored to the needs of customers; and
4. joint production, with customers having to participate in the production process.

As the conventional definition of trade—where a product crosses the frontier—would miss out on a whole range of international transactions, the WTO defines trade to span four modes of supply:

- *Mode 1—Cross-border*: services supplied from the territory of one country into the territory of another.
- *Mode 2—Consumption abroad*: services supplied in the territory of a nation to the consumers of another.
- *Mode 3—Commercial presence*: services supplied through any type of business or professional establishment of one country in the territory of another (i.e., FDI).
- *Mode 4—Presence of natural persons*: services supplied by nationals of a country in the territory of another.

There are powerful economic reasons to pursue policies to increase the contestability of services markets through all four of these modes. An efficient, competitive financial sector is critical in ensuring that capital is deployed where it has the highest returns.[3] Lower cost and higher quality telecommunications will generate economy-wide benefits, as this service is both an intermediate input and a "transport" mechanism for information services and other products that can be digitized. Similarly, transport services contribute to the efficient distribution of goods within and between countries and are the means through which service providers move to the location of clients (and *vice versa*). Business services such as accounting and legal services reduce transaction costs associated with the operation of financial

[3] See Hoekman (2006) for a survey of the literature analyzing the effects of services liberalization.

markets and the enforcement of contracts. Retail and wholesale services are a vital link between producers and consumers, with the margins that apply in the provision of such services influencing the competitiveness of firms on both the local and international market.

Because many services are inputs into the production of other services and goods, their cost and quality affects the ability of all firms in an economy to compete. Greater competition by opening access to foreign service providers will reduce what Konan and Maskus (2006) call the cartel effect—the markup of price over marginal cost that incumbents are able to charge due to policies that restrict entry; and attenuate what they call the cost inefficiency effect—the fact that in an environment with limited competition, the marginal costs of incumbents are likely to be higher than if entry was open.

In practice, FDI will often be a major channel for foreign providers to supply services and reduce these cost effects. Markusen, Rutherford and Tarr (2005), for example, develop a model where services FDI is a source of new knowledge and competitive pressure, and helps host countries to produce and export more advanced products. In their model, as barriers to trade in producer services fall, costs of imported services drop, and imports (including through FDI) rise and displace domestic firms. However, the additional varieties available to the economy generate positive externalities for final goods production, raising TFP and welfare disproportionately.

Country simulation studies that analyze the likely impact of services liberalization conclude that removing policies that increase costs can have much greater positive effects on national welfare than the removal of trade barriers—see e.g., Konan and Maskus (2006), Jensen, Rutherford and Tarr (2006), and Rutherford, Tarr and Shepotylo (2005). Instead of the "standard" half to one percent increase in welfare from goods liberalization, introducing greater competition on services markets that removes cost inefficiencies raises the gains to the five to 10 percent range or more. These large effects of services liberalization reflect both the importance of services in the economy, the extent to which they tend to be protected, and the importance of incorporating FDI into the analysis as a "mode of supply".

One does not have to rely on casual empiricism or numerical general equilibrium modeling to make the case for services liberalization.

There is a rapidly expanding body of econometric evidence that policy reforms to increase competition in services industries, including through international liberalization, can help boost growth prospects and enhance welfare. Mattoo, Rathindran and Subramanian (2006) analyze the effects of trade and investment openness for the financial and telecommunications sector on growth in a cross-sectional analysis. Controlling for other determinants of growth, they find that countries that fully liberalized the financial services sector grew, on average, about one percentage point faster than other countries. Fully liberalizing both the telecommunications and the financial services sectors was associated with an average growth rate 1.5 percentage points above that of other countries. Focusing on a sample of transition economies, Eschenbach and Hoekman (2006a) explore the impact of financial and infrastructure services policy reforms on per capita income growth of transition economies using time-series data for the 1990-2004 period. Controlling for standard potential explanatory variables, they find that improvements in services policies—infrastructure and finance—have an important, statistically significant positive impact on per-capita growth. Thus, there is a positive relationship between services liberalization, services performance and aggregate performance of the economy. A major channel for the growth effects of services policy reforms is through total factor productivity at the firm level. FDI in services has been found to be an important mechanism through which "good practices" and knowledge is diffused to host countries (Arnold, Mattoo and Narcisco, 2006; Arnold, Javorcik and Mattoo, 2006).

## 2. The Status Quo: GATS

As mentioned, there is no binding EU-U.S. framework governing bilateral services trade and investment-related policies. Although there are sector-specific agreements—e.g., in the area of cross-Atlantic air transport—the primary forum for such cooperation is the WTO. GATS disciplines operate at two levels. First, there is a set of general rules that apply across the board to measures affecting trade in services, of which the most important are transparency and the most-favored-nation (MFN) principle. Second, there are sector-specific commitments by WTO Members on market access and national treatment. Article XVI lists a set of market access-restricting measures that

Members may not maintain or adopt, unless listed in their schedule.[4] Article XVII bans discrimination against foreign services or service suppliers, with the exception of any specific measures a Member schedules. The scope of the specific commitments is determined by which sectors a Member decides to include, and the exceptions it schedules to market access and national treatment. Thus, schedules of specific commitments are made on a sector-by-sector and mode-of-supply basis, with countries having the option of making no commitments, a partial commitment, or a full commitment—i.e., specifying that no limitations are maintained on market access and/or on national treatment.

The resulting complexity makes it difficult to "quantify" the coverage of GATS schedules. Although arbitrary, one simple and transparent way of measuring and comparing commitments is to give a weight of zero to "unbound" type commitments; a weight of 1 to commitments implying no restriction on national treatment or market access (i.e., "none" is scheduled—see Table 6.1), and a weight of 0.5 to commitments where some restrictions are maintained but a service sector has been scheduled. Table 6.1 illustrates the picture that results for the EU (similar data can be compiled for the U.S.). The indices provide a basis for cross-country comparisons and monitoring changes in commitments over time.

In the Uruguay Round no WTO member came even close to locking in all unilateral reforms that had already been implemented—the (weighted average) coverage of specific commitments as of 1995 did not exceed 50 percent for most countries (Hoekman, 1996). Most developing countries have commitments that are well below 50 percent of all services and modes of supply. Adlung and Roy (2005) note that with the exception of commitments by a number of countries to liberalize access to telecommunications markets little progress was made in extending the coverage of the GATS post-1995. They also point out that the provisional (conditional) offers made by WTO members in the 6 years following the launch of new negotiations on services (mandated by the GATS to commence in 2000, and subse-

[4] These include limitations on: (a) the number of service suppliers; (b) the total value of services transactions or assets; (c) the total number of services operations or the total quantity of service output; (d) the total number of natural persons that may be employed in a particular sector; (e) specific types of legal entity through which a service can be supplied; and (f) foreign equity participation (e.g. maximum equity participation).

**Table 6.1 GATS Commitments by EU-15 Member States, by Mode of Supply**

| | Market Access | | | | National Treatment | | | | |
|---|---|---|---|---|---|---|---|---|---|
| Mode: | 1 | 2 | 3 | 4 | 1 | 2 | 3 | 4 | All |
| EU* | 52.6 | 68.1 | 67.1 | 0.0 | 52.3 | 68.4 | 67.4 | 0.0 | 47.0 |
| Belgium | 51.0 | 68.1 | 64.2 | 0.3 | 51.0 | 68.4 | 67.4 | 1.0 | 46.4 |
| Germany | 51.6 | 66.8 | 65.5 | 1.0 | 50.3 | 67.7 | 67.1 | 0.6 | 46.3 |
| Denmark | 51.3 | 67.1 | 65.8 | 2.6 | 51.9 | 68.4 | 65.8 | 3.9 | 47.1 |
| Spain | 51.0 | 68.1 | 59.7 | 1.3 | 52.3 | 68.4 | 67.4 | 1.9 | 46.3 |
| France | 49.4 | 67.4 | 57.1 | 6.5 | 50.6 | 68.4 | 66.5 | 1.0 | 45.8 |
| Greece | 45.2 | 67.4 | 56.1 | 9.0 | 49.4 | 68.4 | 66.8 | 0.0 | 45.3 |
| Italy | 46.8 | 67.7 | 57.4 | 2.9 | 47.1 | 68.4 | 66.5 | 7.7 | 45.6 |
| Ireland | 50.6 | 68.1 | 63.5 | 0.0 | 51.0 | 68.4 | 67.4 | 0.0 | 46.1 |
| Luxembourg | 52.6 | 68.1 | 66.8 | 0.0 | 52.3 | 68.4 | 67.4 | 0.0 | 46.9 |
| Netherlands | 52.6 | 68.1 | 66.8 | 0.0 | 52.3 | 68.4 | 67.4 | 0.0 | 46.9 |
| Portugal | 43.5 | 67.7 | 51.0 | 2.9 | 49.0 | 68.4 | 67.1 | 4.2 | 44.2 |
| UK | 52.6 | 67.7 | 66.1 | 0.0 | 52.3 | 68.4 | 67.4 | 0.0 | 46.8 |
| Austria | 55.8 | 68.7 | 64.8 | 8.7 | 53.5 | 68.7 | 67.7 | 10.0 | 49.8 |
| Sweden | 47.4 | 60.0 | 50.0 | 0.6 | 48.1 | 60.0 | 53.5 | 1.9 | 40.2 |
| Finland | 51.3 | 58.7 | 52.3 | 0.6 | 52.6 | 58.7 | 56.8 | 36.1 | 45.9 |
| Standard deviation | 3.2 | 3.0 | 6.1 | 3.1 | 1.8 | 3.2 | 4.3 | 9.2 | 2.0 |
| Mean | 50.2 | 66.6 | 60.5 | 2.4 | 50.9 | 67.2 | 65.5 | 4.6 | 46.0 |

Source: Eschenbach and Hoekman (2006b).

quently folded into the Doha Round) are not ambitious. Essentially offers were limited to further (still incomplete) lock-in of past liberalization. While not without value, of course, this suggests there is limited interest in using the GATS as a vehicle to push forward liberalization of markets.

Continuing the focus on the EU, Table 6.3 matches the proposals (offers) EU countries made in the Doha Round as of 2003-2004 against the prevailing GATS regime that is summarized in Table 6.1. These data cover the most recent proposals that were made available publicly. The data in Table 6.2 are drawn from an analysis by Langhammer (2005), based on a methodological approach very similar to

**Table 6.2 EU Members GATS Doha Offers by Mode, 2003**

| | Market Access | | | | National Treatment | | | | |
|---|---|---|---|---|---|---|---|---|---|
| Mode: | 1 | 2 | 3 | 4 | 1 | 2 | 3 | 4 | All |
| EU* | n.a. | n.a. | n.a. | n.a. | n.a. | n.a. | n.a. | n.a. | n.a. |
| Belgium | 57.1 | 89.4 | 84.5 | 0.4 | 56.6 | 90.3 | 86.7 | 2.2 | 58.4 |
| Germany | 56.6 | 87.6 | 81.9 | 1.8 | 55.3 | 88.5 | 85.0 | 2.2 | 57.4 |
| Denmark | 60.2 | 89.4 | 85.4 | 2.7 | 59.3 | 90.3 | 84.5 | 4.4 | 59.5 |
| Spain | 57.5 | 89.8 | 78.3 | 1.3 | 57.5 | 90.3 | 86.7 | 1.3 | 57.8 |
| France | 51.8 | 88.5 | 79.2 | 9.7 | 54.0 | 90.3 | 84.5 | 2.7 | 57.6 |
| Greece | 55.8 | 89.4 | 83.6 | 4.9 | 54.9 | 90.3 | 85.8 | 0.9 | 58.2 |
| Italy | 50.4 | 88.9 | 77.0 | 5.3 | 49.1 | 90.3 | 85.4 | 9.3 | 57.0 |
| Ireland | 56.6 | 89.9 | 85.8 | 0.0 | 55.8 | 90.3 | 86.7 | 0.9 | 58.3 |
| Luxembourg | 61.5 | 89.8 | 86.7 | 0.4 | 60.2 | 90.3 | 86.7 | 0.9 | 59.6 |
| Netherlands | 59.7 | 89.8 | 86.7 | 0.0 | 58.4 | 90.3 | 86.7 | 0.9 | 59.1 |
| Portugal | 54.0 | 89.9 | 74.8 | 2.7 | 53.1 | 90.3 | 84.1 | 6.6 | 56.9 |
| UK | 60.6 | 89.9 | 86.7 | 3.5 | 59.3 | 90.3 | 86.7 | 0.9 | 59.7 |
| Austria | 65.5 | 87.2 | 82.3 | 6.2 | 62.4 | 88.1 | 85.0 | 1.8 | 59.8 |
| Sweden | 57.5 | 80.5 | 74.3 | 1.3 | 56.6 | 81.4 | 74.8 | 3.1 | 53.7 |
| Finland | 58.8 | 77.0 | 74.3 | 0.9 | 58.8 | 78.3 | 75.2 | 57.1 | 60.1 |
| Standard deviation | 3.8 | 3.8 | 4.7 | 2.8 | 3.3 | 3.7 | 3.9 | 14.2 | 1.6 |
| Mean | 57.6 | 87.8 | 81.4 | 2.7 | 56.8 | 88.6 | 84.3 | 6.3 | 58.2 |

Source: Langhammer (2005).

that used to construct Table 6.1. The EU offer substantially increases the average "coverage ratio" from 46 to slightly above 58 percent. At the aggregate level the standard deviation would fall from two to 1.6, indicating an increase in uniformity at the EU member state level. In terms of the various modes, commitments in mode 4 improve but remain far below that in other modes. Only Finland's offer on mode 4 is far-reaching, but only for national treatment. In relative terms the smallest expansion in commitment levels occurs for mode 1, possibly reflecting concerns about offshoring. In contrast to mode 1, the increase in the proposed level of bindings for modes 2 and 3 is significant, rising to over 80 percent. For mode 3 market access commitments the variance across EU members would fall, but the structure of commitments remains similar to the pre-Doha status quo, i.e., the "lagging" countries are mostly the same—only Greece would converge to the EU average as a result of the offers that were on the table as of 2004. However, in all cases where national sensitivities on mode 3 appear to remain, the level of proposed commitments on mode 3 is substantially higher than for mode 1.

## GATS: Why So Little Progress?

The EU and the U.S. have among the most comprehensive GATS schedules. Most other WTO members have made substantially fewer commitments. One hypothesis for the limited performance of the GATS is that the forces (export interests) that have been harnessed to allow the reciprocal liberalization of trade in goods do not prevail sufficiently in the services context. Another possibility is uncertainty: binding commitments may need to be preceded and/or complemented by actions to improve the regulation of service markets and ensure that social objectives are met. Yet another possible explanation is that services lend themselves better to bilateral/regional cooperation, reflecting either political or economic considerations (similarity in income levels, geographic proximity, etc.). What follows first briefly discusses the hypotheses just mentioned.

The basic mechanism that makes trade negotiations "work" is that exporters are given incentives to oppose import-competing industries seeking to maintain protection. Negotiations alter the prevailing political economy equilibrium that has generated the status quo set of policies in each country. Insofar as the services agenda revolves around market access, standard reciprocity dynamics should work as well or badly as they do in the case of trade in goods, i.e., resistance to welfare-improving reforms by those currently benefiting from restrictive policies can be overcome by offering export interests better access to foreign markets. Trade agreements can also be a vehicle for improving services regulation and help prevent regulatory capture, through both surveillance and setting rules of the game that make such capture less likely– e.g., a requirement that regulators be independent.

The lack of progress in expanding the coverage of the GATS suggests that reciprocity is not working its magic for services. One potential reason is that the export side of the mechanism may be weaker than in the case of goods. In the case of developing countries—the majority of the WTO membership—most are small and therefore not of great interest to the large players in the WTO, constraining their prospects of negotiating significant additional access to major markets.[5] Moreover, many developing countries are not or do not do not perceive themselves to be (potential) services exporters. A relatively skewed pattern of export interests also prevails in many higher-income countries.

It is helpful to explore the pattern of export interests across "types" of countries across each of the four modes of supply. In the case of mode 1, developing countries tend to be net exporters, while OECD countries engage in substantial two-way trade. A major feature of this type of trade is that it has not been subjected (yet) to major policy barriers. Often mode 1 trade is not constrained at all, although policy can certainly disrupt mode 1 trade. A recent prominent example is on-line gambling. Clearly importing countries may reserve an activity to the State or ban it altogether. But most of the business process outsourcing, call centers, etc. that are growth areas for many countries are not constrained by trade policy measures in the destination or importing country. While there is increasing opposition to mode 1 trade in the EU and U.S. driven by a fear of job losses, outside of government contracts currently little is done to restrict such activities from being "offshored." As discussed further below, the potential for expansion of mode 1 transactions is reduced by existing regulation relating to licensing etc. of service providers. The policy question here is whether there is much scope to agree to mutual recognition or harmonization of regulatory requirements.

Turning to mode 2, most of the export action revolves around travel/tourism. Tourism is frequently a major source of foreign exchange earnings for developing countries, but is also important for the EU and the U.S. However, there are relatively few barriers imposed by "importing" (i.e., the source) countries on tourism. The key policy determinants of tourism performance are under the control of the exporter (the destination country). Export revenue generated depends primarily on measures that the tourism destination country puts in place itself. An exception concerns air travel, as monopoly on bilateral routes can greatly increase the price of air travel and reduce exports of tourism services.[6]

---

5 Note that in contrast to goods, developing countries do not have nonreciprocal preferential access to OECD service markets. That is, there is no GSP for services.

6 In practice the charter industry has offset this constraint to some extent.

Turning to mode 3, most developing countries do not have significant "offensive" interests, in contrast to high-income economies. Both the EU and the U.S. are demandeurs on mode 3, with emerging markets the primary targets. The EU and the U.S. are of course the dominant sources of FDI in services, accounting for both the lion's share of North-North and North-South flows/stocks. Given that both the EU and the U.S. are relatively open to FDI, including in services, the bilateral issues here revolve around specific sectors that are deemed sensitive, and where progress in market opening has been impeded for many years: e.g., aviation, cabotage, and audio-visual services. In contrast, the North-South agenda is much broader, and thus more interesting to a wider set of industries in both countries.

The one mode where all developing countries do confront particularly high barriers and that is therefore of great relevance to potential exporters is mode 4. It is unlikely however that much can be achieved on mode 4 access to high-income country markets, especially for less skilled services activities. Mode 4 is very politically sensitive and in practice, insofar as importing countries are willing to consider relaxing barriers, experience suggests they will do so only on a bilateral basis in a bilateral setting. However, the lack of serious prospects for mode 4 liberalization in the GATS framework effectively removes many potential export interests in many poor developing countries from the process.

The foregoing suggests that a key dimension of the reciprocity mechanism—services exporters—is either missing or much weaker in many WTO members—especially many developing countries—than is true for goods. Exceptions are the large service firms headquartered in high-income economies, in particular the EU and the U.S. These have clear interests in selling more services to both OECD and to the larger developing countries. This is mostly a mode 3 agenda. Another exception is the developing country export interest in mode 4. Thus, if trades are to be restricted within the services arena, it would have to involve deals that are limited to mode 3 exchanges (largely an intra-OECD/large emerging markets affair) or that involve access to developing nations for mode 4 in the OECD (i.e., EU and U.S.) in return for mode 3 access for European and American firms. As mode 4 liberalization on an MFN basis is currently a non-starter, the reciprocity constraint implies that large service firms from the EU and U.S. must be willing to throw their weight behind efforts to reduce protection of agriculture and manufactures to "buy" better access to developing countries. To date, there has been little evidence of such a dynamic emerging in the EU or in the U.S.

There are two other reasons why reciprocity may be a weaker instrument. First, the incentives for domestic political engagement by a variety of groups to favor unilateral liberalization are likely to be stronger for many services. Second, there are likely to be incentives for sector regulators to resist international cooperation on regulatory measures that is anchored in a trade agreement/motivated by trade concerns.

Because inefficient service industries generate costs for downstream users in many sectors, unilateral reform incentives may be larger than for trade in goods and be less susceptible to roll-back, reducing the need to use international commitment mechanisms such as trade agreements. Allowing high cost, low quality services to dominate on a market will be detrimental to almost everyone in an economy, with large users having strong incentives to push for measures—such as deregulation, privatization, and liberalization—that generate more competition in the provision of these upstream suppliers of inputs (Hoekman and Messerlin, 2000). With the exception of the EU—where the Single Market initiative and on-going efforts to integrate markets have played an important role—in practice most reforms implemented by countries since the 1980s have been autonomous. Although for much of this period multilateral commitment mechanisms did not exist and thus were not an option, the extent of unilateral reform that has occurred suggests such mechanisms may not be needed as much as in the case of goods trade.[7]

Hoekman and Messerlin (2000) also argue that the scope for traditional reciprocity-driven services market access negotiations may be more limited than for goods because of concerns relating to regula-

---

[7] Recent research helps explain the unilateral reforms that have been observed in many countries. Grossman and Rossi-Hansberg (2006) develop a model of offshoring of services in which all factors, skilled and unskilled, gain. Markusen, Rutherford and Tarr (2005) conclude that trade in services may be a general equilibrium *complement* for unskilled local labor (in that it fosters overall demand for such labor). Konan and Maskus (2006) find that adjustment costs associated with service-sector reforms may be lower because most services will continue to be produced locally (for technical or economic reasons), after liberalization there will still be demand for labor in services. These results do not imply that there are no losers from services liberalization, but do suggest that there may be fewer losers and more gainers than in the case for goods liberalization.

**Table 6.3 Post-2000 PTAs that Include Services**

| PTA | Entry into Force | Date of Signature | WTO Notification | Negative or Positive List? | GATS-type Market Access Obligation for Mode 3? |
|---|---|---|---|---|---|
| New Zealand—Singapore | Jan '01 | Nov '00 | Sept '01 | Positve | Yes |
| EFTA—Mexico | July '01 | Nov '00 | Aug '01 | Positve | Yes |
| EC—Mexico | Mar '01 | Oct '00 | June '02 | Positve | Yes |
| Chile—Costa Rica | Feb '02 | Oct '99 | May '02 | Negative | No[1] |
| Japan—Singapore | Nov '02 | Jan '02 | Nov '02 | Positve[2] | Yes |
| Singapore—Australia | July '03 | Feb '03 | Oct '03 | Negative | Yes |
| U.S.—Chile | Jan '04 | June '03 | Dec '03 | Negative | Yes |
| U.S.—Singapore | Jan '04 | May '03 | Dec '03 | Negative | Yes |
| Chile—El Salvador | June '02 | Oct '99 | Mar '04 | Negative | No[1] |
| Republic of Korea—Chile | April '04 | Feb '03 | April '04 | Negative | No[1] |
| EC-Chile | Mar '05 | Nov '02 | Nov '05 | Positve | Yes |
| EFTA—Singapore | Jan '03 | June '02 | Jan '03 | Positve | Yes |
| China—HKC | Jan '04 | Sep '03 | Jan '04 | Positve[3] | Yes |
| China—Macao China | Jan '04 | Oct '03 | Jan '04 | Positve[3] | Yes |
| EFTA—Chile | Dec '04 | June '03 | Dec '04 | Positve | Yes |
| U.S.—Australia | Jan '05 | Aug '04 | Dec '04 | Negative | Yes |
| Thailand—Australia | Jan '05 | July '04 | Jan '05 | Positve | Yes |
| Panama—El Salvador | April '03 | March '02 | April '05 | Negative | No[4] |
| Japan—Mexico | April '05 | Sep '04 | April '05 | Negative | No[4] |
| U.S.—Bahrain | Aug '06 | Sep '04 | — | Negative | Yes |
| U.S.—Oman | — | Jan '06 | — | Negative | Yes |
| U.S.—CA + DR | Mar '06 | Aug '05 | Mar '06 | Negative | Yes |
| U.S.—Morocco | Jan '06 | June '04 | Jan '06 | Negative | Yes |
| U.S.—Peru | — | April '06 | — | Negative | Yes |
| Japan—Malaysia | — | Dec '05 | — | Positve | Yes |
| Korea—Singapore | Mar '06 | Aug '05 | Feb '06 | Negative | No |
| U.S.—Colombia | — | Feb '06[5] | — | Negative | Yes |
| Singapore—India | — | June '05 | — | Positve | Yes |

[1] nor for mode 1; [2] Japan used negative list for mode 3 NT; [3] for China; [4] neither for mode 1; [5] conclusion of negotiations.

Source: Roy, Marchetti and Lim (2006).

tory autonomy—a perception that harmonization may not be optimal, and that marginal "quid pro quo" changes to domestic regulatory policies will not enhance welfare, and indeed, could easily lower it. The situation here is very different from that applying to merchandise trade liberalization, where marginal, reciprocal reductions in tariffs will be welfare improving for small countries and the world as a whole, and where reciprocity is needed for large countries to gain from liberalization. Sectoral regulators can be expected to be less than enthusiastic about efforts to negotiate their turf. An additional complicating factor is that successful liberalization in developing countries will often require substantial strengthening of domestic regulatory institutions and infrastructure.

The upshot of all this is that traditional, mercantilist bargaining on a country-pair basis through a request-offer process may not do much to generate additional liberalization and policy reform. Moreover, the limited incentive for many developing countries to use the reciprocity mechanism suggests a shift to a small group, plurilateral approach may be more fruitful. As discussed further below, this may be one way EU-U.S. cooperation on services could support multilateral progress.

## 3. Preferential Trade Agreements: an Alternative?

International cooperation on trade in services is of course not limited to the GATS. Preferential trade agreements (PTAs) to liberalize international transactions in services became increasingly prominent starting in the 1990s. One reason may be the slow progress achieved in the WTO. Although many early PTAs did (and do) not go much beyond the GATS, more recent vintage agreements often do. Roy, Marchetti and Lim (2006) conclude that the substance of the disciplines (rules) that are included in recent PTAs are not dissimilar to those in the GATS, but that many of the PTAs covering services reported to the WTO since 2000 tend to have a sectoral coverage that greatly exceeds the commitments the countries involved made in the GATS (see Table 6.3). This applies both to the existing GATS commitments and the offers that were on the table in the Doha Round as of mid 2006 when the talks were suspended. They also find that PTAs that involve the U.S. have the most comprehensive coverage and deepest levels of commitments. As can be seen from Table 6.3, the U.S. figures much prominently in the list of recent PTAs than does the EU, reflecting the decision of the EU to put new negotiations on PTAs on hold during the Doha Round. However, the 2006 trade strategy of the EU puts great emphasis on regional integration, suggesting that the share of the EU in such PTAs will rise in the future. Historically the EU has accounted for the majority of PTAs notified to the WTO.

Lack of progress in Latin America (the FTAA), the large number of exceptions in many PTAs, and the resistance inside the EU to fully liberalizing intra-EU services trade all illustrate that the challenges to services liberalization may not be that much easier to address regionally than multilaterally. It continues to be the case that most services policy reforms tend to be implemented unilaterally. The experience of the EU—by far the deepest regional initiative to date—illustrates that achieving regional liberalization of services markets is difficult. To a large extent the 1992 Single Market initiative revolved around actions aimed at integrating services markets. Numerous papers have documented how national regulatory regimes continue to segment EU services markets. Kox and Lejour (2006) for example analyze the impacts of remaining policy heterogeneity on trade and investment costs for EU service firms doing business in other EU countries. Complying with idiosyncratic national regulations generates fixed market-entry costs for each export market. They develop an indicator for bilateral policy heterogeneity—based on an OECD dataset of product market regulation—that is used to explain bilateral services trade and services FDI in the EU using a gravity model. They find a strong negative impact of policy heterogeneity costs on intra-EU services trade and FDI. Kox and Lejour project that the original 2004 Services Directive could increase intra-EU services trade by 30 to 62 percent and direct investment in services by 18 to 36 percent.

That said, when it comes to the regulatory agenda, it may be easier/more feasible to implement strategies such as mutual recognition —as done in the EU Services Directive—to lower the costs of regulatory heterogeneity and redundant or duplicative regulatory requirements. That there are potential gains from this is clear, but equally clear is that making progress is difficult. As mentioned, even in the EU there still remains much scope for further liberalization of trade in services.[8] Progress in other regional agreements is much less than in

[8] See, e.g., Kox and Lejour (2006) and Lejour and Palma Verheijden (2004). The latter compare the intensity of intra-EU trade in services with that observed in Canada and find that trade in the latter is two times higher as a share of GDP than in the former.

**Figure 6.1 U.S. Services Exports and Sales by U.S. Foreign Affiliates**

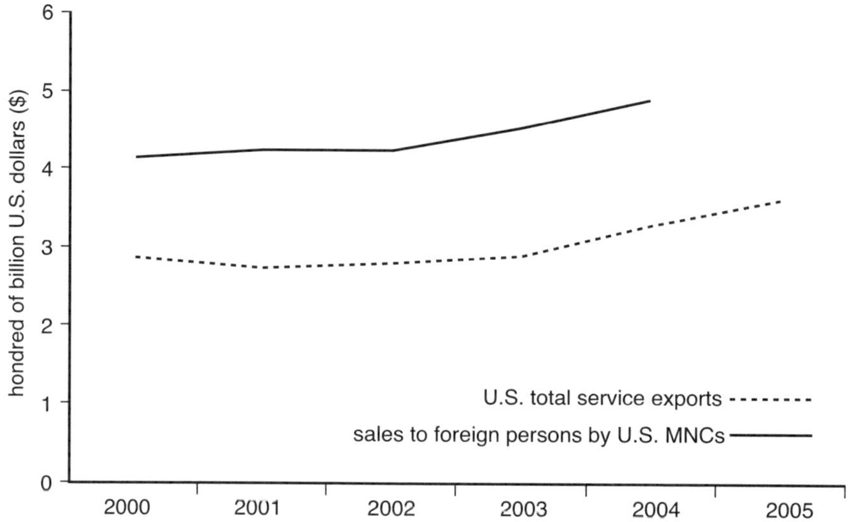


**Figure 6.2 U.S. Services Exports to EU and Sale of Services by U.S. MNCs**

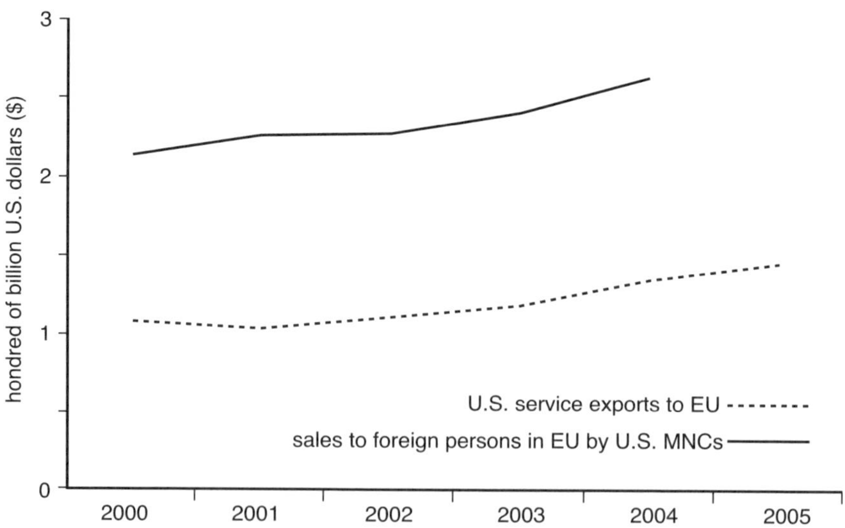

the EU. Park (2002), for example, employs a cross-section gravity analysis of services trade flows and finds that the EU is the only arrangement where intra-regional trade is more than predicted. For other Agreements such as Mercosur, NAFTA, and the Andean pact, trade in services is less than what would be predicted.

The extent of transatlantic integration (more precisely, contestability) of services markets is already significant. About 40 percent of all U.S. cross-border service exports go to the EU-25, while some 35 percent of all EU service exports go to the U.S. These ratios are much higher than for goods trade: 21 percent of U.S. exports of goods go to the EU, whereas the U.S. accounts for 24 percent of EU exports. Shares in EU-U.S. FDI flows and stocks are similarly higher than merchandise trade shares: some 40 to 45 percent of total annual outward and inward FDI flows for the EU-25 go to (come from) the U.S. These FDI flows and stocks in turn generate a significant amount of "foreign affiliate trade in services" (FATS). In the case of the U.S., which collects and publishes detailed data on both cross-border trade in services and sales by affiliates of U.S. services firms in host countries, the overall value of FATS dominates cross-border services trade, illustrating that although services have become more tradable in recent years, geographic proximity remains crucial for the provision of many services. The ratio between FATS and cross-border trade in services for sales to the EU is significantly greater in the bilateral relationship with the U.S. than it is for overall U.S. exports of services (Figures 6.1 and 6.2). This suggests that the EU is more open to FDI from the U.S. than the rest of the world. It is likely that the same is true for the EU-25, although equivalent detailed data on FATS is not available.

## 4. Possible Multilateral Implications of Transatlantic Cooperation on Services

Although the data reveal that transatlantic trade and investment in services is already relatively high, other contributions to this volume make clear that there are still numerous policies that restrict access or violate national treatment in both markets. In the U.S., abstracting from policies that restrict foreign ownership of or participation in specific sectors such as air transport and maritime cabotage, many of these operate at the state level, while in the EU most of the issues concern policies applied by member states, many of which also figure on the agenda of the intra-EU effort to further integrate the European services markets. Recent research on the potential gains from further regulatory reform and harmonization/ mutual recognition initiatives in the EU and the U.S. services relationship concludes that in principle there is a significant incentive to pursue such reform—e.g., OECD (2005) estimates comprehensive services reforms could raise per capita GDP by over 3 percent in the EU and U.S. A key question however is what could be done through *bilateral* cooperation to realize these potential gains—i.e., to implement the needed reforms. To what extent can bilateral EU-U.S. cooperation be an effective means of implementing the needed *domestic* reforms?

Past experience suggests it may be very difficult to harness bilateral cooperation to remove remaining restrictions on market access and national treatment. These barriers are mostly in sensitive sectors where there are long-standing concerns in both the EU and the U.S. about liberalization, partly motivated by cultural and security objectives. To crack these "hard nuts" it is necessary—as is true in the WTO setting—that there be enough on the table to mobilize the internal political forces needed to overcome the opposition of those groups that support the status quo. Given that both the EU and the U.S. are very open to trade in goods (agriculture being of course an exception), and insofar as strongly felt non-economic considerations enter into the equation—as is the case in a number of remaining protected sectors (e.g., audiovisual, maritime cabotage)—putting together an agenda that will allow major progress in further opening remaining services markets is a substantial challenge.

A relevant consideration here is that for large services firms that operate globally—most of them European or American—many of the prevailing regulatory requirements are a cost of doing business that can be overcome relatively easily by hiring locally certified professionals. It is something they would do anyway for good business reasons. The firms that are most affected by regulatory differences are the smaller ones. That suggests it is these firms that will have to organize and push for/support reforms. But their characteristics—small, dispersed, etc.—and the high degree of uncertainty they confront regarding likely benefits for them makes it difficult for the required organization to materialize.

Yet another factor that will affect the power of bilateral cooperation to support national regulatory reform—which is a large part of the proposed transatlantic agenda—is that dealing with regulatory costs (and reducing the associated rents where these exist) will be good for consumers on each side of the Atlantic, but may not do much to increase trade. Instead, the main effect is likely to be more domestic entry into the markets concerned. Not only are there transactions costs associated with international competition, the need to employ local labor and other factors of production in order to sell services—many of which remain difficult to trade via mode 1—may imply that EU (U.S.) firms may not have that much of an advantage over U.S. (EU) firms in newly opened market segments. If so, this will have implications for the political economy dynamics—it may reduce the incentive for service firms to lobby for/support bilateral opening/cooperation.

Progress to date on the services agenda under the Transatlantic Economic Partnership has been limited. Perhaps the most important element of this agenda—an EU-U.S. air services agreement—has yet to be achieved, although the 2006 phased open skies agreement suggests that progress towards the realization of free trade in aviation services may emerge over time. Little progress has been made on mutual recognition of professional qualifications. All this suggests that the return to bilateral efforts to open services markets further—if defined as the removal of explicit discriminatory restrictions—may be relatively low. If the EU and U.S. are unlikely to achieve much more than they have already implemented unilaterally and what they have committed to (will commit) in the GATS, perhaps the rest of the world has little need to worry about EU-U.S. cooperation in this area. At the same time, the implications of this scenario for EU and U.S. citizens are that there would be little in the way of additional benefits from cooperation.

Much of the discussion on the possible content of transatlantic cooperation in the services area has centered on differences in regulatory regimes for specific sectors or activities, as opposed to relaxing discriminatory barriers to trade. Greater acceptance of the principle of mutual recognition—agreement that regulatory standards in an area are essentially or substantively equivalent—could do much to enhance the contestability of markets and reduce compliance costs by eliminating duplicative and redundant requirements. Achieving progress on this front is difficult and will take time and mutual trust and understanding of regulatory systems and compliance—a precondition is not just agreement on the equivalence or adequacy of the substantive norms that apply in each market, but also that these norms are enforced. The approach being proposed in the Framework for Advancing Transatlantic Economic Integration (EU-U.S. Summit, 2007) stresses dialogue: the establishment of joint mechanisms and processes to assess the impact of regulatory regimes and to enhance timely access to information on proposed regulations, and a Transatlantic Economic Council to guide the process and review progress. From a multilateral perspective, progress towards reducing redundant regulatory costs through the type of "soft law" and non-binding cooperation will clearly benefit the EU and U.S. However, only a number of issues relating to financial markets are mentioned as a "lighthouse priority project" in the 2007 Summit: accounting standards (mutual recognition of U.S. GAAP and the IFRS), auditor oversight, reinsurance regulation, and mutual recognition in the filed of securities regulation ("where appropriate"). Other services do not figure as a priority.

What would be the effect of transatlantic regulatory cooperation and recognition on the rest of the world? As long as regulatory cooperation is not explicitly discriminatory, firms that have established in either the EU or U.S. will be able to contest the other market more easily, whatever their "nationality." The same will not necessarily be true for cross-border trade, however, as home country regulation in third countries may not be accepted by either the EU or the U.S., even if equivalent to what is required by regulators in those markets. Thus, a bias towards FDI/mode 3 trade may emerge. However, on balance the type of regulatory cooperation and "learning" that is envisaged in the proposed EU-U.S. framework is unlikely to be detrimental to the rest of the world, as long as the EU and the U.S. apply policy reforms on a nondiscriminatory basis whenever this is feasible. This will depend on what the precise nature of an agreement is—e.g., recognition of qualifications or home country licensing and regulatory supervision can only be extended to other countries if they satisfy the substantive requirements (minimum standards).

## 5. Transatlantic Cooperation in Support of Multilateralism

While there clearly are potential gains from deeper transatlantic cooperation for EU/U.S. firms and households, arguably most of the potential gains from cooperation are to be found at the global level, along the lines discussed previously—better access to emerging markets (through FDI—mode 3) and enhanced access to the EU and U.S. markets through modes 1 and 4. Just to give one example: lack of portability of health insurance in the EU and the U.S. that limits reimbursement of medical expenses to certified national facilities imposes both a major cost and reduces trade opportunities significantly. The potential impact of permitting portability of insurance could be substantial. Mattoo and Rathindran (2006) find that extending health insurance coverage in the U.S. to overseas care for just fifteen types of tradable treatments could produce savings of over $1 billion a year even if only one in ten American patients travel abroad for treatment. The lower costs of health services abroad offer not just cost savings but the opportunity to extend medical benefits to people who currently are not insured. However, the likely destination countries for such services are more likely to be Mexico, Central America or India than the EU. Similarly, there is great potential for increasing trade through mode 1, given that the current magnitude of international outsourcing/offshoring is only a few percent of the overall extent of outsourcing of services tasks—most of which remains intra-national.

This economic argument for taking a broader (global) view of the services liberalization/reform agenda can be complemented by—and be complementary to—the realization of the non-economic objectives that reportedly may motivate EU and U.S. policymakers in pursuing transatlantic cooperation: to overcome some of the major policy differences between the EU and U.S. in recent years (global warming; national security). Shifting the focus of cooperation to complement the pursuit of narrow economic bilateral interests through actions to bolster the multilateral trading system and the ability of developing countries to exploit trade opportunities and improve domestic regulation may help to achieve shared foreign policy/security objectives. What follows sketches out some areas where EU-U.S. cooperation could support both the global good and shared bilateral interests.

Three specific actions could be pursued by the EU and U.S. to attain both economic and non-economic objectives

1. engage in the WTO along plurilateral lines in a way that generates economically meaningful results for both the EU-U.S. and the rest of the world;

2. develop a joint approach to provide financial and technical assistance to low-income countries to improve service regulation and enforcement; and

3. join forces on financing a global initiative on transparency of services policies and performance/outcomes.[9]

## *Nondiscriminatory Plurilateralism*

It was mentioned in section two that moving forward in the GATS context—which arguably offers the greatest potential gains for both the EU and the U.S.—might best be pursued on a plurilateral basis where the outcome is extended to all WTO members on a MFN basis. Analogous to what was done in the Information Technology Agreement, agreement could be sought among a subset of WTO members regarding the sectors that are of common economic interest and the types of commitments to be made. The idea is to create a focal point for liberalizing commitments—either by agreeing on a certain threshold level of commitments or via a "zero-for-zero" analogue—e.g., the number of sectors or sub-sectors without any national treatment exceptions.[10] The prospects for small group approach were enhanced by the Hong Kong ministerial meeting, which explicitly put forward the option of "plurilateral" negotiations among a subset of willing members. Past experience suggests that for liberalization agreements to be applied on a MFN basis, the "internalization" ratio needs to be fairly high—on the order of 90 percent of total trade. As the EU and the U.S. dominate many (most) service sectors, cooperation between them would already greatly facilitate satisfying this constraint.

---

[9] The focus here is only on services. As noted in Burwell (2007), there are other areas in which joint action could make a difference in assisting developing countries, e.g., agreement on adopting rules of origin for beneficiaries of trade preferences that offer the greatest degree of market access.

[10] See e.g., Mattoo and Wüntsch (2004). As noted previously, the rationale for a small group approach is not to let poor country governments "off the hook" but to recognize that there is little they can do to influence the outcome of market access negotiations. As they have few incentives to play this game, they will find it hard to argue domestically that the *quid pro quo* received justifies potentially painful domestic reforms.

## *National Treatment vs. Disciplines on Domestic Regulation*

As reciprocity dynamics depend on export interests, the focus should be on policies that most directly restrict access to foreign markets. A corollary "benefit" of targeting such policies is that it permits accepting whatever general regulatory requirements are in place in a market. If so, regulatory agencies should be much less concerned about the outcome of the negotiating process.

The provisions of the GATS dealing with domestic regulations are weak. The reason is straightforward: effective multilateral disciplines can rapidly encroach upon national sovereignty and could unduly limit regulatory freedom. The weakness of the disciplines on domestic regulation is often argued to reduce the relevance of the GATS as a pro-competitive instrument. Stronger disciplines for domestic regulations could be beneficial in enhancing the contestability of service markets and lowering the costs and increasing the quality of services. Indeed, as domestic regulation applies to all firms whatever their nationality, it may be a more important source of inefficiency/costs than policies that discriminate against foreign suppliers.[11]

That said, dealing with regulatory differences is much more difficult that identifying discriminatory policies. The EU demonstrates how hard it is to pursue policy harmonization and mutual recognition. Pursuing effective horizontal disciplines for regulation in the GATS is orders of magnitude harder, even if limited to a small group setting, given the absence of a clear commitment to pursue market integration and the absence of the types of supra-national institutions that exist in the EU. This observation applies equally to the EU and the U.S., where the 50 states are the loci for much of the regulation that affects the ability to provide services (and the costs of doing so). While making discriminatory policies the primary discipline to be negotiated would cover only a share of the prevailing restrictions, it is not trivial. Thus, national treatment implies the right of establishment as long as domestic firms are permitted to contest a market. Given that FDI in

[11] That is, the "rectangles" associated with regulations that raise costs for all users, limit entry possibility for all new service firms independent of nationality, or are simply redundant because similar but different rules already apply to foreign firms in their home market may be much larger than the "triangles" generated by the efficiency losses from (the tariff equivalent of) discriminatory policies. See Prowse (2006) for an in-depth discussion of aid for trade issues and options.

services will create employment and is often subject to less opposition than efforts at regulatory harmonization or recognition (Messerlin, 2006), this can be an effective way to increase competition on markets.

While the proposed approach will certainly generate gains from international cooperation that are less than if cooperation were to extend to regulatory measures that segment markets, it is not that clear in any event that much can be done through the GATS on domestic regulation. By removing one, important, reason for regulators to oppose their governments making commitments in "their" area, resistance from a powerful set of interest groups in all countries could be greatly reduced. A focus on policies that discriminate would not only diminish fears of the intrusiveness of the GATS, it would also reduce uncertainty regarding the implications of making commitments.

### *"Aid for Trade" and Adjustment Assistance: Complementing the GATS Framework*

Benefits from liberalization—and thus GATS commitments—may be limited or nonexistent in the absence of appropriate regulation. In many developing countries governments confront substantial uncertainty as what complementary measures may need to be put in place to support liberalization. Developing countries also confront resource constraints—the needed institutions and human capital may not be available or in very short supply. Substantial uncertainty may also prevail as to the size and distribution of the (adjustment) costs and likely benefits of reforms. The increasing tradability of services (through offshoring and international outsourcing) will also generate adjustment costs, the prospect (fear) of which has already generated calls for limiting liberalization and restricting trade, in both developed and developing countries.

Addressing such concerns is important in both maintaining the existing level of openness to services trade and in further opening markets to services trade and investment. Policy advice and assistance for regulatory reform and public investments in services infrastructure is of course provided by international financial institutions and specialized agencies. However, there is virtually no link between these processes and services negotiations in the WTO. This disconnect persists even though it is clear that improved regulation—ranging from prudential regulation in financial services to pro-competitive regulation of network-based services—may be critical to realizing the benefits of services liberalization. Weaknesses in existing mechanisms for prudential or pro-competitive regulation, the need to alleviate adjustment costs, and the desire to ensure universal access in liberalized markets are all examples of potential good reasons to hold back on making binding liberalization commitments. Such considerations may help explain the limited use that has been made by poor countries of the GATS and their resistance to making additional specific commitments to open/guarantee access to their markets.

Development assistance that focuses on strengthening domestic regulation and attaining social objectives such as universal access to a specific service could do much to change this situation. Both the EU and U.S. have supported the call for an increase in "aid for trade" that has been made in recent years, most recently at the 2005 Hong Kong WTO ministerial.[12] It is noteworthy that services have not attracted much attention in the aid for trade discussions to date. Much of the aid for trade agenda at the country level revolves around improving the quality and cost of services. It goes far beyond technical assistance to help countries make market access commitments, and extends to assistance for regulatory strengthening and resources to strengthen services-related infrastructure. To benefit from trade opportunities, many developing countries need to bolster the competitiveness of their firms and farmers by lowering the cost of, and increase access to, services such as transport, finance, and communications. This in turn requires a mix of policy reforms—including liberalization—as well as investments in infrastructure, training, and institutional strengthening. A joint effort by the EU and the U.S. to channel more assistance to these areas would help increase the benefits that accrue to these countries. A concerted aid effort does not imply ceasing to seek to negotiate binding disciplines. Instead it would put greater stress on the improvement of service sector performance and the use of (need for) assistance to attain such improvements.

[12] See Prowse (2006) for an in-depth discussion of aid for trade issues and options.

## *Transparency—Documenting Services Policies and Their Impacts*

The functions of the WTO extend beyond rulemaking and enforcement. One of its tasks is to increase the transparency of member trade policies through the Trade Policy Review Mechanism (TPRM) (Art. III WTO). The objective of the TPRM is "...achieving greater transparency in, and understanding of, the trade policies and practices of Members... [through] the regular collective appreciation and evaluation of the full range of individual Members' trade policies and practices and their impact on the functioning of the multilateral trading system. It is not, however, intended to serve as a basis for the enforcement of specific obligations under the Agreements or for dispute settlement procedures, or to impose new policy commitments on Members." (Annex 3, WTO). Annex 3 WTO, Section B states further that "Members recognize the inherent value of domestic transparency of government decision-making on trade policy matters... and agree to encourage and promote greater transparency within their own systems, acknowledging that the implementation of domestic transparency must be on a voluntary basis and take account of each Member's legal and political systems." Services are included in the ambit of the TPRM. Indeed, the WTO is currently the only multilateral body that has the mandate to review all the services trade-related policies of countries.

In practice, despite the TPRM, rather little is known about national services trade-related policies.[13] The same is true of services "performance". The WTO could be a much more effective focal point for regular interactions on and monitoring of the services policies that are applied by its members. No other organization has as strong an incentive to do so. The absence of a comprehensive effort to document and monitor national service sector policies is in part a reflection of the revealed preferences of WTO members, which in turn reflect a mix of resource constraints and a desire to prevent regular and multilateral scrutiny of policies. Only the former is a legitimate reason for the status quo. A concerted effort by the EU and U.S. to finance a global data collection effort would remove the resource constraint.

[13] One reason for this is the positive list approach that was chosen to determine the coverage of GATS specific commitments. In contrast to the negative list approach applied in U.S. free trade agreements, a positive list does not generate full information the extent to which applied policies discriminate against foreign firms.

Financing a major effort to compile data on applied policies, prevailing market structures and indicators of service sector performance may do more to promote global reform in the medium term than a focus on (bilateral) market access negotiations. Reform requires domestic constituencies to implement and sustain it—comprehensive data on policies and outcomes will allow think tanks, industries, NGOs, etc. both to compare their own countries to others and let researchers assess the effects of prevailing policies, and the impacts of liberalization. At present no such comprehensive data on policies or performance exists. It is a global public good, which helps to explain why it is underprovided. Joint EU-U.S. leadership in providing this public good could do much to promote further market access and related reforms in all countries.

More frequent and in-depth analysis of services trade policies in WTO members—as well as the extent to which high-income countries have provided assistance to address priorities that were identified by developing countries, mentioned earlier—could support more constructive engagement of business and NGOs with the WTO and the GATS. If WTO members were to expand the transparency mandate of the organization to make the WTO a focal point for multilateral discussions and assessments of the state of members' service sectors, the institution could do much to help address the needs of its poorer members by raising the policy profile of the services agenda in these countries and identifying where investments/assistance are needed. By combining its commitment and monitoring "technologies" to mobilize liberalization commitments that are conditional on assistance, and monitoring the delivery and effectiveness of such assistance, the process could play a useful role in both helping members improve the performance of service sectors and expand the coverage of the GATS.

While ideally pursued through the WTO, the proposed transparency initiative can be implemented (i.e., financed) bilaterally, with the actual process outsourced to one or more organizations that have the capacity to manage the collection and compilation of the required information. The effort should involve research and public interest bodies in all the countries concerned. These bodies can do much to help shed light and build consensus by identifying good (better) policies, their economic impact, including distributional effects within and across countries, and whether alternative instruments exist that could attain governmental or societal objectives (more) efficiently.

## 6. Concluding Remarks

Increasing the contestability of service markets is likely to generate significant welfare gains for all countries. This applies as much to the EU and the U.S. as it does to lower-income nations. In contrast to many other WTO Members, both the EU and the U.S. are already relatively open to international competition in services. Both parties have among the most comprehensive commitments in the GATS. Bilateral trade and investment flows of services are already large. This is not to deny there are barriers to bilateral trade in services. Several important sectors remain relatively closed. However, the main factor that segments markets is regulatory in nature. This is clearly recognized in the 2007 Framework for Advancing Transatlantic Economic Integration. However, although well worth pursuing, making concrete progress to towards convergence and/or mutual recognition will not be easy. The EU experience illustrates that this is a difficult process that will take substantial time and require concerted attention from policymakers.

From a narrow economic perspective, a case can be made that greater potential gains from international cooperation between the EU and the U.S. that targets services are to be found in other markets, in particular emerging markets. That suggests attention and resources should also be directed to the WTO. A joint effort by the EU and U.S. to cooperate in moving the multilateral liberalization agenda forward could generate not just larger benefits in terms of improved access to markets for EU and U.S. firms, but also generate benefits for developing countries—where the potential gains from services reforms are very large. To date, the GATS has not been a very effective mechanism to promote greater liberalization. Bilateral agreements are sometimes more ambitious, but even if they are more effective—the jury is still out—they constitute a piecemeal approach. A concerted effort by the EU and the U.S. toward nondiscriminatory plurilateralism; directing "aid for trade" to the services agenda in developing economies; and investing in global transparency, monitoring and evaluation could do much to build and maintain support for liberalization and open markets, not just in developing countries but, as importantly, in the EU and the U.S. The challenge is as much to keep markets open as it is to further open them.

## References

Arnold, Jens, Beata Smarzynska Javorcik and Aaditya Mattoo. 2006. "The Productivity Effects of Services Liberalization: Evidence from the Czech Republic," Policy Research Working Paper 4109. World Bank, Washington, D.C.

Arnold, Jens, Aaditya Mattoo and Gaia Narciso. 2006. "Services inputs and firm productivity in Sub-Saharan Africa: Evidence from firm-level data," Policy Research Working Paper 4048. World Bank, Washington, D.C.

Adlung, Rudolf and Martin Roy, 2005. "Turning Hills into Mountains? Current Commitments Under the General Agreement on Trade in Services and Prospects for Change," *Journal of World Trade*, 39:1161-1194.

Burwell, Frances. 2007. *Transatlantic Leadership for a New Global Economy.* Atlantic Council Policy Paper (April).

Eschenbach, Felix and Bernard Hoekman. 2006a. "Services Policy Reform and Economic Growth in Transition Economies, 1990-2004," *Review of World Economics*, 142(4).

Eschenbach, Felix and Bernard Hoekman. 2006b. "Services Policies in Transition Economies: On the EU and WTO as Commitment Mechanisms," *World Trade Review* 5(3): 415-43.

Grossman, Gene and Esteban Rossi-Hansberg. 2006. "Trading Tasks: A Simple Theory of Offshoring," Princeton, mimeo.

Hoekman, Bernard. 1996. "Assessing the General Agreement on Trade in Services," in Will Martin and L. Alan Winters (eds.), *The Uruguay Round and the Developing Countries.* Cambridge: Cambridge University Press.

Hoekman, Bernard. 2006. "Liberalizing Trade in Services: A Survey," World Bank Policy Research Working Paper 4030.

Hoekman, Bernard and Aaditya Mattoo. 2007. "Services, Economic Development and the Doha Round: Exploiting the Comparative Advantage of the WTO," in Donna Lee and Rorden Wilkinson (eds.), *The WTO after Hong Kong*, London: Routledge.

Hoekman, Bernard and Patrick Messerlin. 2000. "Liberalizing Trade in Services: Reciprocal Negotiations and Regulatory Reform," in Pierre Sauvé and Robert Stern (eds.), *Services 2000: New Directions in Services Trade Liberalization*, Washington D.C.: Brookings Institution, 487-508.

Jensen, Jesper, Thomas Rutherford and David Tarr (forthcoming), "The Impact of Liberalizing Barriers to Foreign Direct Investment in Services: The Case of Russian Accession to the World Trade Organization," *Review of Development Economics.*

Konan, Denise Eby and Keith E. Maskus, 2006. "Quantifying the Impact of Services Liberalization in a Developing Country," *Journal of Development Economics* 81:142-62.

Kox, Henk and Arjan Lejour. 2006. "The Effects of the Services Directive on Intra-EU Trade and FDI," *Revue Economique*, 57(4): 747-69.

Langhammer, Rolf. 2005. "The EU Offer of Service Trade Liberalization in the Doha Round: Evidence of a Not-Yet-Perfect Customs Union," *Journal of Common Market Studies* 43(2), 311-25.

Lejour, Arjan and Jan-Willem de Palva Verheijden. 2004. "Services Trade within Canada and the European Union," CPB Discussion Paper 42, The Hague, Netherlands.

Markusen, James, Thomas Rutherford and David Tarr. 2005. "Trade and Direct Investment in Producer Services and the Domestic Market for Expertise," *Canadian Journal of Economics* 38(3): 758-77.

Mattoo, Aaditya and Randeep Rathindran. 2006. "How Health Insurance Inhibits Trade in Health Services," *Health Affairs* 25(2): 358-368.

Mattoo, Aaditya and Sasha Wünsch. 2004. "Pre-empting Protectionism in Services: The WTO and Outsourcing," *Journal of International Economic Law* 7: 765-800.

Mattoo, Aaditya, Randeep Rathindran and Arvind Subramanian. 2006. "Measuring Services Trade Liberalization and its Impact on Economic Growth: An Illustration," *Journal of Economic Integration* 21:64-98.

Messerlin, Patrick. 2006. *Europe after the 'No' Votes.* London: Institute of Economic Affairs.

OECD, 2005. "The Benefits of Liberalising Product Markets and Reducing Barriers to International Trade and Investment: The Case of the United States and the European Union," Economics Department Working Paper 432, Paris, June.

Park, Soon-Chan. 2002. "How Far has Regional Integration Deepened? Evidence from Trade in Services," KIEP Working Paper 02-17.

Prowse, Susan. 2006 "Aid for Trade: Increasing Support for Trade Adjustment and Integration—A Proposal," in S. Evenett and B. Hoekman (eds.), *Economic Development and Multilateral Cooperation* (Palgrave-McMillan).

Roy, Martin, Juan Marchetti and Hoe Lim. 2006. "Services Liberalization in the New Generation of Preferential Trade Agreements: How Much Further than the GATS?" WTO Staff Working paper ERSD-2006-07.

Rutherford, Thomas, David Tarr and Oleksandr Shepotylo, 2006. "The Impact of WTO Accession and the DDA: The Importance of Liberalization of Barriers against FDI in Services for Growth and Poverty Reduction," in Thomas Hertel and L. Alan Winters (eds.), *Poverty and the WTO* (Palgrave and World Bank), 467-96.

# *Chapter 7*

# Deepening the Transatlantic Economy: The Key Role of Services

*Daniel S. Hamilton and Joseph P. Quinlan*

Service activities are the sleeping giant of the transatlantic economy—an economic factor that, if awakened and unbound, would further deepen the commercial stakes between the United States and Europe and enhance the global competitiveness of both parties. At present, however, the full potential of the transatlantic services economy remains hampered by internal barriers, regulation, and obstacles in the U.S. and in Europe.

## The Size and Nature of the Transatlantic Services Economy

Services sector reform offers such potential benefits to the U.S.-European economic relationship because of the size and nature of the transatlantic economy. No global commercial artery is as large and as thick as that which the United States and Europe. Though often overlooked, the transatlantic economy remains the most important global economic entity in the world due in part to the transatlantic convergence in such key areas as industry deregulation (media, energy and telecoms), technology use, and financial market liberalization. Similar stages of economic development and commonly shared economic principles have also played a part in making the transatlantic economy the leading player in the global economy. Bolstered by all of the above, the majority of U.S. and European foreign investment flows continues to be directed toward each other, rather than to low-cost developing nations or "big emerging markets."

Indeed, despite market liberalization measures in India, robust economic growth in China, the economic revival of central Europe, or sweeping privatization measures in Latin America —the majority of U.S. and European foreign direct investment throughout the 1990s, and throughout this decade, have been directed at each other.

Over the 1990s, for instance, six countries in Europe were among the top ten destinations of U.S. foreign investment. The United Kingdom ranked first again, followed by Canada (2), the Netherlands (3), Switzerland (4), Mexico (5), Ireland (6), Germany (7), Singapore (8), Japan (9) and Italy (10). Moreover, U.S. investment stakes in Europe have expanded sharply this decade, with Europe attracting over half of all total U.S. foreign direct investment over the 2000-06 time frame. The bias towards Europe runs counter to the hype and angst associated with U.S. outsourcing to such low-cost locales like China and India, and the common belief that it is the low-cost destinations of East Asia that have attracted the bulk of U.S. investment.

U.S. foreign direct investment to China and India has jumped dramatically this decade, notably to China. Total U.S. investment to China, for instance, surged to nearly $11 billion (on a cumulative basis) in the first half of this decade, nearly double U.S. flows to China in the second half of the 1990s. Although that represents a dramatic rise, it is important to put this in perspective. U.S. investment in the tiny European country of Ireland over the same period ($36 billion), for instance, was three times larger than U.S. investment in China. Similarly, although U.S. foreign investment to India doubled in the first half of this decade to $2.5 billion, over the same period U.S. firms ploughed more capital into such smaller European economies like Norway ($3 billion), Denmark ($5 billion) and Belgium ($6 billion).

The discrepancy in U.S. investment flows to Ireland, Denmark and other European nations on the one hand, versus U.S. investment in China and India on the other, reflects many impediments that plague inflows to developing nations. A nation such as Ireland, on the other hand, remains attractive due to its low-cost, English-speaking labor force, first class infrastructure, and access to the larger European Union market. U.S. firms have been drawn to Denmark on account of its technological skills, to Norway due to its natural resources, and to Belgium for a variety of reasons, including its world-class infrastructure, access to the EU market and Brussels' position as the center of political power within the European Union. In contrast, securing an investment stake in India and China, while attractive on paper, is a much more laborious process, requiring more time, due diligence and investment capital, on account of the many deficiencies still plaguing both nations.

## Europe's Investment Bias Towards the United States

The collapse of the Berlin Wall and the demise of communism opened new markets right in the backyard of western Europe, and not unexpectedly, European multinationals jumped at the opportunity. Europe's leading firms ploughed billions into Hungary, Poland and the Czech Republic over the 1990s, drawn by the region's cheap labor, raw materials, and new market opportunities. Late in the decade, the prospects of EU enlargement sustained healthy investment inflows to central Europe.

Yet, despite western Europe's investment push into central Europe over the 1990s, the amount of capital sunk in such places as Hungary, Poland and others pales in comparison to the amount of capital sent across the Atlantic over the same period. After averaging $22.2 billion over the first half of the 1990s, foreign direct investment inflows to the U.S. from Europe soared to an annual average of nearly $110 billion in the second half of the decade, marking one of the most explosive periods of inward foreign investment in U.S. history. For the entire decade, European firms sank nearly $660 billion into the United States, accounting for roughly three-quarters of total U.S. investment inflows over the 1990s. European investors accounted for a similar percentage again in the first half of this decade, with the United Kingdom, Switzerland and France ranked as the top three foreign investors in the U.S. over the 2000-04 period.

Many variables lie behind the large and expanding European investment stake in the United States. As the largest and wealthiest markets in the world, the U.S. is considered too important to neglect. As Krish Prabhu, chief operating officer of Alcatel at the time, put it to the *Financial Times*," So much of company strategy is driven out of the United States today. No serious player can afford not to have a presence there." In addition to market access, many European firms have entered the U.S. to obtain U.S. technological capabilities, or so-called "created assets." Other firms have crossed the Atlantic to gain greater market access in U.S. services sectors like utilities, financial services and telecommunications. Indeed, greater service linkages between the United States and Europe have been at the heart of greater transatlantic deepening.

## Deeper Transatlantic Convergence through Services

Cross-border investment in services has been a particularly important factor powering the surge in transatlantic investment over the past decade and a half. Once national in character, various service activities in the United States and Europe have been fused and are now more transatlantic in nature. Functions that were once considered nontradable (data processing, education, medical services) are now being traded regularly. Activities long classified as domestic endeavors (advertising, legal services, consulting) today easily take place across borders. Industries in both the U.S. and Europe that were once the domain of the public sector (telecommunications, insurance, electric utilities) have been privatized and opened to foreign competition. Both the European Union and Switzerland opened and deregulated their telecommunications markets at the start of 1998, which came on the heels of industry deregulation in such sectors as utilities, insurance and financial services.

Many of these national efforts to liberalize service activities in both the U.S. and Europe were encouraged and advanced in part by supporting multilateral trade agreements. The General Agreement on Trade in Services (GATS), for instance, was chief among them. The agreement, reached in 1995, was the first multilateral deal to provide enforceable rights covering trade and investment in the services sector.

Meanwhile, under the auspices of the World Trade Organization, GATS and two other seminal multilateral deals—the Information Technology Agreement (ITA) and the Basic Telecommunications Agreement—were concluded in the second half of the 1990s. The ITA helped eliminate tariffs on a range of information technology products and promote trade in computer hardware, software, and semiconductor manufacturing equipment and other products. The Basic Telecommunications Agreement, meanwhile, was the first multilateral telecommunications trade package ever reached and was signed by 69 nations, which accounted for more than 90 percent of world telecom revenue. In particular, the agreement paved the way for more foreign investment and participation in telecommunications services and facilities in both the United States and Europe. In general, the Information Technology and Basic Telecommunications agreements helped construct an information highway linking the United States with Europe.

The agreements came into effect at the end of the decade and have subsequently underpinned robust levels of transatlantic cross-border foreign direct investment in telecommunications, software, semiconductors, scientific instruments, banking, insurance and the securities market.

Another critical element promoting more transatlantic services linkages was the European Union's Single Market program, announced in the second half of the 1980s and implemented in the early 1990s. The program triggered a wave of EU-wide restructuring and deregulation of services, fostering greater U.S. foreign investment in services across Europe. Intra-EU services investment also rose as the Single Market was implemented. This helped create even larger and more competitive European service giants that ultimately targeted the United States as a primary source of growth area in the late 1990s.

Transatlantic services investment in such sectors as electricity, telecommunications, water, and various business services (like advertising and legal services) soared over the 1990s, with mergers and acquisitions the most widely used mode of entry by transnationals. Indeed, massive deal making between and among the services giants of the transatlantic economy fueled the global boom in M&A over the second half of the 1990s. According to the United Nations:

> On average, more than three-quarters of global M&A transactions in the services sector took place among developed countries during 1987-2003. Intra-Western Europe transactions (the bulk of which comprise intra-EU transactions) and transatlantic transactions dominated the picture. Led by U.S. and European service leaders, services accounted for 64 deals among the top 100 cross-border M&A deals over the 1996-2003 period, versus 36 deals of the top 100 over the 1987-1995 timeframe. Viewed in another way, roughly three-quarters of U.S. foreign investment to Europe in the first half of this decade was in service activities. Services also accounted for nearly 80 percent of total European investment in the U.S. over the same period.

The role of services in underpinning transatlantic investment flows has also been shaped by the accelerating pace of technological change. In Europe and many other parts of the world, technology advances have appreciably lowered the cost of communications, making it more feasible and efficient to retrieve process and disseminate multiple forms of information. Just as container ships made the physical export of goods possible in the past, fiber-optic cables have made it possible to export more data, information and other knowledge-based services that used to be considered non-tradable. In short, communications technology increasingly allows firms to split and disperse parts of service functions to foreign affiliates or to non-equity joint partners.

As communication costs have fallen, the information infrastructure has expanded and the internet has proliferated, knowledge-based services of both the United States and Europe have become more linked, promoting more trade and foreign investment in services. Industry deregulation, a more liberal investment environment and falling communication costs all converged in the 1990s to drive a transatlantic investment boom in services. Other variable supporting transatlantic services investment include the rising share of services in economic activity on both sides of the Atlantic; the growing services intensity of the production of goods; and greater competitive pressures in services markets that have pushed firms to seek markets abroad and strengthen their competitiveness.

Today, the services economies of the United States and Europe have never been as intertwined as they are today, notably in such activities as financial services, telecommunications, utilities, insurance, advertising, computer services and other related functions.

## Enhanced Economic Integration through Services

Following in the footsteps of manufactures, U.S. and European services companies now deliver their services more through foreign affiliate sales than through trade. In the 1970s and 1980s, firms delivered services primarily via trade. In the 1990s, however, foreign affiliate sales became the chief mode of delivery.

Sales of services by U.S. foreign affiliates in Europe soared from $85 billion in 1994 to roughly $264 billion in 2004, the last year of available data. That marks more than a three-fold increase from the early 1990s, and was about double the $134 billion in U.S. services exports to Europe in 2004.

**Figure 7.1: U.S.-Europe Services Linkages**

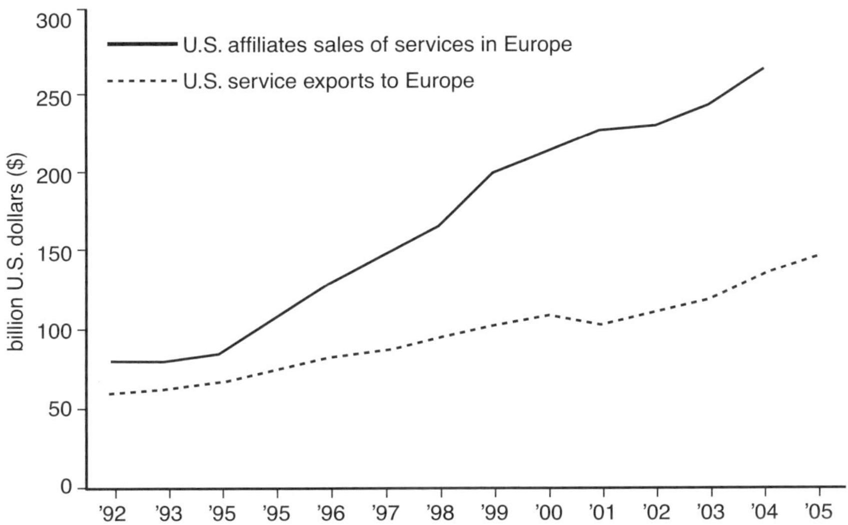


Source: Bureau of Economic Analysis, U.S. Department of Commerce

Europe is the most important market in the world for U.S. foreign affiliate sales of services, just as it the most important market for U.S. foreign affiliate sales of goods. Indeed, of total affiliate services sales of $490 billion in 2004, Europe accounted for 54 percent of the total, with Asia (with a share of 23.3 percent) and Latin America (11.7 percent) a distant second and third, respectively.

By country, the United Kingdom, whose various services sectors are most aligned with those of the U.S. accounted for the largest share of U.S. affiliate sales not only in Europe but also the world. In fact, foreign affiliate service sales in the UK in 2004 ($105 billion) were nearly as large as total foreign affiliate services sales in all of Asia ($113 billion). In Europe, Germany ($29.6 billion), France ($28 billion), and the Netherlands ($19 billion) trailed the UK.

Sales of services by U.S. affiliates of European firms have also soared over the past decade. As Europe's investment position in services has expanded in the U.S., so have foreign affiliate sales of services in the U.S. The latter totaled $260 billion in 2004 versus $86 billion in 1994, a three-fold increase. U.S. services imports from Europe expanded over the same period, by roughly 120 percent, well below

**Figure 7.2 Services Sales of U.S. Foreign Affiliates Abroad – Europe vs. China**

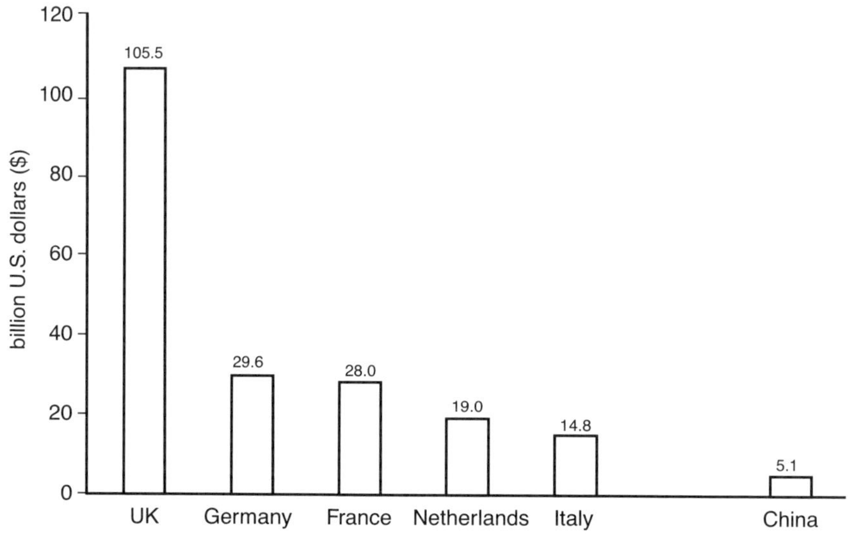


Source: Bureau of Economic Analysis

**Figure 7.3 Sales of Services to Europe by U.S. Affiliates, by Country, 2004**

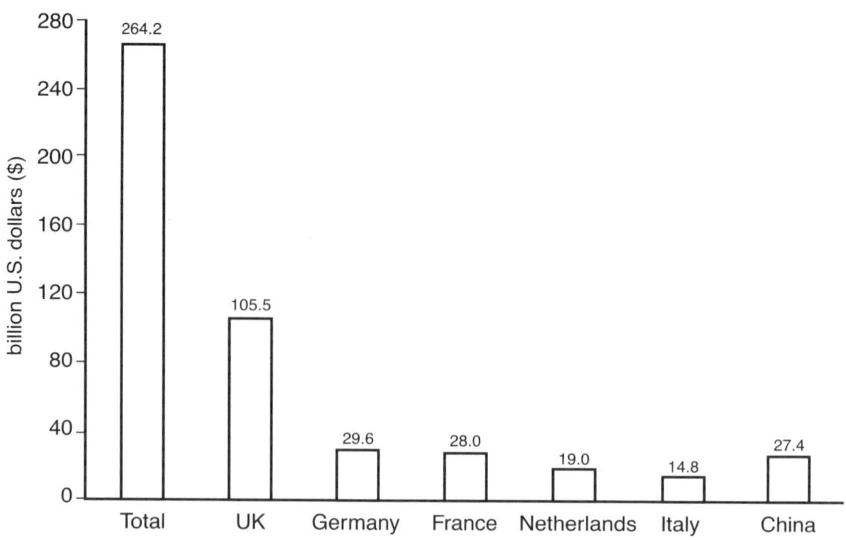


Source: Bureau of Economic Analysis

**Figure 7.4 Sales of Services to Europe by U.S. Affiliates, by Industry, 2004**

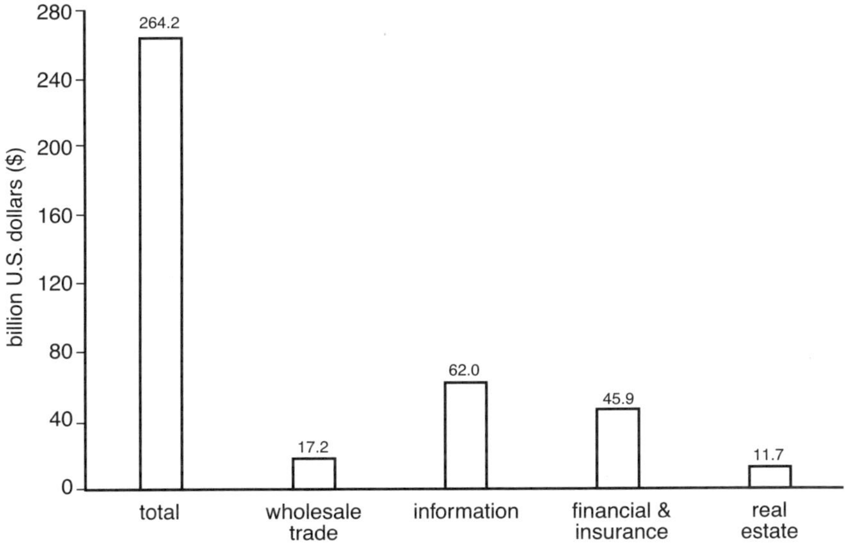


Source: Bureau of Economic Analysis

**Figure 7.5 Europe-U.S. Services Linkages**

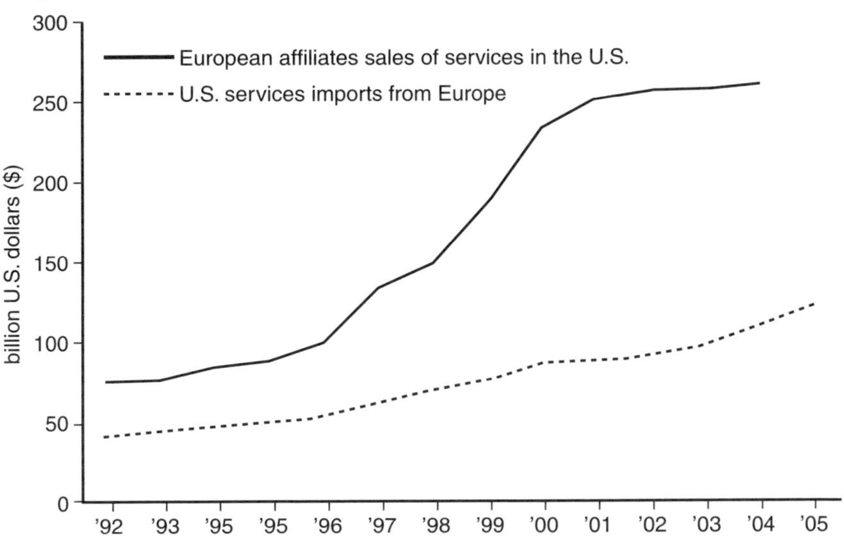


Source: Bureau of Economic Analysis

**Figure 7.6 Sales of Services to U.S. by European Affiliates, by Country, 2004**

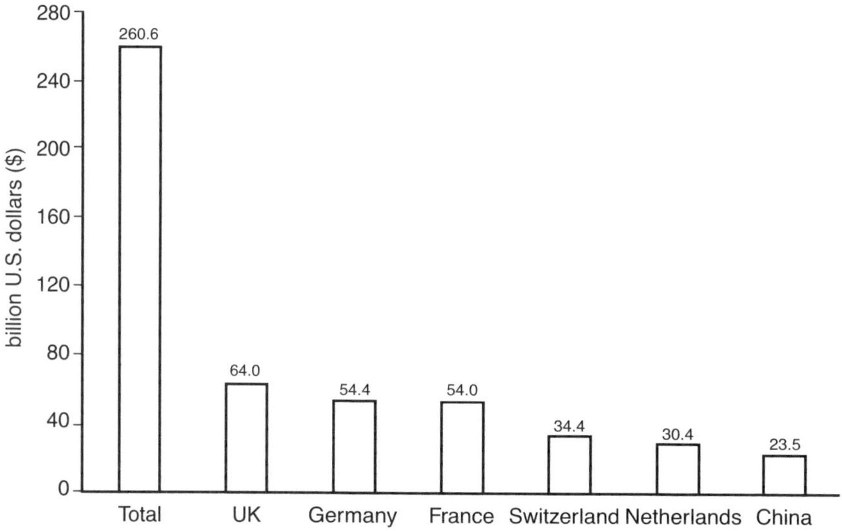


Source: Bureau of Economic Analysis

**Figure 7.7 Services Sales of Foreign Affiliates in the U.S.— Europe vs. China, 2004**

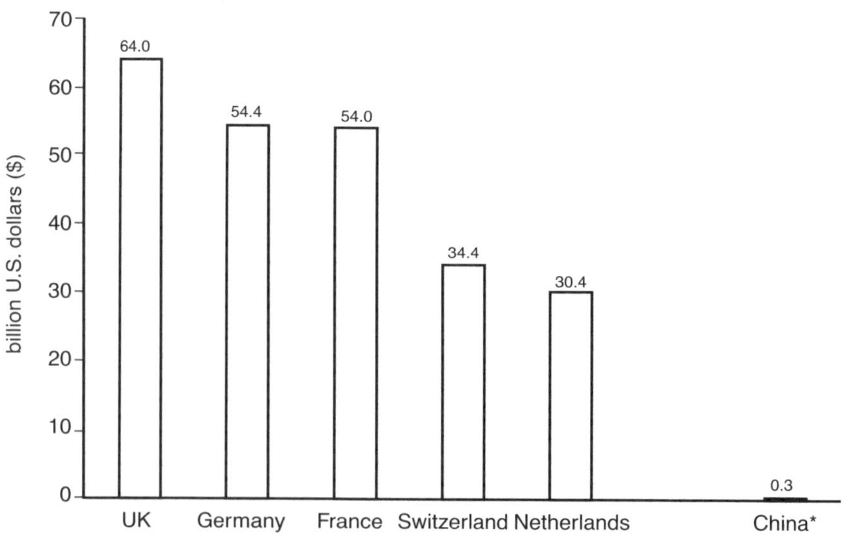


*Data for 2002

Source: Bureau of Economic Analysis

**Figure 7.8 Sales of Services to U.S. by European Affiliates, by Industry, 2004**

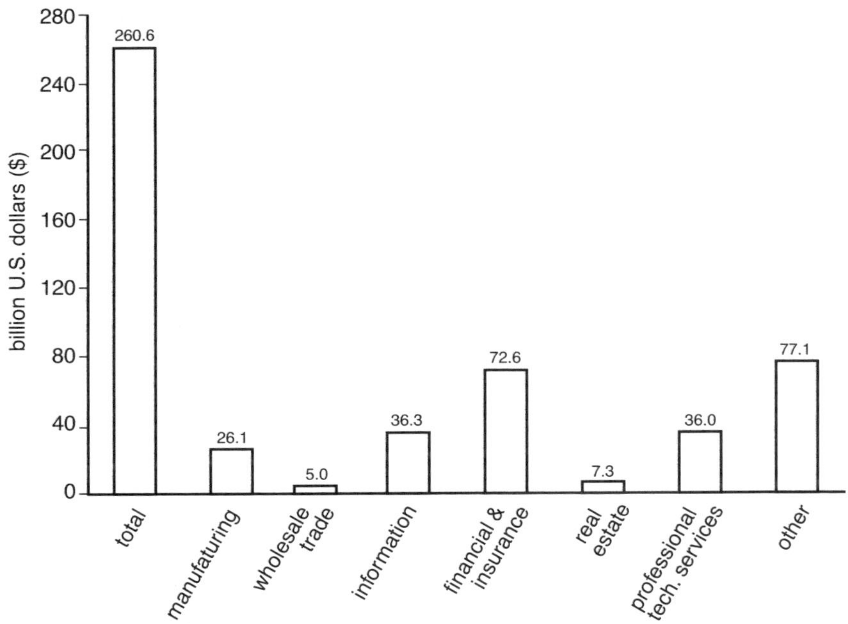


Source: Bureau of Economic Analysis

the rate of growth of affiliate sales of services. Services imports totaled $110 billion in 2004.

Leading the way were British services firms, whose U.S. affiliate sales in services totaled $64 billion in 2004, or roughly a quarter of total European affiliate sales. German, French and Dutch affiliates in the U.S. posted substantial sales of services as well, totaling $54.5 billion, $54 billion, and $30.3 billion, respectively, in 2004.

Financial and insurances services accounted for nearly 28 percent of total services sales in the U.S. by European affiliates, with sales totaling $72 billion in 2004. This was followed by information services ($36.3 billion), manufacturing services ($26 billion), professional and technical services ($23 billion), and a variety of other services sectors.

In short, foreign affiliate sales of services on both sides of the Atlantic have exploded over the past decade. In fact, affiliate sales of services have not only become a viable second channel of delivery for U.S. and European multinationals, they have become the overwhelming mode of delivery in a rather short period of time. Moreover, nations where services accounted for close to 60 percent of overall employment—such as the UK, the U.S., and the Netherlands and Norway—had the best record of job creation within the OECD.[1]

## Europe's Services Directive and the Impact on the Transatlantic Economy

Despite the major significance of the transatlantic services economy, barriers remain on both sides of the Atlantic. U.S. barriers are most prominent in maritime, legal, engineering, architectural and accounting services. In the EU-15 as a whole, barriers appear highest for domestic and foreign firms in accounting, maritime and legal services, and higher for foreign firms relative to domestic firms in distribution and maritime activities.[2] The key issue, however, remains the continued existence of services barriers within the EU itself. Liberalization of inner-EU services would be the single most important stimulus to the transatlantic services economy.

The EU has been committed to a common market for services and goods since its inception in 1957. The EU Single Market was supposed to come into effect on January 1, 1993, providing freedom of movements in goods, capital, people, and services. Seven years later, EU leaders announced a strategy for the removal of barriers to services, although progress has been very slow and piecemeal. Relatively speaking, goods move across the Union largely without difficulty; however, services remain hampered by 27 different sets of national rules and regulations—even though services account for almost 70 percent of GDP and jobs in the EU.

Through an initiative called the Services Directive, the EU commission seeks to break down services barriers all at once, rather than by tackling liberalization sector by sector. The Directive was adopted

---

1 Tobias Buck, "OECD stresses services market reform benefits," *Financial Times*, April 27, 2005.

2 OECD, *The Benefits of Liberalising Product Markets And Reducing Barriers to International Trade and Investment: The Case of The United States and the European Union, Economics Department Working Paper 432*, (Paris: June 2005).

at the end of 2006; member states have three years to implement it. While some elements of the Directive were widely opposed by EU members, analysts estimate that it could be an important initiative to improve the continent's competitiveness and employment, and deepen the linkages of the transatlantic economy.

Implementing the Services Directive would be akin to waking the sleeping giant of the transatlantic economy—services—and ultimately producing a number of benefits and gains for the U.S. and EU, including the following:

- *Boosting transatlantic foreign direct investment flows.* Like the Single Market program, which trigged a sharp rise in more foreign direct investment, the elimination or reduction of barriers to services activities in Europe would attract more foreign direct investment from leading services firms in the U.S. Under such a scenario, Europe would most likely remain the top destination of U.S. foreign direct investment, continuing the trend of the past half-century. Services deregulation would also promote more intra-European foreign investment.

- *Lowering prices while raising productivity and growth.* Services reform and deregulation would trigger greater cross-border competition in services, which would ultimately lead to lower prices, benefiting both consumers and businesses. Productivity levels would rise as costs declined and as firms leveraged more competitively priced services. Since services are a critical component of many manufacturing industries, greater service deregulation in Europe would yield a competitive boost to Europe's manufacturing sector. Finally, falling prices, combined with rising productivity would help boost real economic growth in the EU and a rise in European corporate earnings.

- *Improving wages and creating jobs.* The services sector of the EU already accounts for nearly 70 percent of total employment; a new regulatory framework that removes tariffs and non-tariffs to services would drive the percentage even higher. Net employment gains would be most noticeable in the new enlargement members, where services jobs (as a percentage of the total) lag the EU average.

- *Stimulating grater cross-border trade in services.* A more deregulatory environment for services would promote greater cross-border transactions in services, helping to boost not only intra-EU trade in services but also cross-border transatlantic trade in services. Cross border trade in services is already quite robust but would become even stronger under a more deregulatory climate.

## The Way Forward

Removing barriers to trade and investment in services represents a key opportunity for the transatlantic community. While services presently account for the largest share of gross domestic product in virtually all of the nations that comprise the transatlantic economy, the role of services could be even larger and growth-enhancing if the political will was present to push ahead with even more services deregulation and reform.

At this juncture the lack of services reform represents a significant opportunity cost to the U.S., EU and the transatlantic economy. The lack of reform could very well undermine the growth and attraction of the transatlantic economy. On the other hand, services reform would only embellish and fortify the transatlantic economy's leading global role. The EU Services Directive is one step in the right direction, but others should follow—on both sides of the Atlantic—if the full potential of the transatlantic economy is to be realized.

# About the Authors

**Chiara Bonassi** is a Research Fellow of CERM, Center for the Economic Analysis of Competitiveness, Markets and Regulation.

**Daniel Hamilton** is the Richard von Weizsäcker Professor and Director of the Center for Transatlantic Relations at the Paul H. Nitze School of Advanced International Studies (SAIS), Johns Hopkins University; and Executive Director of the American Consortium on EU Studies (ACES), designated by the European Commission as the EU Center of Excellence Washington D.C. He leads the international policy work of the Johns-Hopkins-based U.S. National Center of Excellence on Homeland Security. Dr. Hamilton has held a variety of senior positions in the U.S. Department of State, including Deputy Assistant Secretary for European Affairs and Associate Director of the Policy Planning Staff. He and CTR Fellow Joseph Quinlan have written a series of publications on the transatlantic economy, including *Deep Integration: How Transatlantic Markets are Leading Globalization* (2005) and *Partners in Prosperity: The Primacy of the Transatlantic Economy* (2004), that have become standard references for government, business and the media. They are recipients of the 2007 Transatlantic Leadership Award from the European-American Business Council and the 2006 Transatlantic Business Award from the U.S. Chamber of Commerce to the EU.

**Bernard Hoekman** is the manager of the international trade team of the Development Research Group of the World Bank. He has worked extensively on trade related projects and lending operations in the Middle East and North Africa and economies in transition. His research focuses on the functioning of the multilateral trading system (WTO), international transactions in services, the relationship between competition and trade policy, the economics of regional economic integration, and channels of international technology diffusion. Between 1988 and 1993 he was on the staff of the GATT Secretariat in Geneva, where he worked as a research economist and provided support to the Uruguay Round negotiating group on services.

**Arjan Lejour** manages the European Analysis Research Program in the International Economics department of the Netherlands

Bureau for Economic Policy. Current and recent research areas include the conduct of trade in services, jobs and growth in Europe and the Lisbon agenda, subsidiary in Europe, EU enlargement, international trade, and competing welfare states. He has numerous publications to his name in journals, books and the working papers of research institutes. Prior to his current position he was a researcher in the International Economics department of the same institute.

**Fabio Pammolli** is Director of the IMT Lucca Institute for Advanced Studies and a Professor of Economics and Management at the University of Florence. His research interests are in the fields of economics of innovation, industrial dynamics and market regulation, processes of industrial growth in markets and networks, economic analysis of the pharmaceutical industry. He is the author of many publications. He is a Member of the Commission on Intellectual Property Rights, Innovation and Public Health at the World Health Organization in Geneva; Director of European Pharmaceutical Innovation and Regulation Systems; and President of the Centre for the Economic Analysis of Competitiveness, Markets and Regulation.

**Joseph P. Quinlan** is a Fellow at the Center for Transatlantic Relations, Paul H. Nitze School of Advanced International Studies, Johns Hopkins University. He has extensive experience in the U.S. corporate sector. He is a leading expert on the transatlantic economy and well-known global economist/strategist on Wall Street. He specializes in global capital flows, international trade and multinational strategies. He lectures at New York University, and his publications have appeared in such venues as *Foreign Affairs*, the *Financial Times* and the *Wall Street Journal.* He and co-author Daniel Hamilton have written a series of publications on the transatlantic economy, including *Deep Integration: How Transatlantic Markets are Leading Globalization* (2005) and *Partners in Prosperity: The Primacy of the Transatlantic Economy* (2004), that have become standard references for government, business and the media. They are recipients of the 2007 Transatlantic Leadership Award from the European-American Business Council and the 2006 Transatlantic Business Award from the U.S. Chamber of Commerce to the EU.

**Randal K. Quarles** has served in a variety of public positions involving financial institutions policy, most recently as Under Secretary of the Treasury for Domestic Finance. From 2002-2005 he was

Assistant Secretary of the Treasury for International Affairs, where he had lead responsibility for the U.S.-EU Financial Markets Dialogue, which became the principal governmental forum for addressing transatlantic tensions concerning financial market regulation. He also served as the U.S. Executive Director of the International Monetary Fund from 2001-2002. In the early 1990s he played a significant role in the efforts of the George H.W. Bush Administration to reform financial services legislation, which began the legislative process that culminated in the Gramm-Leach-Bliley Act of 1999. In the private sector, he has been a partner at Davis Polk & Wardwell, the New York law firm, and co-head of its Financial Institutions Group. He is a frequent speaker and author on policy and legal issues concerning the financial sector.

**Andrea Renda** is a Senior Research Fellow at the Centre for European Policy Studies in Brussels. His areas of expertise include competition policy, intellectual property, regulatory impact assessment, new media and telecommunications, consumer protection and industrial policy.

**Massimo Riccaboni** is Associate Professor of Economics and Management at the University of Florence and a Senior Research Fellow of CERM, Center for the Economic Analysis of Competitiveness, Markets and Regulation. His research interests are in the fields of economics of innovation, industrial dynamics, processes of industrial growth in markets and networks, economic analysis of the pharmaceutical industry. He has published in, among others, *The Proceedings of the National Academy of Sciences*, *The Journal of the European Economics Association*, *The International Journal of Industrial Organization*, *Management Science*, *Economics Letters*, *Health Affairs*, *E. Journal of Health Economics*.

**Lawrence J. White** is the Arthur E. Imperatore Professor of Entrepreneurial Studies and Professor of Economics at New York University Stern School of Business. He is currently the Deputy Chair of Stern's Economics Department. Professor White has been with NYU Stern for almost 30 years. His primary research areas of interest include financial regulation, antitrust, network industries, international banking and applied microeconomics, and he has published numerous articles in publications such as the *Journal of Business*, the *Journal of Economic Perspectives*, the *Journal of Political Economy*, the *American Economic Review*, the *Review of Economics and Statistics*, and the *Quarterly Journal of Economics*. He is the author of *The S&L Debacle:*

*Public Policy Lessons for Bank and Thrift Regulation*, among other books, and he is the co-editor of *The Antitrust Revolution*. While at Stern, Professor White has taken three leaves of absence to serve in the U.S. Government: on the Senior Staff of the President's Council of Economic Advisors (1978-1979); as Chief Economist of the Antitrust Division of the U.S. Department of Justice (1982-1983); and as a Board Member of the Federal Home Loan Bank Board (1986-1989).